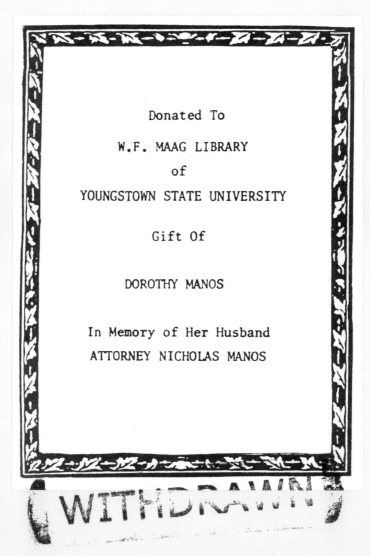

FORGING AHEAD

THOMAS JAMES WISE

Hon. M. A. (Oxon.), and Honorary Fellow of Worcester College

FORGING AHEAD

....

THE TRUE STORY OF THE UPWARD PROGRESS

OF

THOMAS JAMES WISE

PRINCE OF BOOK COLLECTORS,

BIBLIOGRAPHER EXTRAORDINARY

AND OTHERWISE

By

WILFRED PARTINGTON

....

It ain't by princerples nor men
My preudunt course is steadied,—
I scent wich pays the best, an' then
Go into it baldheaded.—J. R. LOWELL

NEW YORK
COOPER SQUARE PUBLISHERS, INC.
1973

Originally Published, 1939
Reprinted 1973 by Cooper Square Publishers, Inc.
59 Fourth Avenue, New York, N. Y. 10003
International Standard Book No. 0-8154-0442-5
Library of Congress Catalog Card No. 72-89409

Printed in the United States of America

To

P. E. O'N.

ACKNOWLEDGMENTS

I am greatly obliged to Dr. Philip Gosse for the unrestricted use of his father's letters and for other help; and to the Brotherton Collection Committee of Leeds University for putting the MSS of the Gosse-Wise Correspondence at my disposal—an arrangement in which Dr. R. Offor, the University Librarian, has been most considerate.

To the officials of the British Museum Library—especially to the Keeper of Printed Books, Mr. Wilfred A. Marsden, and also Mr. A. S. Johnson—for their courteous assistance over a long period my indebtedness cannot be too warmly conveyed.

Special thanks are due to Mr. Herbert E. Gorfin for his unsparing efforts to supply data, and for checking relevant parts of my MS.

To Sir John Murray, Messrs. Cecil Clay (R. Clay and Sons), C. S. Evans (Heinemann Ltd.), F. S. Ferguson (Quaritch and Co.), S. F. Sabin (Frank T. Sabin), Stanley Unwin (Allen and Unwin), *The Times,* and the Library Staff of Texas University (in particular William H. McCarthy), my inquiries have involved no little trouble which has been readily and generously undertaken.

The considerable contribution of Thomas James Wise himself is acknowledged in the text.

For letters of information and facilities, I am hardly less obliged to the Viscount Esher and Sir Sydney Cockerell; to Miss Olivia R. Garnett, Miss Sylvia Gosse, Mrs. Flora V. Livingston (Widener Memorial Library, Harvard University), Miss Irene Cooper Willis, Miss Audrey Lucas, and the late Mrs. Clara Watts-Dunton; to Messrs. H. F. B. Brett-Smith, A. E. Calkin (Rivières), John Carter, H. M. Cashmore (Birmingham City Librarian), Richard Curle, Allan Dobson, C. G. Des Graz (Sotheby and Co.), Frederick H.

viii   ACKNOWLEDGMENTS

Evans (Jones and Evans), M. Buxton Forman, John Kelly, P. R. Kimber, John Kirkby, Dr. R. B. McKerrow, the late Benjamin Maggs (Maggs Bros.), W. Marshbank, Dr. Alexander Mitchell, Harold G. Mitchell (Brontë Society), de V. Payen-Payne, Professor A. W. Pollard, Graham Pollard, Sydney E. Preston, Seymour de Ricci, William Roberts, George Bernard Shaw, Percy Simpson, M. H. Spielmann, Harold Strauss (Covici-Friede, Inc.), George Sutcliffe (Sangorski and Sutcliffe), W. E. Redway, O. P. Rubeck, C. H. Wilkinson, and Herbert Athol Wise; to the Ruskin Literary Trustees, the executors of the estates of the late Mrs. T. J. Wise and the late Mrs. Florence Hardy; to the proprietors of *Punch* (for permission to quote the verses of E. V. Lucas), Wm. Blackwood and Son, Methuen and Co., the Oxford University Press, and the Bibliographical Society; and to any others I may have been unable to reach.

I think it fair to add that the assistance here acknowledged has been given from the disinterested motive of assisting my researches, and without reference to my views or conclusions regarding the subject.

WILFRED PARTINGTON.

LONDON: 1939.

CONTENTS

Chapter 1. INTRODUCING THE SECRET EMPEROR OF BOOK
FORGERS AND SOME OF HIS FORERUNNERS   3

My first meeting with Thomas James Wise—The curious things he showed—£3,000 to save Swinburne MSS getting into wrong hands—The careers of famous English literary forgers—Wise and the genesis of this book —A savage censorship attempted.

Chapter 2. EARLY AND EVENTFUL YEARS   10

Wise's reticence about his biography—His parents and education—Book collecting in his youth—His essay as a poet—Essential-oil and sugar—The successful clerk —George Bernard Shaw's recollection of him—Story of a pin as a clue—Tracking down descendants of the famous—He becomes a private dealer in rare books—A Dickensian scene.

Chapter 3. ROBERT BROWNING, HIS "PAULINE," AND
OTHER AFFAIRS   25

The Browning vogue—The poet's joke against himself —A society to study him—Fecund Furnivall—His revealing flair—Wise's story of his introduction to the poet— Sequel to a calf love—"Pauline" reprinted—Wise experiments with types—How his facsimiles were faked —A cool "friendship"—Wise traps the poet—A story of a lock of hair—The collector's omnivorousness—His strange psychology.

Chapter 4. WORDSWORTH ADVENTURES AND A NEW FAKE
REVEALED   36

Curious story of Wise's first interest in Wordsworth— Sequel to an evening over pipes and books—His pas-

*sion for morocco—Dark secret of a black tulip—His
"unique" issue of "Lyrical Ballads" a fake—What else
is wrong in the Ashley Library?—Errors concerning
a Wordsworth manuscript—A spurious edition.*

Chapter 5. SHELLEY STORIES: THE PIRATE IN FULL SAIL   46
*Furnivall fathers another society—Andrew Lang's fun
and its sequel—Richard Garnett and Wise—The triumphs, profits, and evils of type-facsimiles—The collector's romantic book finds—Wise adopts an alias—
The sarcastic professor—A mystery solved from two
sources—Two false New York imprints—How Wise recovered his Shelley losses.*

Chapter 6. REVELATIONS OF THE CONTEMPORARY DIARY
OF MR. Y. Z.   64
*When did the forgeries begin?—Clays' destroyed rec-
ords—Unexpected evidence from a diary—Cost price of
the frauds—A surprise plea for secrecy—Wise's bitter
anger with a provincial bookseller—Clever marketing
of the forgeries—What the British Museum paid—Ironical reflections.*

Chapter 7. WOMEN, WINE, & FRIENDS: THE ROLES OF
BUXTON FORMAN AND EDMUND GOSSE   71
*Relaxations—The girl who stole his pin—Whisky, and
songs in manuscripts—The real Shelley pioneer—
Shabby treatment of a useful friend—Buxton Forman
and the forgeries—Wise's meeting with Swinburne,
and a mystery—Edmund Gosse's bon mot—What
he did for Wise—Miss Gosse's drypoint—A painful affair—Swinburne secret revealed—Gosse's moving protest
and appeal.*

Chapter 8. MARRIAGE, SECRET PUBLISHING, AND RUSKIN
RUSES   82
*Wise's first bride—House that gave name to his famous
library—His ingenious publishing scheme explained—
Record of 250 privately printed books—The law
flouted—Profits and a café rendezvous—How a severe
censor laid himself open to censure—Some of his pub-*

lications stopped—Misleading certificates—Ruskin's aloofness—Suspicions of Wise—Suppressions—Machia-vellian maneuvers—Deceiving the public.

Chapter 9. THREE MEN AND A BOY   97

The "Wee Cham of Literature"—How Clement Shorter offended Thomas Hardy—Charlotte Brontë's husband tracked down—A great haul of MSS—Humors of expurgating—Picture of the "twin souls"—Authors' letters in payment for lunches—Robertson Nicoll and the "Bookman"—Employed to boost the forgeries— William Roberts's pointed attack—Great American book collectors—John H. Wrenn—What he was worth to Wise—Mystery of "Dr. Underwood"—The innocence of William Harris Arnold—Wise as a packer—Herbert Gorfin's Great Expectations.

Chapter 10. "RUSKIN'S ROMANCE" AND THE ARCHIVIST'S DISILLUSION   114

Wise's society of autograph collectors—Guidance against forgeries—Books versus babies—Domestic shadows—The "Grace Darling" piracy—Wise beats Shorter by 23 years—A remarkable Ruskin letter— Divorce—A disguised catalogue—Swinburne's poem on Burns—Exposure of two Wise pamphlets in the "Athenaeum"—Bibliographies projected and aban-doned.

Chapter 11. REMARRIAGE, AND THE WRITING ON THE WALL   127

Wise's career opens out—His new bride—He secures his choicest books—Battle for Elizabethan quartos— Richer prizes than he knew—Comedy of a gibe against the Scotch—Treasure bricked up in a chimney corner— Unmasking of Ruskin forgeries in 1903—Sequel to Ruskin's amorous offering—Danger of discovery passes —Wise's first catalogue and its subtle uses—Mr. Otto P. Rubeck—Bulls and books—Mrs. Browning's love song in the original version.

Chapter 12. THE TRIO AT THE PINES AND THE SECRETS
OF THE VATICAN VENUS 142

*Swinburne's Bohemian days—A new reminiscence—
The rescue by Watts-Dunton—Mystery of the Pines—
Clearing up Algernon's library—Wise's profitable coup
—John Wrenn introduced—More deals—72-year-old
Watts-Dunton's marriage to his secretary—The comedy
of the Swinburne "Juvenilia" myth—How it was ex-
ploded—Gosse in trouble, but Wise escapes.*

Chapter 13. THREATS, COUNTER-THREATS, AND MORE
MYSTERIES ILLUMINED 154

*Watts-Dunton damns three pamphlets—How Wise re-
taliated—The Old Man quashed—A faked presentation
copy—Telltale alteration—The Hell at the Pines—
Wise's self-revelations in his letters—Gosse's severe
chastisement of his protégé—Rubbing the dust off the
butterfly's wings—Wise deceives his literary partner—
Gosse's perplexity about mysterious pamphlets—Destroyed correspondence.*

Chapter 14. PAYING OFF OLD SCORES AND FINDING A
SCAPEGOAT 172

*The final home at Heath Drive—When E. V. Lucas
was befogged—Sir Edmund Gosse's reproof—R. L. S.
bargain missed—Putting the coping stones on his
career—The bibliophilic merry-go-round—A highly
exciting pursuit—Wise looks back—A committee of enthusiasts—How Furnivall, his master, was repaid—
Kicks for a bookseller who sold him a £3,000 book for
£22.10—A scapegoat for emergencies—The sad story of
Richard Herne Shepherd—The story behind Swinburne's "Unpublished Verses."*

Chapter 15. REVELATIONS GRAVE AND GAY 188

*A haul of George Borrow manuscripts—Comedy of
Lockhart and the Romany lad—An erroneous description—Little "Herby" sets up as bookseller—His savings
laid out on the forgeries—Wise behind the scenes—The
Charlotte Brontë revelations—He issues a piracy in
1914—King Shorter snubbed by "The Times"—All fair*

in bibliography and war—Specimen revelations from the Ashley manuscripts—When William Morris burst his trousers—Curious pastimes of Pre-Raphaelites.

Chapter 16. WAR AND EXPLOITATION   202

Orgy after the World War—The boom—America swoops down on English treasures—Historic collecting —Silly limits in the book boom—Evil days in stately homes—The boom spreads Wise's fame—The exploitation of Joseph Conrad—Mockery of presentation copies—Unmasking a forgery—Chancey affair of "Chance"—More writing on the wall.

Chapter 17. PORTRAIT OF A DICTATOR   215

When Joseph Conrad was angry—Wise withdraws a threat—Raising the devil in the book trade—Lyceum drama in his library—The man and his books—Binding folly and the sequel—His private printing comes to an end.

Chapter 18. FIRSTS AND SUPER-FIRSTS   225

Why Wise "spread himself" on his magnum opus— John Drinkwater's lament—G. B. Shaw adds to the Ashley abundance—On Michael Sadleir and Trollope —Wise and an author's widow—Notable rarities—A £380 book for £10—"A trick to catch the old one"— Amazing inconsistency — Honors — Did Wise meet George Eliot?

Chapter 19. BYRON ROMANTICS   235

Wise "discovers" a new Byron love affair—Miss "L" and her child—A delicate investigation by mail—Why the sensational claim is a myth—£100 offer for a fake.

Chapter 20. A REVISED STORY ABOUT MRS. BROWNING'S LOVE SONNETS   246

Wise's fame as the enemy of forgers—He receives a disturbing visitor—An interview with his old printer— Giving himself away—The romantic story of Mrs. Browning's love sonnets—A false tale and how it was uncloaked—Meeting an attack before it was launched—

Amazing audacity—Forgeries and piracies bought back from Mr. Gorfin.

Chapter *21.* THE EXPOSURE AND SOME SURPRISING SEQUELS   254

The "Enquiry" published—Its aim and methods—Big headline sensation for the newspapers—Wise's statement to an interviewer—Why his Herne Shepherd theory can be ruled out—Another reply, then silence— Mr. Gorfin gives the lie direct—Lord Esher's challenge unanswered—The Browning episode cleared up—A private inquiry—Question of a confession—Wise not always too ill to refute the charges—Curious corrections made in the British Museum's copy of a Wise book.

Chapter *22.* WHY WERE THE FORGERIES DONE?   269

Death of Wise—Inadequate obituaries—"The Times" notice resented—Changed plans for the Ashley Library —Purchase by the nation and cost—Important books and MSS missing from the collection—A grievous loss —Fourteen of the forgeries done away with—Wise's "wild career"—The secret known—Why were the forgeries done?—Theories examined—The real reason— The true psychological interest in the case—Coincidence of a quotation—Wise's three claims to fame.

APPENDIX: THE BIBLIOGRAPHY OF THE BIBLIOGRAPHER   285

INDEX   305

ILLUSTRATIONS

Thomas James Wise, Hon. M.A. (Oxon.)   *frontispiece*

FACING PAGE

Reproductions of two pages of a letter from Wise to the author   6

Dr. Frederick James Furnivall   26

Wise and Clement King Shorter   40

Reproduction of page 97 of *Lyrical Ballads* and of the faked *cancellans*   40

Harry Buxton Forman   74

Thomas Hardy and Edmund Gosse   100

Wise's portrait, the frontispiece to Vol. II of *Ashley Library Catalogue*, 1905-8   138

Swinburne and Watts-Dunton in the garden at The Pines   166

Herbert Gorfin; Wise at the age of 40; Wise's Book Device and Bookplate   192

Joseph Conrad   216

Reproduction of pages from two other letters from Wise to the author   240

Corrections made by Wise in the British Museum copy of his *A Browning Library*   266

CHAPTER 1

INTRODUCING THE SECRET EMPEROR
OF BOOK FORGERS AND SOME OF
HIS FORERUNNERS

I

I WAS VERY CURIOUS to see him—this successful business man looming into such prominence in the world of books; already something of a dictator, spoken of with the familiarity of fame as "Tommy" Wise. And he, as was later revealed, was anxious to meet me. But our reasons were different.

There is nothing unusual in a man of commerce taking up book collecting as a hobby. For the weary and disillusioned fugitive from the daily round and the damned office, it is of all relaxations the happiest, most enthralling, most honored. But here, one reputed to have spent a strenuous if obscure career in the City amassing his wealth, was such an expert in rare books as only a lifetime of study could make him, and was the author of a most imposing array of instructive works. No bookman had ever before produced such a mass of valuable and fascinating information. How was it done? Where was the mystery? What manner of man was he?

It was on a late and darkening autumn afternoon in 1919 that I was shown into the already widely known Ashley Library. My first impression was of a pink bald head bent over a large handsome desk against a background of books shining in the gay parade of new gilt and many-colored moroccos. Then a short, chubby figure, bespectacled and smiling, approached briskly and greeted me also briskly. My second impression was of the keenness of the eyes twinkling behind their large lenses, and how ferret-like they became searching mine—as if trying to read their imprint. My third impression was that this plump, alert, confident man of sixty years looked remarkably shrewd and determined.

I was also curious as to what of his famous treasures he would select to show me. First was a case preserving Mary Shelley's long account of the shipwreck and cremation of the poet, locks of hair of Shelley and Mary, and some of his ashes "snatched . . . from the funeral pyre," and given to Byron's former mistress, Jane Clairmont, by Trelawny when that old adventurer and satyr was pressing his affections on her. The few dead cinders seemed unimpressive compared with the moving pathos of Mary Shelley's living epistle. And I did not care to comment on the surprising absence of reference to them in the accompanying detailed Deed of Sale of Jane Clairmont's effects. Already I divined that under his joviality Wise was a testy man, brooking no argument.

The owner next showed me, with pride and obvious anticipation of my astonishment, some of Swinburne's manuscript aberrations in verse and prose on the subject of flagellation.

"Amusing, are they not?" he asked.

"No! They strike me as being puerile and pitiable."

"Eh?"

Was he going to privately print this stuff? He discussed the matter vaguely. They were safe with him, he assured me. When he told me, with many laughing asides, how he had spent some three thousand pounds to save the poet's unpublished manuscripts getting into wrong hands and to preserve them for posterity, I was deeply impressed. That favorable impression remained for many years until my researches brought out the truth to be told here.

During the years I was editing the *Bookman's Journal* (1919 to 1931) and afterward writing the book-collecting section of the American *Bookman* (1931-1933), almost to the time of his death in 1937, I was in the habit of meeting Wise pretty regularly and also of being in correspondence with him in rare-book and kindred discussions. In the boom that made those years memorable, the increasing prevalence of fabricated first editions and manuscripts became a subject of anxiety to those concerned for a hobby so delightful and valuable to literature. Wise, when he became aware of my views, enthusiastically pressed me to "block the forger's path"—to use his own words. "Carry on the good work," and "You ought to expose this," he would urge. The support of his great authority and world-wide reputation at the time it was offered would naturally be regarded as worth having. And so I innocently regarded it. Little did I suspect that the man who sometimes provided me with powder and shot for the campaign against fakers, whose clarion cry against fraud was heard afar, was himself the secret Emperor and Grand Lama of Forgers: that he would go down to history in the line of succession to William Henry Ireland, John Payne Collier, and De Gibler.

For after the boom came the bomb. In 1934 it was revealed that a considerable number of purported first-edition pamphlets of writings by Victorian authors, copies of which were in the Ashley Library of Thomas James Wise, were forgeries; others were condemned as of very doubtful authenticity. The classification of these highly esteemed pamphlets as first editions, their reputed literary and bibliographical importance, and their commercial value as rarities, had depended almost solely upon the authority of Wise. He was not then accused of being the fabricator of these forgeries, though the implications of his intimate connection with the things were obvious. The bomb bursting in the charming stillness of the libraries of the collecting and literary worlds was the sensation of the time. Then followed a great silence.

It is perhaps advisable to say something of the genesis of this study and its development. In 1932 I had designed to devote a considerable article in the American *Bookman* to Wise's career as a collector and bibliographer; and for that purpose he at some of our meetings told me certain things incorporated in this book. But in 1933 the article (which was being built up at leisure) was still uncompleted when the *Bookman* ended its long career. In the following year came the sensation concerning those spurious first editions in the Ashley Library.

In 1936 I informed Wise of my plan to extend my article into the present study, expressing my wish to use certain correspondence. He was then preserving an obstinate silence in the face of the exposure of his rare pamphlets. His reaction to my request was both surprising and revealing. He promptly placed an embargo upon the use of any of his letters to me. The copies I had sent to him were returned with passages viciously and heavily scored out in blue pencil in an effort at censorship which was abandoned for the embargo. That embargo, however, has been without the intended effect, and has not prevented me from setting forth what I have considered it a duty to write of a man who so amazingly won for himself a threefold claim to fame.

The object of this biographical and critical study of Wise is to present fresh information and to give new and hitherto unpublished evidence of Wise's responsibility for the forgeries, to trace the curious and little-known ramifications of his career, to show the inner character of the man in relation to his work and ambitions, and generally to indicate the extent and value of his achievements. In these respective aims I hope to do him impartial justice. For my aim is to preserve Thomas James Wise as he was: not to present him changed and furbished up after his own habit of rebinding things that ought to have been left in their original condition—all decked up in scarlet, apple-green, and royal-blue moroccos, like his lamented Byrons and desecrated Wordsworths.

25, Heath Drive
N. W. 3.
7. 3. 4. 31.

My dear Partington,

Here's another chance for
you to carry some more,
or block the path of the
forger. You will doubtless remember
from in the Catalogue —

And why did his son find known
nothing whatever about it? And
where was it him hidden all these
years? And where was Poultney
it now?

Very truly yrs
T. J. Wise

Reduced reproduction of the first and last pages of a letter from Wise in which
he urges the author to block the forger's path.

II

It is almost certain that the earliest literary forgeries were of religious writings, a fact which induces some amusing reflections. After the religious fraud came the political forger, who, even if he made statecraft the excuse for his methods, was more usually concerned to secure for himself or his associates some valuable consideration. But neither religion nor politics has had much to do with the activities of later practitioners, in their making of forged manuscripts, spurious printings, piracies, faked first editions, and the like. These mainly developed in the latter part of the eighteenth century (though there were earlier ones); for it was by then that collecting had ceased to be confined to learned institutions and wealthy noblemen, and was becoming more and more developed through the spread of education and wealth.

As the numbers of book collectors have increased, so have these "wrong" books and manuscripts been multiplied to cater for them. Almost every country has produced literary fabricators. Their annals are adventurous, gay, sad, and generally incredible; and of all the bold and clever gallery, taking ability with offense (and the two often coincide), the English breed must surely be awarded first place—notwithstanding that France can claim Lucas Vrain, who confessed to manufacturing 25,000 spurious autographs for a wealthy dupe, including letters by Cleopatra, the resurrected Lazarus, and Mary Magdalene—and all in modern French!

The Irelands, father and son, were a curious pair. Sam, the father, had a passion for collecting; and William Henry (1777-1835), the boy, likewise picking up many rare books, studied medieval literature, and amused himself writing verse in imitation of early authors. How this led to his producing, in his 'teens, the "newly discovered" Elizabethan manuscripts that he rained upon a delighted father, is too well-known to need retelling. In 1795 proud Samuel held at his house in Norfolk Street, London, an exhibition of his clever son's "finds." The pundits, sublimely hoaxed, lifted up their voices in wonder and gratification; and Boswell went down on his knees in his best breeches to kiss the relics! Eventually the Irelands were exposed; and Samuel died broken-hearted, still protesting the innocence of his son, who had already confessed the forgeries and disappeared.

It is never too late to repent; though later book-world forgers, perhaps not relishing the fate of the Irelands, have tended either to brazen out their deeds or to lie low, hoping doubtless that they will go down to posterity as beautiful mysteries.

Contrary to the case of William Henry Ireland, life did not become exciting for John Payne Collier (1789-1883) until he was 63 years old, at which time he was enjoying a Civil-List Pension of £100 in recognition of his bibliographical work and scholarly services to learned societies. Then he surprised the world by producing a copy of the Second Folio Shakespeare (1632) bearing annotations which, if genuine, provided a corrected text earlier than any other known. Shakespearean students of repute declined to accept these; and, while the ink was flying in another battle of books, he added sensation to sensation by bringing forward documents concerning Shakespeare and his contemporaries. All were proved to be spurious; and it was also found that he had planted forgeries in the Dulwich College Library and even in the British State Paper Office. Collier fought back and managed to find a few optimistic champions, such as are usually at hand in a case of the kind.

The cases of Ireland and Collier are only mentioned by way of brief introduction to our subject and as prominent figures in the gallery of delinquents. It is usually extended to include poor Thomas Chatterton (1752-1770), the one genius of them all, who committed suicide at the age of 18 after producing immortal verse attributed to a fifteenth-century "Thomas Rowley." Pity for the tragedy of Chatterton, however, prompts the plea that his case is arguable: he was no worse than Horace Walpole, who so badly treated him, and who put out a novel purported to have been done by someone else. Yet Walpole is never included in the infamous gallery.

But there is another figure of whom it is necessary to say something. In the middle of the nineteenth century there was operating in London, and for a time also in America, a clever scoundrel named De Gibler, who was to sow a great deal of trouble. His specialty in delinquency was the forging of what probably totals hundreds of letters purporting to be by Byron and Shelley (but chiefly the former) and making faked association books. This De Gibler called himself George Gordon Byron, claiming to be the illegitimate son of Lord Byron by a Spanish lady—a claim that has been denied. He is said to have been remarkably like the poet; and that fact, the "peculiar circumstances" he had to relate, and his astute little wife's [1] ability to embroider the tale, must have made his career a lively one, and provided a never-ending source of amusement to the De Giblers in their connubial chamber. The alleged Don Juan Junior remains a mysterious person. But he will reappear later in these pages, for his misdeeds were constantly coming under the rake of Thomas James Wise, whose life and character affords a study even more remarkable than those of the delinquents mentioned and whose achievements include a new departure in literary frauds.

[1] Wife or mistress? Mary Russell Mitford, in a valuable and amusing letter of gossip written to Mrs. Ouvray (April 7th, 1852), gives an account of the De Giblers that she had received from Dr. W. C. Bennett, who figures here in connection with Wise. De Gibler's partner is described as a most elegant young woman, who was educated at a finishing school at Blackheath: and "Mrs. Byron, it is now said, was not his wife."

CHAPTER 2

EARLY AND EVENTFUL YEARS

Full many a time and oft my soul
Has nursed upon its faltering breast,
The light of some long cherished goal,
Yet vainly clutched the wished-for rest!
Oft bursting on the heart's cold strand,
Hope's wave has borne a gladder ray;
But full as oft my eager hand,
Missing the wave, clasped but the spray!

From *Verses*, by Thomas J. Wise.

I

REMARKABLY LITTLE has been recorded, or seems to be known among many who might be expected to know, about the family, upbringing, and early career of Thomas James Wise. Modern fashion favors the supply of biographical information, even by the subject of the biography. The dearth in this case is largely due to Wise's own determined reticence. In the few statements he made about himself and his career, biographical details were always lightly skirted. He was once offered handsome terms—"a thousand down on account before putting pen to paper," as he told me—to write a book about himself and his experiences. Asked why he had not done so when assured of commanding wide attention, his reply was: "All that's of interest about me is in my books. My life is in the bibliographies I've compiled and the books I've collected. The rest doesn't matter to anyone."

This modesty, or contempt for biographical fashion, is hardly in keeping with the character. Nevertheless, it is true enough that there is much that is revealing of their author to be gained, at the cost of some study, from his specialized works—so much indeed that he was speaking either with cynicism, or with that surprising naïveté that makes his strange psychology stranger.

II

Thomas James Wise was born on October 7th, 1859, at 52 Wrotham Road, Gravesend, the first-born of Julia Victoria Wise, formerly Dauncey. His father, Thomas Wise, was a "manufacturing traveler"—a description which, although it may appear unusual, was his own—and subsequently he became a tobacconist. He has been otherwise described as a builder, and a London general merchant. The son invariably stated his father's rank or profession to be that of "Gentleman." Three other children were born to Julia Victoria and Thomas Wise—two sons and a daughter. The daughter Julia died in infancy. One son, Henry Dauncey, died in 1915; the other, Herbert Athol Wise, enlisted in the army in 1891 and served most of his time abroad, retiring with the rank of acting sergeant. He was twelve and a half years junior to Thomas James, the eldest of the family, and survived him. The mother died of consumption in 1881. The widower was afterward twice married: first to Hannah Waldock (who predeceased him); and then, at the age of 70, to his nurse, Jeannie Donald Carden (or Garden). He died in 1902, leaving his estate of £2,362 entirely to his relict, who was remarried to one Avenell. These facts correct the misstatements made in usually accurate quarters as to Thomas James Wise's parents. It is not true that he inherited any family business; or that he derived wealth from his parents. He was a "self-made" man, who gained fortune and fame in divers extraordinary ways.

Wise senior was a Baptist; and young Thomas James's upbringing, if not very strongly influenced, was at least under the auspices of that denomination. Among the two or three recollections of boyhood he permitted himself to give, one was of his devotion to his invalid mother, whose interest in literature led to his reading poetry to her—especially that of Shelley, for which he developed a partiality. Shelley readings in a Baptist home sounds rather incongruous, but the readings may have been selected and such as would have appeared innocuous to the Brethren—one of whose leading tenets is the confession of sins. Maternal leanings to literature guiding a child's taste and career is a circumstance fairly common in biography; but it cannot be recorded in this instance that mutual affection and kindred tastes between mother and son was ever commemorated by the latter in outward sign such as a book dedication or written tribute.[1]

The Wise family early left Gravesend for North London. The elder son, Thomas James, in later life was wont to describe himself as having been educated privately.[2] His schooling was, according to another statement of his, received at the City of London School, in Milk Street off Cheapside, where he stayed until the age of 16; but the present headmaster, Mr. Francis Richard Dale, states that there is no record of his being there. His brother says that Thomas was educated at home owing to his delicate health. He was early placed in a junior capacity with the firm of Rubeck & Co., of 14 Mincing Lane, E.C., and afterward of 59 Mark Lane, E.C.3, an essential-oil merchant. The beginning of the lad's career was not auspicious. At the end of six months he was sacked by Hermann Rubeck, the proprietor—who, however, on the representations of the father agreed to give Tommy another chance. Little could Hermann have guessed the surprising sequel to his clemency. With Rubeck & Co., Wise

[1] The headstone on the "family grave of Julia and Thomas Wise" in Highgate Cemetery was left neglected after the burial of Julia, the mother of Thomas James Wise, and the lower inscriptions are partially illegible. The tombstone also records that buried in this family grave is one "Amelia Groseman, died July 13th, 1874, aged [10 or 19] years." The Registry of Deaths at Somerset House contains no entry for 1874 respecting this Amelia Groseman.

[2] For example, the *Who's Who* for 1925 (the issue to which Wise first contributed his biographical entry) and for the years following. It was in that same work that for fourteen years the information supplied by him gave a wrong year—1901—for his second marriage (see Chapter 11).

was to be associated for the whole of his city career. There was little, if anything, he did not come to know about essential oils; but the products Hermann Rubeck specialized in (according to the encyclopedias) possess an aromatic smell, and as a rule leave no permanent grease spots.

Most boys at some time collect something or other—birds' eggs, black eyes, stamps, vermin, etc. Tommy, who had soon shown inclination for literary pursuits, at seventeen began book collecting. The stories which have been printed about the lad's starving in order that he might buy books are inventions, although it is true that on occasions he walked to and fro from his work to put the fares thus saved toward the cost of some particularly desired volume—a little economy not unfamiliar among keen youngsters. The favorite hunting ground of Thomas was at first the Farringdon Road, where book-laden barrows and stalls still line the streets. Afterward he adventured into the picturesque old bookshops up Fleet Street and along the Strand and in its more dubious backwaters that have now fallen before palatial offices and gorgeous cinemas plastered with their grotesque "lovelies." If priceless treasures in Elizabethan manuscripts and old books were not to be found "plenty as blackberries" as in the London of Halliwell-Phillips, nevertheless the city's bookshops were still El Dorados for the wise. Thomas, of that ilk, was a stocky lad, and a shrewd. Not only did he browse and occasionally buy a volume, but he began paying visits—naturally shy at first—to the better-class antiquarian shops further West, noting their prices, and the finer condition of the books as compared with those of the dirty untidy piles on the street stalls and barrows. He was learning: ideas were fertilizing—ideas that were to lead to the acquisition of wealth and fame.

His visits to the old bookshops became more frequent as he grew more familiar and confident with their proprietors. Sometimes he would make a much debated purchase; at other times, to raise his funds, he would sell to a bookseller a volume picked up cheaply from a rival shop close at hand. But at all times he asked questions. Young Wise in quest of wisdom was as quick as a ferret after a rabbit.

One never-to-be-forgotten day, when aged eighteen, he spent no less than twenty shillings on Thomas Moore's *Epicurean* and Shelley's *Cenci* (this was the order in which he mentioned them); and these he declared to be the foundation of the Ashley Library now honored in the British Museum with its own special room. The price made our young epicurean wince, but he was wise; they were both first editions. The antiquarian booksellers on their part were only too ready to encourage the intelligent, pert young man, neatly dressed in his black cloth and bowler hat—a book collector obviously determined to go far in a delightful pursuit. His inquisitiveness was already remarked. He would start as many queries as a good researcher with his nose in a bad catalogue. Among other things that impressed him in this early stage of his private education was that the more entertainingly a bookseller talked about a particular work he was showing, the more desirable the volume seemed to become, and the higher its price.

That observation was to have a result affecting the whole of book collecting and book selling; for he had now determined to form a fine library for himself, and also to supply others forming libraries.

III

In 1881 there settled in London a middle-aged merchant who for some years had been interesting himself in literary subjects and contributing to the transactions of learned societies: James Dykes Campbell. To him literature was more than Mammon; and now at forty-three he retired from business on a moderate competency to become a man of letters—devoting himself largely to the study of Coleridge, whose biography he wrote. Young Wise was an admirer of Campbell and was much impressed by his example. He was not to be such an idealist himself: for him Literature was too often spelt with a £ for the first letter—that plan of his to build a fine library required capital. Nor was he ever equal in scholarship to Campbell or those other contemporaries whose critical abilities he was to use, as we shall see, to such advantage and so unscrupulously.

But he had all the energy and determination necessary to achieve the ambitions now clearly before him; he had also plenty of patience when he chose to exercise it. If any man's life ever exemplified what triumphs can be effected, what revenges taken, by watchful, silent biding-the-time, it is that of Thomas James Wise.

For all his materialistic outlook, however, he had his romantic moments, the results of which were seen when in 1883 he printed his *Verses*. Of this, his first publication, 35 copies (including six on special paper) were produced. The twenty-three-year-old author took for his title-page quotation this from Martin Tupper:

> "Thoughts that have tarried in my mind, and peopled
> its inner chamber."

Wise's poetry was pretty much of the *Keepsake* variety, and contained the usual sprinkling of "last Trumps," "throbbing bosoms," and "Fancy's ears." He came to be very shy of his little book of *Verses;* it appeared for sale in his disguised bookseller's list of 1895, but he never admitted it to his *Ashley Library Catalogue*. Three examples of his poetizing have been selected for their peculiar appropriateness—one at the head of this chapter, and two which will be given later.

The most interesting points about this booklet are the printer of it, and that limitation of edition which was to become so famously associated with Wise's publications. The man chosen for the honor of printing Thomas James's muse was [William?] Fullford, of King's Cross, which place was within easy reach of Holloway. He was little more than a jobbing printer; but he hitched up his trousers and did his best with red and black inks and ruled borders to please his new customer—who hinted at lots of work to follow. For among other thoughts peopling Wise's "inner chamber" were some exceedingly novel ones requiring the services of a printer who would do just what he was told without asking a lot of questions.

Fullford's next job for his new customer, a few months later, was to make a reprint of Keats's *Ode to a Nightingale* in an edition of 29 copies, including a few on vellum. Perhaps there wasn't much difference between the two poets for William Fullford, to whom the cash result was eminently satisfactory—for Wise was always prompt in paying his accounts, and settled without a quibble those for printing and binding. But the result was not so satisfactory for the customer; who soon realized that Fullford was not the man for his purpose.

Wise needed a printer with a large range of types—an adept who could print anything, match anything. For what reasons will transpire in the next three chapters.

IV

Wise's commercial instincts were in keeping with his shrewd character. He was always on the lookout for profit, however small. Any mission in the city was keenly explored for its commission. Even visits to restaurants had to yield their return, according to the recollection of a later colleague. On returning from a meal in a neighboring café, Wise was noted invariably to go to a shelf in the sample room, take down a large tin used as a container for saffron, and drop into it a few lumps of sugar. When filled, the tin disappeared, and an empty one took its place. There is nothing very original, it is true, in this practical application of the old saw that many a pickle makes a mickle: the mickle fortunes of some of our most prominent snobs have been built up by surreptitious collecting of lumps of sugar, evasion of penny fares, and by such means.

But if the keen, short-statured clerk was something of a hustler, he was also a thoughtful young man—even a man of vision. At this period he had a number of inspirations which, opportunist as he was, were to be exploited to the full. One of these was the realization of the collecting possibilities in the galaxy of early nineteenth-century authors that included Scott, Wordsworth, Byron, Shelley, Keats, and Leigh Hunt. After all, he was not so far removed from their time. When he was twenty-one, that hardy adventurer Trelawny [3] was still alive telling tales of his friend, Lord Byron, discussing how much should be suppressed of the affair of Jane Clairmont,[4] whom he liked (she had been kind to him!), lauding his "ever glorious Shelley," and abusing that poet's widow, whom he hated (she had refused to marry him after all he had done!!).

When Wise in his early hunts saw the first edition of *Endymion* and also the Pisa *Adonais* procurable for ten guineas or less, he pondered deeply. There could not be so many of these treasures about—especially in fine condition and in the original boards. The time would come, and that soon, when the world would be seeking them and willing to pay high prices for them (he was actually to see them realize as many hundreds as they had once been priced in pounds). Here was his immediate field, then, with Shelley in the center. It says much for his imagination and courage that at twenty-five, earning a salary well under £4 a week, he gave what was then the record sum of £45 for a superb copy of the Pisa *Adonais;* and a little while afterward another £40 for a set of two Shelley items (from the Glasgow booksellers, Kerr and Richardson)—all original issues. These then-high prices caused a stir in the antiquarian world and gave Wise a reputation. Such bidding required pluck; it also required resources.

---

[3] At 87 years of age he was still walking the earth "without greatcoat, stockings, or underclothing this Christmas," as D. G. Rossetti recorded in 1879.
[4] Mother of Byron's Allegra.

Although at first only earning a young clerk's salary, he had the advantage of living at home—127 Devonshire Road, Holloway, N.[5]—with his parents, as he continued to do until thirty years of age. This meant a substantial economy: Thomas James was a careful sort. Assisted by occasional book deals and other sideline earnings, he was able both to pursue his collecting and to save money for that great chance which comes sooner or later for the commercially ambitious—and which, seized with the cash in hand, leads on to fortune. Sometimes when he had his small but slowly growing capital tied up, he was hard-pressed to meet the demands of his book buying. But he never faltered. He could afford to tease the booksellers about his impending insolvency. "I'm stony broke," he would chaff them. "It looks like 4/9 in the pound for you." They, who believed him to be a wealthy young City merchant, joined in the joke.

V

All this time he had been making rapid progress in the essential-oil business—perhaps more rapid than even Hermann Rubeck, his employer, suspected. Young Wise spared no effort to learn all that was to be learned, and a something—it is said—that he was not intended to learn, in the merchant's office. By the most diligent attention to his and everyone else's duties, as well as by extraordinary perception and opportunism, he soon made himself not only indispensable to but the confident of his employer. Before he was 30, he was Rubeck's chief clerk and cashier. He has been described by an intimate friend as one of the shrewdest buyers on the Produce Market. But in office life he has also been compared to an unflattering Dickensian character in very similar circumstances, although Hermann Rubeck was hardly Mr. Dombey.

This was his daily or city life; and although his rare book

---

[5] It was one of a long row of three-storied, single-fronted houses in a dull, somewhat dingy thoroughfare.

activities were allowed to obtrude into his office routine, it was all part of the young man's scheme—a scheme to be pursued with relentless and indefatigable vigor, and to succeed even beyond his wildest dreams. Once the City was left behind him for his home in that dingy Holloway thoroughfare, his evenings and nights were almost entirely given up to his books, to the research involved by them, to occasional literary meetings (all part of the great scheme), and to private and far-reaching projects as to which his friends were told no more than it was strictly useful that they should know.

The privacy of his room in that Devonshire Road home was jealously guarded. It was his habit to shut himself up there, and work far into the nights except when meetings of the Browning and Shelley Societies, or occasional evenings in town or boating on the Thames, brought necessary relaxation. It has been related by a member of his family that he was visited in this upper room by George Bernard Shaw, T. P. O'Connor, Stopford Brooke, Dr. Furnivall, and Harry Buxton Forman. In this reminiscence, however, is possibly some confusion with his literary society contacts; of which, in his later years of celebrity, Wise was never tired of speaking. Mr. Bernard Shaw's recollection, as written for me, is: "I made his acquaintance when we both belonged to Furnivall's Shelley Society. We were both playboys then. . . . I never visited him privately; and when the Society perished I lost touch with him for many years. Later, when we both became famous, we corresponded, as he was keen on collecting rehearsal copies of my plays (I print little private editions for use in the theatre) and I was the only person he could get them from." Of this sidelight it only remains to be said that, however Mr. Shaw's description may apply to himself, Thomas James Wise was not then, or at any time, a playboy. His life and habits were much too purposeful for that.

Of natural qualifications other than those already mentioned, one was his extraordinary memory. Another was his gift of observation, as an illustration of which this story of his later years may be told here. In a discussion with Sir John Murray, a question arose over a disputed document attached to a manuscript. "You have seen the manuscript; I have not," he told Sir John. "You can judge from the appearance of the pin whether it was placed where it is subsequently to 1900, or whether it is a pin of a century or more ago." It is a clue worthy of Sherlock Holmes. How many today would know that the head of the old-fashioned pin was merely stuck on, and was liable to slip down the stem? [6] It was by such pinpoint observation that Wise developed his faculty for examining books and making his bibliographical descriptions.

This period between the ages of 20 and 30 was most fertile for him in ideas. Not only did he realize the great scope in collecting the famous early nineteenth-century authors, but it occurred to him that there must be living some descendants of those romantic figures. What an inspiration! They would be sure to possess interesting relics, perhaps unpublished pieces, certainly letters; and letters from and to those passionate lovers and erratic geniuses would be revealing. There is often dramatic personal history behind inspired writings. For all the parade of critical commentary in Wise's books, the truth is that he was generally more captivated by the story behind the story than by the work itself.

So he set to business, putting out cautious inquiries here, burrowing like some human mole there, in order to reach the quarries. Bold as he was, not even Wise could have anticipated the harvest he reaped from time to time. Those descendants were doubtless amazed to find themselves traced by the prim, business-like little man who knew so much about their family heroes, of whom he could usually tell some new and amusing stories. What an enthusiastic collector to go to so much trouble! How nice to be so wealthy and to want to buy these old papers and books of which (one suspects in some cases) the possessors were rather tired! And the

[6] Of the kind that the proverb spoke: "It takes ten men to make a pin."

dear man was so generous; at least, that is what some of the descendants thought, knowing nothing about the rare book market.

In 1886, when he was twenty-six, he found out Mrs. Cheltnam, and bought from her Shelley's *Epipsychidion,* which the poet had given to her father, James Henry Leigh Hunt. Next, he traced the son of Sir John Bowring, to whom Mary Shelley gave the MS of her husband's *Hellas;* and this changed hands in the following year. Also he acquired through Harry Buxton Forman (who had bought them from Jane Clairmont's heiress and executrix) Shelley letters and relics of the first importance, and Jane's own series of diaries —so enthralling, and still mostly unpublished.

A few years later he secured one of the seven copies saved from destruction of the suppressed *Œdipus Tyrannus* as the result of finding Lieutenant Colonel Call, the husband of the daughter of the ubiquitous Trelawny, to whom the author had presented the copy. This happens to be one of the comparatively few instances in which Wise recorded the price he paid—£36; and he adds that in 1920 a copy (apparently with far less interesting association) was sold for $6,100 (say £1,220). This last example evidences the shrewdness of his buying. But his reward in hunting down these single items was nothing compared with his amazing scoop when Swinburne's library came to be cleared at The Pines, and with his deals with Charlotte Brontë's husband and George Borrow's daughter—the revealing stories of which will be told later.

VI

It was not only as a book hunter and book buyer that he was keen and farsighted. I remember, at the time he had retired from business and was immersed in the compilation of his great catalogue, telling him of a reader who had written to me asking where or how a copy of one of Wise's privately printed bibliographies could be obtained. I inquired what he did with his spare copies, whether he sold them, and could the reader be advised to write to him? I shall not forget the momentary scene that followed. We were in the room that housed his famous library. Wise leaped off his seat as if he had been severely bitten there, exclaiming: "Sell my books? Never! I am NOT a bookseller." From his extraordinary indignation, and in that sumptuous room surrounded as we were by bookcases crammed with gold-tooled, morocco-garbed treasures, I supposed that I had uttered an incongruity. I murmured an apology: Wise calmed down in an instant; and in the next he was telling me the firm to which he sold all copies beyond those he required himself.

The fact is—although it was not known to me then, nor to 95 per cent of the book world—that for the most of his career Wise was a bookseller. He was the equivalent of what are called in some of the highly commercialized sports the "professional amateur"—the person who makes money out of his playing engagements and connections while posing as unpaid. In other words, he was a private dealer in rare books and manuscripts. The business was done by negotiation—often as "friendly offices" for acquaintances, especially Americans—mainly from his home addresses. Apart from one deceptive instance, he issued no catalogues: there was no need to do so, for he dealt not so much in quantity as in quality. This phase of his activities was kept *sub rosa* with the same skill that he showed in other enterprises.

There is nothing derogatory in dealing in books and manuscripts: on the contrary, it is one of the most esteemed trades, of whose fortunate members many an author has declared his envy. But some explanation (for his clients immediately, and the world ultimately) was later necessary to account for a reputedly wealthy collector of his vaunted independence and character engaging in deals. So there was propagated the plausible fiction that he sold duplicate copies acquired in the process of collecting and improving his collections. If this was truly the case, then Wise had an abnormal number of duplicates, and did amazingly well out of their resale. No doubt he did dispose of a few: most collectors do; but the explanation in general was as fictitious as are the imprints of some of his pamphlets. Light will be thrown in later chapters on his dealings, the full scope of which will probably not be revealed for many years. The subject is introduced now because, although it was in the nineties that the business flourished, it began in the period now under consideration.

VII

A haunt of Wise's in his twenties was the shop of Bertram Dobell, who is now fittingly canonized as one of the illustrious of antiquarian booksellers for his literary discoveries, and for being a good Samaritan to poor poets. This worthy had his shop (started as a stationer's and news agent's on a capital of £10) in Queen's Crescent, Kentish Town—which was convenient for Wise. It was also convenient for Harry Buxton Forman, Wise's very friendly rival in collecting. So handy for both that it was "damned awkward," as Thomas James exclaimed one early morning when both men, laughing to hide their chagrin and confusion, met outside the shop waiting for Bertram to open. They had received one of his catalogues by that morning's post, and were there after the same bargain!

On another occasion Wise called at the bibliopole's shop just before closing. The Dobells were giving a Christmas party for their children. Bertram used to recall the scene: the shrewd hustling young "merchant," attracted by the gay lights and glad tumult from the interior, going to the glass doorway separating shop from domesticity, opening the curtains a few inches, and peeping into the cheery room where the infant Dobells and their school friends were playing. After a long silent contemplation, he turned hurriedly, and with a subdued "Good night" plunged into the darkness of the snow-carpeted street—to make his way to the grim terraced house in Holloway.

The picture supplies another Dickensian hint. Perhaps for a while the busy ambitious young bachelor felt that there was something else in life besides the scramble to find and sell rare books and manuscripts, his daily strivings for mastery with old Hermann Rubeck, and those secret projects now filling his thoughts every spare minute. But the reflection would soon pass. No! He was not ready to settle down in a home of his own. There was so much to do. He had so many irons in the fire.

And there were those literary circles he was getting into. What scope they offered him!

CHAPTER 3

ROBERT BROWNING, HIS "PAULINE," AND OTHER AFFAIRS

Thanks, unwise Wise.
Browning's comment when Wise told him the price
paid for an original *Pauline.*

I

IN THE EIGHTIES poetry was still being read. If the Victorians of that decade did not devour it with the same whole enthusiasm and feeling that their parents and grandparents did, nevertheless cultured taste included not only appreciation of the classic Muse, but an admirable desire to do justice to contemporary poets. Among these was Robert Browning, whose works, with their strange mixture of religious expression and of daring originality of thought, attracted two opposite camps of admirers and fascinated both by some obscurities of meaning. He himself, when asked to explain a passage in one of his early poems, said, so the anecdote goes: "When that poem was written, two people knew what it meant—God and Robert Browning. And now God only knows what it means." Well! if the poet was uncertain, his admirers could excuse themselves for their doubts. But those doubts made them more curious. Why should not they get together and debate them? There were literary societies for the study of dead master poets like Chaucer and Shakespeare. Why not one for a living poet? And so it came about that in 1881 was founded the Browning Society—the forerunner of a series of societies associated with later living writers. It was an immediate success, drawing to it not only those who revered Robert, but also those who loved Elizabeth Barrett Browning

and her *Sonnets* with their revelation that never varies—
whether in an age of stuffy bonnets and crinolines or in one
of shorn hair and short skirts.

The official founder of the society was Frederick James
Furnivall. Any such institution simply had to owe its birth
to him; for had he not the prestige of having formed the
Early English Text, the Chaucer, the Wiclif, and the New Shak-
spere Societies? Dr. Furnivall's record as the fecund father
of literary societies is unique. But he was much more than
that: a fruitful scholar and philologist to whom we owe the
Oxford English Dictionary, a practical idealist, a hard-work-
ing pioneer, a magnificent oarsman who was adored by the
young ladies he taught to row. Something more than a passing introduction of him is necessary here because he figures
pretty considerably and astonishingly in the story of Thomas
James Wise.

The big cheerful bearded scholar was as fearless as he was
industrious. He had a revealing flair for inconvenient truths,
and an inconvenient flair for revealing them. For example,
he was one of the most ardent admirers of the verse of Browning, and an esteemed friend of the man himself, for whom
he did much. When the poet died, his biographers were concerned to make the most impressive show of his pedigree,
giving credence to Browning's fond and often vaunted belief
that he was descended from a noble Anglo-Saxon family that
bore in Norman times the name of De Bruni. This snobbery
was intolerable to Furnivall, whose regard for truth caused
him to make researches which traced the poet's family back
to a great-great-grandfather who was a footman-butler. He
published a long and interesting protest against the biographical suppression of the worthy footman "for the sake of
the contemptible vanity of successors," adding that readers
could not help asking themselves in how many other cases
this kind of thing had been connived at.

DR. FREDERICK JAMES FURNIVALL

Prolific father of literary societies, founder of the *Oxford English Dictionary,* and magnificent sculler. He befriended Wise, taught him his bibliography, but was ill-rewarded.

II

Wise was soon influenced by the vogue for the Brownings and began collecting their writings in 1880. When the Society was founded, he early became a member, taking—young as he was—as active a part in its affairs as the older and more influential members allowed. In 1883 (when he was twenty-three) the committee recorded their regret that the calls on their funds precluded them from publishing the Browning concordance he had undertaken, so they "released him from his promise." In the following year he was elected to the committee, much to his satisfaction. He would henceforth have a voice in its activities. Subsequently he became the Society's secretary for a short time.

The references he was wont to make in later life to his friendship with Robert Browning rather tended to give the impression that it was a long and intimate one. Dr. Thurman L. Hood says it began through membership of the Society, the collector "often calling on Sunday afternoons with questions from his colleagues for the poet to answer (that, at least, was the excuse)."[1]

The introduction was apparently made in 1886 through the kindly interest of Dr. Furnivall; the first of the poet's few brief letters to Wise concerns the visit at which it was made. Wise's own account of the meeting is instructive.[2] One spring morning Furnivall took his young protégé to call on Browning at his home, 19 Warwick Crescent. The aged poet—he was then seventy-six—was found burning letters and documents from an old trunk dragged from the top of the house. How this destruction lacerated the collector's feelings is conveyed. Then Browning fished out two copies of the extremely rare first edition of his *Pauline* (1833), his original essay into print. The little eyes of the visitor widened. "Had I upon the instant asked Browning for one of them, I am convinced

[1] See *Letters of Robert Browning Collected by Thomas J. Wise*. Edited by Thurman L. Hood, Dean of Trinity College, Hartford, U. S. A. (1933).
[2] See his *Browning Library* (1929).

he would have given it to me. But delicacy forced me to hesitate, and I allowed the opportunity to pass," he says. After he had left the house, however, he began thinking how he could make good the regretted lack of enterprise. Furnivall, he declares, suggested that he should write asking for one of the copies, and offering to pay to charity such subscription as might be named. But before the suggestion was acted on, Wise was again in the company of Browning—this time with Dykes Campbell as host—when the poet, walking round the room looking at the books, observed: "I see you have everything of mine, Campbell." "No," was the reply, "I still lack *Pauline*," upon hearing which, Browning promised to send one of the two copies he had just found. "Here," continues Wise, "was an opportunity for me to ask for the other copy. But once more modesty restrained me." But next day modesty was overcome. He wrote to Browning, who replied that, having given one to Campbell, he was keeping the other for his son.

Wise, whenever he talked about the authors he had met, used to lay stress on his friendship with Browning, and to describe him as "a charming man, without any 'side.' You would have taken him for a well-to-do stockbroker." The indications, however, are that the "friendship" was somewhat one-sided. The poet was affectionately demonstrative to friends like "my dear Gosse," and Furnivall, and Dykes Campbell. He kept a strictly correct and "neutral" attitude toward the Society of his admirers (who were "fair game for criticism," as he told Edmund Yates), although he appreciated its usefulness when a little book of his verse had "got itself sold ... at the rate of 2,000 copies very early, and is now reprinting. It all comes of the Browning Societies." [3] Likewise, supposedly wealthy enthusiasts such as our book

---

[3] Furnivall's Browning Society had a family of no less than twenty little (or branch) societies! Both the Browning and Shelley Societies were wound up in 1892. The branch at Girton College had half-a-crown cash in hand, and this the dear girls liquidated in chocolate creams. How perfectly sweet! Browning, very partial to the fair sex, would have approved such a liquidation of assets.

collector were not to be discouraged. But the poet's dozen communications to "Dear Mr. Wise" are either short notes of thanks for the never-failing presentation copies, or slightly longer ones that are mostly courteous, but formal and strictly confined to answering questions.

III

When Robert Browning was a boy, playing "at verses and letters, instead of cricket and trapball," he had a calf love for one Miss Sarah Flower Adams, who was to secure celebrity as the authoress of the hymn "Nearer my God to Thee." She was the inspiration of some verses which the youthful poet wrote, showed to her, and then destroyed. One of them began:

> *Pauline, mine own, bend o'er me—thy soft breast*
> *Shall pant to mine—bend o'er me—thy sweet eyes*
> *And loosened hair, and breathing lips, and arms*
> *Drawing me to thee......................*

A few years later he printed this poem under the title of *Pauline; A Fragment of a Confession* (1833)—the very book that Wise's modesty failed to get for him from the author.[4] "Robert Browning told me," he was never tired of recalling, "that not a single copy of *Pauline,* his first book, was ever sold. A relative gave him £30 to pay for the production and advertising of the little work in a small edition. But not a single copy was sold." There is some evidence to corroborate that Wise was told by the poet of this experience of his first appearance in print. But not content with the telling, Wise—now so keen a collector of autograph material—must needs have it in writing! In consequence we find Browning replying to the request: "If it really does interest you to have my statement 'in black and white,' I willingly repeat that to the best of my belief no single copy of the original edition of *Pauline* found a buyer."

[4] How he obtained his copy of this rarity and the remarkable sequel to the event is told in Chapter 14.

In 1886 the Browning Society—doubtless at the instigation of their energetic young member, Thomas James Wise—produced, in an edition of 400 copies, a "type-facsimile" reprint of this same *Pauline*. It was prepared under the superintendence and editorship of Wise, who asked the author to write an introduction. Browning jibbed, replying dryly: "I really have said my little say about the little book elsewhere, and should only increase words without knowledge"; and he also declined to see the proofs. It is clear that he disliked the idea of the reprint, but consented to it as (in his own words) "a concession to the whim of the more than friendly members of the society." Was such a distinction for this piece of juvenilia distasteful to him (it was in his *Collected Works*)? Or did he suspect that trouble might result from facsimile reprinting? Previously, according to the Society's report for 1884, he had "withdrawn his leave" for the reproduction of *The Ring and the Book*. He was a shrewd man; he knew more about the ways of forgers, pirates, and fabricators than most people. He knew all about Powell, the American forger. He had been taken in by the forged Shelley letters of De Gibler. Wise himself provided examples of Browning's readiness to suspect: as in the case of the purported 1849 printing of *The Runaway Slave*, the story of which is told later. Incidentally, of the *Pauline* edition done by his special permission for members only, Wise was selling a bundle of copies to his agent, Mr. Gorfin, for £2 as late as 1910. But the Society was dead by then.

It was the page-for-page type imitating of the 1833 *Pauline* and of first editions of Shelley that started Wise on his remarkable series of typographical forgeries. We have seen Fullford in 1884 reprinting for him Keats's *Ode to a Nightingale,* but not attempting typographical imitation—no doubt owing to his lack of material. But the idea was in Wise's mind. Now he had taken his work to Richard Clay and Sons—a well-known firm of printers, then in Bread Street Hill, E.C., with almost unlimited type equipment and with men skilled in using it. What ardor he applied to this task of imitating *Pauline* may be gathered from his triumphant comment in his preface: "In all respects save the paper, which it has been found absolutely impossible to match exactly, the present reprint may be considered a very good and precise representation of it." Evidently feeling that there was some call for defense of such efforts at close imitating, he says:

There is a sentiment attaching to the very form in which a book of this description first appeared which is entirely wanting if the same work is perused in another dress; and therefore, failing the original, we are only too glad of the opportunity of providing ourselves with a good likeness of it. It is in this sentiment that the true book lover finds his pleasure, and not in the mere massing together of many volumes, simply because they are "curious" or "scarce," as persons who are not collectors frequently suppose.

The pleading here is specious. But with Wise it is nearly always a case of sufficient for the day is the argument thereof. Keats, sitting in the garden of the Grove at Hampstead, weak in body but with soul inflamed with poetic fire, did not listen less enraptured to the nightingale because it sometimes sang from a neighbor's tree. And his ode to the "Light wingéd Dryad" is not less beautiful, nor less appealing to our sentiment, when read in an edition having a stanza to a page instead of a stanza and a half, as in the first edition. The absurd craze for imitative reprints, that Wise encouraged, will be referred to again. Strangely enough it was himself who, 38 years later, revealed the fraudulent uses to which his own facsimiles were put. In the March (1924) number of the magazine I was editing he made public a long statement, of which the chief part is as follows:

Sir,—May I be permitted, through the columns of *The Bookman's Journal*, to enter a warning against two impudent forgeries of rare books, of which a number of copies appear to have been planted upon the unwary, and which are certainly enjoying an unfortunate success? The two books in question are the first editions of Shelley's *Adonais,* printed in Pisa in 1821, and *Hellas,* printed in London in 1822. The forgeries now circulating have been prepared by taking copies of the very close reprints issued by the Shelley Society to its members in 1886, removing my own introductions, and then rubbing them in dust to impart an appearance of age. That the result is sufficiently misleading is testified by the fact that among the persons who have fallen victims to the fraud are two of the foremost and most widely experienced antiquarian booksellers in London, each of whom was misled by the apparently genuine appearance of the books. How many of the smaller dealers and private collectors have been likewise defrauded, and how many copies of the books have crossed the Atlantic, it is impossible to say. Both books are valuable (the *Adonais* in mint condition is now worth about £350), so the temptation to the fabricator to do his best—or worst—is a strong one.

In the spring of 1886 I produced for the Browning Society a facsimile reprint of Browning's first book, *Pauline.*[5] Almost immediately copies of this reprint, "faked up," were offered as originals. . . .

Coincident with the experimental work on close imitating of *Pauline,* he had still more opportunity in 1886 for typographical experience and for getting acquainted with the range of types of Clay and Sons when he produced the Shelley reprints, which will be dealt with in Chapter 5.

IV

While never encouraged by any warmth in Browning's letters, Wise was extraordinarily thrustful in his to the poet. One contained three queries regarding Robert's poem, *The Statue and the Bust* (1855), that Wise said had been raised by a member of the Society who signed himself—it was averred—"Ball-goer." To this Browning replied: "Dear Mr.

[5] Actually, apart from the papers used, a comparison of Wise's reprint with the original *Pauline* reveals easily distinguishable differences between the types employed. But the fabricator of copies of the reprint to pass for the valuable original would trust that the fake would be bought without expert, or even close, comparison. Long before Wise's warning, both J. H. Slater and H. B. Wheatley exposed the faking of the *Pauline* reprint, the latter commenting: "The forger is abroad whenever prices rule high."

Wise, I have seldom met with such a strange inability to understand what seems the plainest matter possible: 'ball-goers' are probably not history readers, but any guide book would confirm what is sufficiently stated in the poem." He then appends some notes to show what a stupid fellow (whoever he might be) the inquirer was, the last of which concludes: "My vagueness leaves *what* to be 'gathered' when all these things are put down in black and white? Oh 'ball-goers'!" Browning would have been still more sarcastic and pointed had he known that young Mr. Wise, the sender of the queries, made a spurious edition of *The Statue and the Bust.*

Then there was the still more surprising correspondence in August, 1888, when the determined young collector-dealer wrote to the poet about a 28-page printing dated 1849 of Elizabeth's poem, *The Runaway Slave*—to receive the disappointing reply: "I never heard of a separate publication, and am pretty certain such a circumstance never happened. I fear this must be a fabricated affair." Wise, desperately anxious to get the aged [6] poet's authoritative acceptance of the printing as genuine, came back with a clincher—sending a copy of the pamphlet for inspection. Shrewd as Browning was, his suspicions were lulled by the appearance of the print; for he returned the pamphlet with this comment: "I daresay the fact has been that, on the publication of the Poem in America, the American friends (in London) who had been instrumental in obtaining it, wrote to the Authoress (in Florence) for leave to reprint it in England, and that she of course gave her consent—probably wrote the little advertisement. The respectability of the Publisher and Printer is a guarantee that nothing surreptitious had been done." But the fact that it gave the name of Edward Moxon as publisher and Bradbury and Evans as printers did not prove they had produced it. Browning's first opinion that it must

[6] Browning was 76. He died the following year.

be fabrication was correct. The imprints were fictitious. The thing was one of Wise's forgeries.

As a relief to these unpleasanter aspects of Wise's activities, two stories of his collecting of Browning first editions and manuscripts may fittingly come here, although out of their chronology. In 1914, Mrs. Fanny Browning, the widowed daughter-in-law of the poet, sent a tiny lock of Browning's hair to the collector. He had it enclosed under a glass panel let into a superb binding to adorn his copy of another of his forgeries—Elizabeth's *Sonnets* (Reading: 1847)—thus adding value and association interest to a pamphlet whose Day of Judgment had yet to come. Fanny Browning accompanied the lock of hair with a letter in which she wrote in all seriousness: "You remember I said I had sent it to be cleaned, as I fancied it had got moths in it."

Some time after the death of Sir Edmund Gosse in 1928, his son, Dr. Philip Gosse, was having lunch with Wise in the hotel of a Southern seaside resort. A discussion on books led to talk about the Brownings—a natural turn of the conversation because the party included Fanny Browning. Dr. Gosse recalled that when a small boy he, together with his sisters Teresa and Sylvia, always visited 19 Warwick Crescent (which was close to their own home) on Robert Browning's birthdays, taking bouquets. The young visitors were received with delight by the poet, who promptly found chocolates for them. After tea together, Browning, to amuse his little guests, drew pigs for them on scraps of paper. "Those sketches would be even more interesting now," added Dr. Gosse reflectively. "I often wonder where they have got to."—"Oh," replied Wise promptly, and with a laugh, "I can tell you that. They are in the Ashley Library. Your father showed them to me, and I persuaded him to let me have them." Dr. Gosse tells the little story as an example of the collector's omnivorousness.

V

When Robert Browning had passed from the scene of his triumphs and Wise was at the height of his, the book collector and dealer was fond of saying, both in conversation and in print: "I am one of the few persons still living, and I believe the sole remaining man, who broke bread at Browning's table." Again, in his introduction to his *Browning Library*, he speaks of his love of the poet's books and concludes: "Robert Browning was a great poet and a great gentleman, and one of the kindest and most noble-hearted of men."

How strange the psychology of the man who, while writing thus of his affection for Browning and living in his Ashley Library in the daily presence of the bust of the poet, yet knew that he had fabricated five spurious editions of the Brownings! [7]

[7] They were Robert's *Cleon* (1855), *The Statue and the Bust* (1855), and *Gold Hair* (1864); and Elizabeth's *Sonnets* (Reading: 1847) and *The Runaway Slave* (1849). Of two of these forgeries, mention has already been made. The most sensational of the five, however, is the *Sonnets*, the story of which is reserved for Chapter 20.

CHAPTER 4

WORDSWORTH ADVENTURES AND A
NEW FAKE REVEALED

*The occasion is the first upon which a really full & faultless set of
the original editions of the writings of either master has been drawn
together. I very much doubt whether the achievement will ever be
repeated.*

Wise's Introduction to his
Two Lake Poets.

I

IT WAS IN 1884 that Wise turned his attention to Wordsworth. Behind the circumstance is a highly curious story.

In that year, he has recorded in his somewhat affected account,[1] he began the "frequent" habit of paying after-dinner
visits to the home in Manchester Square of the Reverend
Stopford Brooke, whom he had got to know through the
Shelley Society. That ardent bookman's study, on the top
floor of his tall Victorian house, had volumes lining every
wall, heaped on the tables, and piled up on the floor. The
friendly atmosphere and charming disorder probably both
attracted and irritated the young, smart business man; whose
own ideal library was to be a museum-like exhibition of
serried ranks of sumptuous bindings, behind ornamented
glass doors. Anyhow, there in his host's delightful room "we
smoked our honest pipes"—a pretty touch.

One evening Stopford Brooke handed to Wise a description he had received from John Pearson the bookseller, of
a clean, uncut first edition in the original boards of Wordsworth's *Poems* (1807), saying: "This is a book you ought to
take." Wise continues: "I replied that I never bought a book

[1] See *Two Lake Poets* (1927).

36

I could not read with satisfaction, and that, with few exceptions, I derived but little pleasure from the shorter poems of
Wordsworth, whilst the longer ones attracted me not at all."

In reply to this sweeping pooh! pooh! so typical of Wise,
came the kindly host's over-optimistic prophecy: "One day
you'll read nothing else." But that day had not dawned
when Wise, over seventy years of age, added: "The time
when I shall feel driven to revel in the poetry of Wordsworth
to the exclusion, even the comparative exclusion, of the
works of other great poets, is never likely to arise." [2] Could
the poet have known of his bibliographer's intolerance, he
would probably have said that lack of enthusiasm from one
who required to be *driven* to revel in his poetry was no great
loss. To turn one of the *Peter Bell* satires:

> *This Wordsworth verse that did from Nature rise*
> *Mere books of numbered pages were to Wise,*
> *And they were nothing more.*

Notwithstanding the plain hint that his literary taste forbade his buying the rare first edition of Wordsworth's
Poems, he was round at Pearson's the next morning, and
bought the strongly recommended item for three guineas (a
price which was low enough then and makes the mouth
water now). The commercial instinct working after the
smoking of "honest pipes" would tell him that he certainly
ought to overcome his exquisite literary prejudices when
such a bargain was to be had.

The incident is typical of Wise's opportunism. In a way,
he deceived Stopford Brooke, who, hearing the almost indignant protest of his guest against buying anything other than
what it pleased him to read, might well have presumed the
rarity would still be available for himself or another of his
friends. As for the treasure itself, the old drab boards cover-

---

[2] Incidentally, this is not one of the best illustrations of the theory advanced by Mr. Richard Curle (in one of his eulogistic introductions to Wise's
catalogues) that "Mr. Wise collects an author primarily because his literary
sense is appealed to and his literary instinct aroused."

ing what Wise himself describes as "this very satisfactory example of the 1807 *Poems*" were broken. So instead of preserving the book in its original state (as he learned to do subsequently), he had it bound in apple-green levant morocco.

At that time he could no more resist apple-green morocco than Adam could refuse Eve's green apple. He later acquired another copy of Wordsworth's *Poems, in Two Volumes.* This had been in Robert Southey's library, and was still in what is now punningly known as the original "Cottonian" binding with which Edith Southey was wont to clothe her husband's books out of her castoff petticoats and dresses. Was this jolly binding preserved? No! Away it had to go, for the binders to replace it by morocco and gold. So-ho! for the apple-green levant. Much smarter than Edith's faded old petticoats.

But much less interesting.

II

Poets are reputed to be, and indeed often are, the most careless and happy-go-lucky of men—except where their own work is concerned. Then they can be as exacting and meticulous as anyone—plagues to their printers, terrors to their publishers. Of such was William Wordsworth, who must very nearly hold the record for having leaves reprinted (now known as *cancellans*) to alter or correct his work before it went out to the world.

For example, there was his pamphlet, the *Convention of Cintra* (1809), the production of which had its amusing aspect —although Wordsworth was probably far from seeing it at the time. The pamphlet, one of the poet's prose writings inspired by his love of justice, was in the printer's hands. One day, in an idle moment, Wordsworth picked up an old magazine and read a paragraph which made him start. It told of a pamphleteer having been fined £100 and imprisoned in Newgate for a libel "as it was termed" upon a bishop.

The poet was a good deal shaken by the fear that something he had written might be "made a handle for exercising upon my person a like act of injustice." De Quincey was deputed to be the censor of the *Cintra* pamphlet, and if any dangerous passage should be found the printer was instructed to cancel the leaf. "As to expense, that I disregard in a case like this." Such a passage came under the voluntary censorship, and publication was subsequently delayed while the necessary two leaves were reprinted and substituted.

Similar delay occurred in connection with the first publication of Wordsworth's *Lyrical Ballads,* in which Coleridge's *Ancient Mariner* originally appeared. As this is one of the outstanding books in English poetry, the few existing copies of the unamended first edition are naturally classed among the high prizes of book collecting—"the black tulip of that sort of literature," as Swinburne described the rarity that made him "break the tenth commandment into shivers" when he thought of it. Wise, of course, possessed one of the "black tulips."

He also possessed a second copy of the rare *Lyrical Ballads.* It was another tulip, whose blackness now reveals a fake.

III

Wise was very proud of the section of his library devoted to the Lake Poets: on the whole he was right to be proud. Of the five variant issues of the first edition of *Lyrical Ballads* (1798), he possessed three, two of which he claimed to be unique copies. The adventures of the printing and publishing of the ballads make a diverting story. He, with his fondness and ability for pursuing tortuous paths, reveled in it; and his triumphant satisfaction at owning two varieties of the first edition that no one else possessed is not disguised. Some forty pages in his *Bibliography of Wordsworth* (1916) and thirty in his catalogues of 1926 and 1927 are devoted to the "points" constituting the rarity of his specimens. Between 1916 and 1927 he seems to have had his own personal adventure with *Lyrical Ballads;* for only in 1926 and 1927 could he describe the peculiarity of one of his two unique copies—a copy which has since been the object of much inquiry and had the distinction of examination under ultraviolet rays at the British Museum.

This copy, which is of the issue bearing the "J. & A. Arch" imprint, contains a *cancellans*—in this case, a leaf reprinted in substitution for pages 97 and 98. The textual difference between the original issue and the one corrected by the *cancellans* is that on page 97 the second line is altered from "Than fifty years of reason," to "Than years of toiling reason," and on page 98 a poem's title is abbreviated. Wise suggests that this reprinting of the leaf was one of the changes undergone by the book immediately after printing in 1798. To explain why the textual changes made on the reprinted leaf were not followed in subsequent editions, he suggests that the second edition was set up from a copy of the first which had not been corrected by the insertion of the *cancellans*. The alterations thus went unmade, according to Wise, through successive editions until 1836, or 38 years later, when Wordsworth altered the line to read: "Than years of toiling reason."

Wise was the first to call attention to the issue containing this *cancellans* that is apparently peculiar to his collection. If genuine, it constituted one of the most important and valuable of his Wordsworth rarities. But it is a fake—and a bad one at that.

The *cancellans* is printed from a type larger than, and of a face different from, that used for the book. It is a type which had not been designed in 1798 when *Lyrical Ballads* was printed; and therefore the substituted leaf, which could only have been run off at a much later date, is a fraud. With the exception of the paper (which is "all-rag" like that used

Wise (left) and his "twin soul" Clement King Shorter (right)
(see chapters 9, 15, etc.).

97

97

One moment now may give us more,
Than years of toiling reason :
Our minds shall drink at every pore
The spirit of the season..

One moment now may give us more
Than fifty years of reason ;
Our minds shall drink at every pore
The spirit of the season.

(2)

(1)

Reduced reproduction of the upper portion (1) of page 97 of the very rare first issue of the first edition of Wordsworth's *Lyrical Ballads* (1798), compared with the upper portion (2) of the same page of the faked *cancellans,* or substitute leaf, done to alter the second line. The differences in the types are easily discernible, particularly in the page numbers.

for the book), all the other evidence—the appearance of the ink, the size, etc., goes to corroborate that the *cancellans* is a fake.

It happens that the first issue of *Lyrical Ballads* has an admittedly genuine *cancellans* (pages 63-70), which the printer had to produce to substitute for Coleridge's *Lewti; or the Circassian's Love Chant;* and this is in the same type as the remainder of the book. Why should the printer have departed from his practice and the general custom if he really had been called upon to reprint pages 97 and 98 in 1798?

Again it was important that Robert Southey, Poet Laureate and high priest among literary critics, should have both an early and a correct copy of *Lyrical Ballads*. In fact, he received an advance copy containing the genuine *cancellans;* and, true to his book-collecting instinct, he recorded in his copy (now in the British Museum): "The Advertisement [3] and the Circassian Love Chant in the volume were cancelled. R. S." If what may be called the Wise *cancellans* was really produced by Wordsworth's printer, why was it not sent to Southey, as the other was?

The second edition of *Lyrical Ballads* was carefully prepared, the two poets making a number of alterations. There is even documentary evidence of Coleridge warning the printer not to print from an early copy containing the canceled *Lewti.* But he said nothing about any other *cancellans.*

The change of the line to "Than years of toiling reason" appeared in the 1836-7 collected edition of Wordsworth's work. Yet Wise's story is that the poet altered the line in 1798, and for 38 years after allowed edition after edition to come out without the correction—attributing this action to a man so meticulous about his work, which he was constantly revising and reissuing, as Wordsworth was.

Lastly, no other copy of the first edition of *Lyrical Ballads*

[3] I.e., the list of contents, which shows the title substituted for the withdrawn *Lewti.*

with this *cancellans* of pages 97 and 98 is known; and Wise has not a word to say of the provenance of what, were it genuine, would be a copy of the highest importance.

All these considerations are merely supplementary to the main fact that the *cancellans* is condemned on its type. It is possible to theorize that Wise acquired the volume with this faked *cancellans* in the ordinary way of book collecting and was deceived. But it is hardly possible to believe that, when he observed the bibliographical differences and came to consider all the circumstances, he could feel other than suspicious. The question, then, that arises, in view of his connection with the long run of forged pamphlets and pirated editions, is: Why should he lend his authority to establish as genuine this fake *cancellans*, and that by the ridiculous theory that Wordsworth, of all men, had it printed to correct his two poems, and then for 38 years permitted the corrections to remain undone?

Apart from the attempt to fabricate a rarity of great value, the result was that the bibliographical history of such an important book was falsified in the Ashley Library catalogues. Further, that copies of the "J. & A. Arch" issue with pages 97 and 98 uncorrected were forced up to fictitious values—the presumption in the rare-book trade being that naturally, of the copies extant, the majority would bear the *cancellans* or corrected leaf; whereas, in fact, not one is known to exist except Wise's very black tulip.

IV

The discovery in regard to this "unique" issue of the first edition of *Lyrical Ballads* means that other hitherto unsuspected rarities in the Ashley Library will be the subject of investigation in the future. To what extent there has been fabrication of others of the library's rarities may not be known for many years.[4] Nevertheless, Wise's collecting of

4 Another example I have discovered during my researches is described in Chapter 13.

the two Lake Poets was successful in gathering printings and manuscripts of undoubted genuineness and of the highest importance to students of the two authors.

One of his manuscripts is of Wordsworth's nine-line poem on childhood, beginning:

> *My heart leaps up when I behold*
> *A rainbow in the sky:*

and is famous for containing the line which has now passed into everyday language as a saying: "The child is father of the man." But Wise's note on this MS reveals the critical limitations of the bibliographer—and something more.

The manuscript was written by the 72-year-old poet and sent to his publisher, Moxon, in 1842, with the instruction added in faltering script: "The above sonnet I wish inserted first of my Poems refering to the period of Childhood." Comparison of this late script with the definitive printed version shows important differences in four lines. This caused Wise to add the characteristic note to his catalogue description of the MS:

> For some unknown reason Moxon failed to obey the poet's instructions. Not one of Wordsworth's editors has been aware of the revisions, and consequently the text of 1807 has always been reproduced in subsequent editions of the poet's work.

For some equally unknown reason Wise failed to observe —or rather to record—that across the manuscript, in a more faltering script even than the poet's, Moxon (presumably) has written, "Corrected from Mr. Wordsworth's last copy"— indication that the version thus minuted had not been followed.

It is fairly obvious that Wordsworth wrote, from failing memory, the 1842 version only to indicate clearly to Moxon that this was the particular "Childhood" poem to have first place in the series. This hurriedly written script sent with the instruction to his publisher was never intended as a textual revision—as Moxon rightly understood. The four lines as they appear in Wordsworth's imperfectly remembered version are inferior to those in the poem as printed and approved by the poet from time to time.

Which is precisely why, if they knew of what Wise mistakenly calls the "revision," the various editors of the poet have not altered the poem. It was foolish of Wise to boost the importance of this scrap of Wordsworth's writing, with the evidence of what it really was so clearly before him. He had enough MSS of indisputable value in his collection.

V

A privately printed 4-page brochure of Wordsworth's poem, *Grace Darling*, was produced for his own use in 1843. The poem, wrote the poet to Henry Read (March 27, 1843), "I threw off two or three weeks ago ... to do justice to the memory of a heroine whose conduct presented a striking contrast to the inhumanity with which our countrymen shipwrecked lately upon the French coast have been treated." This printing is now a rarity. Because every surviving copy of it that Wise had inspected was inscribed by the author, he states: "There can be no doubt that each example of *Grace Darling* distributed by Wordsworth was given by him personally as a friendly gift."

This is a perfectly reasonable conclusion and in accordance with custom. Authors who go to the trouble of privately printing a piece of their work usually inscribe the few copies and distribute them among their friends. Yet, with the knowledge of what he had written, Wise is silent about the curious feature of that other example of a private Wordsworth pamphlet, the dedicatory verses *To The Queen*.[5] Printed for the author (Kendal, 1846) —"one of the most uncommon of the First Editions of Wordsworth," says Wise. Neither his own nor any other is recorded as being a presentation copy, although the production is of the same class as the *Grace Dar-*

[5] See also Chapter 7, Section III.

ling. That fact is remarkable, though not remarked on. Wise seems to have always a blissful confidence that his readers will accept his conclusions without question or comparison. But there was good reason why a copy of this edition of the verses *To The Queen* had *not* been inscribed by Wordsworth.

It was one of Wise's forgeries, produced long after the poet's death.

CHAPTER 5

SHELLEY STORIES: THE PIRATE
IN FULL SAIL

"By Jove, I will; he was my father's friend!"
Thus Dr. Furnivall, in choice blank verse,
Replied when he was asked by Mr. Sweet
(Sweet of the pointed and envenomed pen,
Wherewith he pricks the men who won't elect
Him a Professor, as he ought to be),
'Twas thus, we say, that Furnivall replied
To the bold question asked by bitter Sweet.
And what that question? Briefly, it was this—
"Why do not you, who start so many things,
Societies for poets live and dead,
Why do not you a new communion found—
'Shelley Society' might be the name—
Where men might worry over Shelley's bones?"
"By Jove, I will; he was my father's friend,"
Said Furnivall: and lo! the thing was done.
                    The Shelley Society, by Andrew Lang.

I

IN THE AUTUMN OF 1885 the idea of a Shelley Society occurred
to Professor Henry Sweet, whose grievance it was that his
services as a philologist were not readily acknowledged. Of
course the fiat of Furnivall had to be obtained for the project.
The father of literary societies must not only be persuaded
to accept the role of paternity, but the literary doctor must
also be the man midwife.

He was as willing as usual—indeed more so in this interesting case. He remembered that his own father, a surgeon,
had attended Mary Shelley at her confinement. The poet,
when he lived at Marlow, had often rowed up the Thames

46

to Windsor, left his man and boat there, and sat on the surgery counter chatting with Furnivall senior. Shelley would refuse all refreshments except a dish of milk and a piece of bread. Although the surgeon did not believe in the poet's theories, he had been delighted with the young man's society.

All this Dr. Furnivall told at the inaugural meeting of the Society at University College on March 10th, 1886. He explained that when Mr. Sweet had asked, "Why not found a Shelley Society," he had replied: "By Jove, I will; he was my father's friend." And proceeded to remark that had the proposal been made with respect to a Tupper or a Gosse [this was a side dig at young Edmund, whose poetical aspirations were once acute] people might naturally have wondered. But as Shelley was one of England's greatest poets, etc., etc., etc.

When Andrew Lang read Furnivall's speech in the newspapers, there followed an incident that led to the production by Wise of one of his most attractive privately printed pamphlets. Like many more of his printings, this one was produced *sub rosa*. It was not until seven years had passed that he revealed his hand by sending Gosse a copy of the pamphlet —drawing from Sir Edmund this reminiscence:

> ... I well recollect that Thursday in March, 1886. I was busy in the garret I used to occupy in the Board of Trade when Lang came in like a whirlwind, and waved a newspaper. He read the report of the Shelley Society's meeting with shouts of laughter, and said "I must do this for the Saturday Review— for Shelley was my father's friend—give me some paper!" "Won't you do it in verse?" I suggested. And right away, seated on the edge of the table and sprawling across it, he scribbled the blank verse, murmuring it out aloud as he wrote. I contributed two or three lines to it as it proceeded. The whole thing was done in fifteen minutes, folded up, addressed, stamped, and sent off with splutters of laughter. You cannot think how delighted I am to possess this charming memorial of a delightful episode....

The opening lines of Lang's amusing poem, with its effective reiteration of Furnivall's "By Jove, I will; he was my father's friend!" preface this chapter, which tells of some strange sequels when "Lo! the thing was done." The poem was promptly printed by Wise in one of his limited editions as *Lines on the Inaugural Meeting of the Shelley Society*. Reprinted for Private Distribution from *The Saturday Review* of March 13th, 1886. The pamphlet appears in Wise's 1895 bookseller's list, which presumably would only be circulated to his clients. He did not include it in his 1905-8 catalogue of the Ashley Library. He had written to Lang about permission to print the *Lines*, but had only received a cold, curt, unfavorable reply.

II

Wise, the 26-year-old bookman, member of the Browning Society, and known to be collecting Shelley, was among the first to be enlisted in the new project. From the beginning, he was one of those who ran the Shelley Society. It was just the field for enterprise that he needed: the activities of the Browningites were rather too circumspectly controlled by men like Furnivall and Dykes Campbell, overwatched by the shrewd and careful poet himself.

This is a very notable period in the development of the Shelley Cult. The poet's sisters were still alive. His son and daughter-in-law, Sir Percy and Lady Shelley, were intensely active—especially the latter—in clearing the poet's name and doing justice to his work. Professor Dowden was nearing the end of long labors on his *Life* of Shelley. Within the Society were two groups: one of scholars like Dr. Richard Garnett, and Dowden, and Furnivall, concerned only with the genius and interpretation of the poet; the other, of collectors like Wise, whose interests were more materialistic.

Something of the division that separated these inner and outer circles is indicated by Miss Olivia R. Garnett, daughter of the British Museum's great Keeper of Printed Books. "My father," Miss Garnett writes to me, "was reticent in this sort of Shelleyan controversial matters, and generally turned off inquiries by non-experts with a humorous expression or a quotation from the Classics. In such a manner he would refer to Mr. Wise, whose cognomen struck him in such connexions as singularly and amusingly inappropriate. Far otherwise was it with reference to Mr. Buxton Forman. . . . If my father met Mr. Wise in person it must have been in the Reading Room." In short, there emerges the conclusion that young Wise's interest in Shelley and Browning was far less that of the student than that of publisher, collector, and dealer. One of the Society's reports even makes the nice distinction. Some of the members of the Committee, including Wise, are grouped as "Shelley Workers"; while others are described as "Students of Shelley." The reading of papers—and admirable many of them were—was a natural feature of both societies. There is no record of a single paper ever having been contributed by Wise. The same observation applies to him in connection with the Browning Society.

But he was at least as active as anyone. The obsession for facsimile reprinting was now upon him, and also the urge to get among the types of Richard Clay and Sons. From the beginning, it was the Society's policy to publish facsimiles of Shelley's writings, and to distribute them to members for the purpose of attracting subscriptions. The printing arrangements were put entirely under the control of Wise. The Reverend Stopford A. Brooke, in an inaugural address, outlined the program, apparently with some misgivings: "It pleases us to have facsimiles of the first editions of Shelley, and other bibliographical curiosities. I do not say that this is a very high ambition, nor that it has anything to do with the love of poetry." Here possibly young Wise or somebody tugged at the clerical coattails, or upset the speaker's glass of water; for the worthy Brooke side-stepped with ecclesiastical agility, continuing: "Yet it is a harmless and innocent fancy. . . . A lover likes everything that puts him in mind of his mistress, even a picture of the room she dwells in." True!

so true!—always providing that the mementos are not faked, nor the picture made by another lover.

Wise lost no time. The Society was launched on March 10th, 1886; and a month later his type facsimile of the first edition of *Adonais* (begun while his Browning Society's *Pauline* reprint was still in preparation) was ready for delivery to members. There followed in the same year type-facsimiles of Shelley's original *Hellas* and *Alastor*, in addition to other publications—all from Clay and Sons; and the program was continued in 1887. The prefatory note to *Hellas* gives an indication of Wise's triumphant feelings about his typographical success: "Of this 1822 edition, the present is as exact a representation as it has been found possible—with types—to obtain ... each 'printer's error,' 'dropped letter,' or other peculiarity of the original being carefully retained."

The young bachelor spent laborious nights in his Holloway home straining over the proofs. He found it fascinating, certainly useful, to make these imitative reprints of rare first editions. What an experience it was for him! Watching for wrong fonts, a comma missing here, a slug (i.e., a space) there; learning the dodges—legitimate dodges—of the printing trade, the publishing trick of working off old edition sheets with new title pages, the canceling of pages, etc., etc. Eagerly he drank of the cup of bibliographical knowledge which was later to bring him fame—the cup now filled at the pumps of the Shelley and Browning Societies from the common well of Richard Clay and Sons.

It is only fair to say that there were other type-facsimiles being produced at this time, although by none to the extent of Wise's manufacturing. That there was money in them, he himself shows in citing the case of Harry Buxton Forman, who, having bought a copy of the elusive first edition of Byron's earliest work, *Fugitive Pieces*, for £70, made a facsimile reprint of it in the same year, 1886. "The profit derived from the sale of the reprint," says Wise, "exactly

equaled the sum Forman had paid for the original copy." [1]
It was a cheap way of acquiring rarities that Wise came to
exploit wholesale.

The Victorian bookmen and collectors were sincere, enthusiastic, and not a little impressionable. The arguments
advanced to them were that the rare first editions of collected poets and prose writers were becoming harder to get
as competition, especially from America, grew; and that it
was the "right thing" to have these facsimile reprints, which
were the best of alternatives and worthwhile substitutes for
the unattainable. In consequence, collectors and librarians
paid their guineas. The reprints multiplied until now they
can be bought in bundles at a shilling a time. The British
Museum and offices of rare-booksellers must echo with the
curses of experts wearied by optimists bringing these type-
facsimiles in the hope that they are rare originals and worth
small fortunes. The same places must also be filled by the
ghostly sighs of the disappointed inquirers.

The production of imitative reprints without proper safe-
guards—i.e., without the use of dated watermarked paper,
and also the facsimile itself bearing a printed statement that
it is a facsimile—is playing into the hands of the unscrupulous. Both the law and printing practice ought to have made
it impossible for such reprints to be made. Whether those
who produced them in 1886 and 1887 appreciated the objec-
tions now made to their work, it is idle to argue. What is
certain is that the typographical experience Thomas James
Wise gained in his considerable share of facsimile reprinting
was utilized in producing the spurious nineteenth-century
pamphlets.

I have met with no evidence of Wise faking his own facsimile reprints. The "doctoring" of individual copies of a
72-page book, for example, the discoloration of paper to give
the appearance of age, would be a long and troublesome

[1] See his *Byron Bibliography* (1932), Vol. 1, page 4.

business, with uncertain results, and possibly immediate risk of discovery. On the other hand, the production of small pamphlets of from 8 to about 24 pages of matter already published, putting on them false imprints, and also dates earlier than those on any printings of the same matter—thus making them appear as rare first editions hitherto unknown —would involve much less labor for far greater return. In the latter case the printers did the work as directed by the clever customer in the background. And that was the highly ingenious idea conceived in the mind of Thomas James Wise about this time. His manufacturing of facsimiles for the Shelley and Browning Societies had now accustomed the printers to accept from him predated title pages.

III

While the young man was now advancing in his business career with Hermann Rubeck and busying himself with the Shelley and Browning Societies, his rare book collecting and dealing went on apace. He surprised me in later years by saying that he had picked up few bargains, explaining that this was due partly to the fact that he insisted on having only the finest specimens, and partly to the fact that he had bought mostly as the result of booksellers reporting rarities to him. He was, however, silent about some of his big coups which, as will be shown, brought him thousands of pounds profit. Perhaps he did not call them bargains.

It was an opportune time for a shrewd, well-informed man like Wise, who realized that books in their original boards and in fine condition, especially books with "points" or association interest, would soon be in greater demand. There were plenty of good things about for those with courage and determination—even bargains. For instance, he called at a bookshop to learn of a man who had just found a first edition of Shelley's *St. Irvyne* in the original state, for which he had paid only a shilling. "Cuss him!" was Wise's comment.

But he had his finds also. An exciting one was in a book auction lot of three volumes containing about 40 tracts on Catholic emancipation. Someone had begun to catalogue the volumes, but had given up the task. Had that cataloguer turned over one more tract he would have come across a rarity—Shelley's *Address to the Irish People* (Dublin: 1812. Price 5d.). Wise's keen eyes spotted it, however; later they stared anxiously at a London bookseller when he in turn examined the volume. Nevertheless, no one else detected the lurking treasure; and presently Wise secured the lot for £2.10. He resold the tracts, with the exception of Shelley's *Address*, to the British Museum for the same sum; so that the Shelley rarity cost him nothing. Subsequently he sold it for £200, when he replaced it by another and finer copy having the association interest that it had been given by the poet to Jane Clairmont.

Another story about Wise, which can be supplemented here, illustrates not only his determination to have the rarest of the rare, but the very romance of collecting. That excessively scarce first edition *Original Poetry* by "Victor and Cazire," Shelley's early work, was suppressed because a poem by "Monk" Lewis was accidentally included in it—and possibly also because the poet's sister ("Cazire") was offended by its publication. *Original Poetry* was so rigidly suppressed, in fact, that for 50 years it was an unknown book. In 1859 a reference to it was found, but 38 more years passed before the first copy came to light at Dorchester in 1898. The find caused a sensation, and Wise captured the unique item—paying £155 for it, according to a letter from him to me. In 1903 a second copy was found at Barnsbury, London; being a slightly taller copy containing words erased in the other. It had been bought for sixpence by an old gentleman who died in ignorance both of its authorship and of its great value, bequeathing it among other effects to his housekeeper. Of course, Wise had to have this one; it cost him £600 at auction (he was well off then), and he sold his original copy

to the American collector, John H. Wrenn. It now reposes
in the Wrenn Library of the University of Texas. Then a
third copy came to light. It was notable for containing the
autograph inscription: "Given to me at Eton by the Author
Percy Bysshe Shelley, my friend and schoolfellow. 1810.
W. W."—i.e., William Wellesley, 4th Earl of Mornington.
Wise was fortunate enough to pay no more than £600 for it,
selling the copy he held to that great American collector
Henry E. Huntington. Thus, the only three copies of this
Shelley rarity with such a romantic history all came into
Wise's hands.

"During the first 20 years of my search for Shelleyana," Wise
recalled, "I met with no opposition I was unable to defeat,
and Mr. [F. R.] Halsey of New York became my first serious
and successful competitor."[2] There in his own words is the
determination of the man.

It was with Halsey that Wise had an auction-room duel
in 1903 for the Shelley political pamphlet, *Proposals for an
Association of those Philanthropists who convinced of the
inadequacy of the Moral and Political state of Ireland ... are
willing to unite to accomplish its regeneration.* Only one
other copy of this rarity was known at the time; and it was
anticipated that there would be a keen fight for this second
copy, which, when Wise was a boy of ten, had been catalogued
for sale at £10. The protagonists did not appear, being represented by agents. Wise left with the auctioneer, Mr. Thomas
Hodge, of Sotheby and Company, an instruction to "bid for
it to an amount limited only by his judgment." Not for a
moment did he anticipate defeat, he says, although why not
it is difficult to see. Anyhow, the fight came on. At £530 the
auctioneer exercised his discretion, and Wise lost the rarity to
his New York rival. His disappointment was acute—although
the auctioneer, who had sacrificed his own interest for the
sake of his client, assured him he was well out of the business,
that the price would have gone soaring up, and that Wise

2 See *A Shelley Library* (1924).

was certain to get another copy at a smaller price. But he never did.

IV

The foregoing stories have been selected as illustrative of the adventure of Wise's Shelley collecting. Two others, of the more involved course his career was now taking, should be told here.

In 1887 Thomas James Wise became Charles Alfred Seymour. The object of this disguise was to mislead any unsympathetic person who might chance upon a copy of *Poems and Sonnets. By Percy Bysshe Shelley. Edited by Charles Alfred Seymour, Member of the Philadelphia Historical Society* (Philadelphia: 1887). Of course it was printed for "Private Circulation Only," and as usual "Limited to 30 copies"; and of course the Philadelphia imprint was false. Wise's long preface is a mixture of cynical humbug and wholesale quotation from Dowden.

These *Poems and Sonnets,* which were originally contained in a manuscript volume, express Shelley's feelings for the comely and seductive Harriet, his first wife, at a time when they were happy in the full ardor of fresh and mutual love. "Thou wert the inspiration of my song," he dedicated the volume to her:

> *Then press into thy breast this pledge of love,*
> *And know, though time may change and years may roll,*
> *Each flowret gathered in my heart*
> *It consecrates to thine.*

The poems remained in manuscript until they came into the possession of Professor Dowden, to be included in his *Life* of Shelley. Now we come to Wise's justification for the imposture. He asserts that "Dowden, Rossetti, Forman, and *other friends* were with me in my desire to have these poems in a convenient form" [the phraseology should be particularly noticed]. "But Lady Shelley expressed dissent (as she did with most projects connected with Shelley not originating directly with herself) although she held no interest whatever in the copyright of the verses." [Then why was Lady Shelley's permission sought—if it was sought?] "To avoid discussion with her Ladyship the name of Charles Alfred Seymour was invented, and Philadelphia was selected as the nominal place of printing."

Wise did not include this Shelley "first edition" in his *Ashley Library Catalogue* of 1905-8; but he described it fully in his big *Catalogue* of 1922-1936, and his chuckling justification also says that the book was printed in London by Clay and Sons, and prepared and edited by him in collaboration with Professor Dowden—who, it is alleged, "elected the mythical Charles Alfred Seymour to the equally mythical Philadelphia Historical Society." But Dowden's life of Shelley, in which these *Poems and Sonnets* were first printed, was issued in November, 1886. For Wise, alias Seymour, to reprint the poems in a separate edition in 1887 and call it a first edition looks like an attempt to manufacture a rarity. Moreover, Dowden's letter to Wise included in the Ashley Library copy hardly confirms his collaboration in the affair. He writes to his "friend":

My dear Sir,   Dublin. Aug., '88.
    You are very good to give me (on behalf of "Mr. Charles Alfred Seymour") the beautiful quarto. When a gentleman of the road makes you stand and deliver, and then courteously hands you back your purse, you can do no less than make a bow and say that he has the manners of a Prince. . . .

No gentleman of the road, wise or unwise, could have mistaken the sarcasm here.

But, having, in the pleasantest way possible, called Wise a highwayman, Professor Dowden evidently thought that there was a more fitting description to be applied. His letter continues:

And so I feel to that amiable member of the Phila. Hist. Soc. He has done his work with the greatest care and correctness as far as I can see, and I hope you will greet him from me in the words of Shelley in his Homeric hymn which tells of the light-fingered doings of the first of pirates . . . I will keep the veil of darkness over his misdeeds, but I fear I cannot help him to the "other songs."

What had happened needs no explanation. Dowden's letter does not even require to be read between the lines. The fact is that now, by 1887, the pirate was in full sail.

V

There is in the Ashley Library a series of six important little volumes of Shelley letters. Their abbreviated titles with the alleged dates of printing are as follows: [1] *Harriet Shelley's Letters to Catherine Nugent* (1889); [2] *Letters . . . to Jane Clairmont* (1889); [3] *Letters . . . to Elizabeth Hitchener,* 2 vols. (1890); [4] *Letters . . . to William Godwin.* 2 vols. (1891); [5] *Letters . . . to J. H. Leigh Hunt.* 2 vols. (1894); and [6] *Letters . . . to Thomas Jefferson Hogg.* Vol. 1 only. (1894). These letters, it should be understood, are by the poet, with the exception of those in the first volume. Although Wise admits in the *Ashley Library Catalogue* (Vol. V, page 104) that all these were his publications, an examination of them shows mysterious characteristics. They are all "Privately Printed," but bear neither publisher's nor printer's imprint. The first four contain no identification with Wise; but the fifth (which came out after a lapse of three years from the date of the fourth) and finally the interrupted sixth work, are identified, and bear the Ashley Library book device at the end.

It is obvious from the volumes themselves that the first four were issued surreptitiously. Why the suppression of the imprints? Why, with the exception of Harriet's letters, the absence of any reference to the source of the material? Why the cataloguing of them in such an inadequate and uncandid way? I was for a long time mystified. Then, in the same week that brought a revealing communication from America,

I was shown a letter written by Wise, dated January 13th, 1893. Both communications refer to Shelley's *Letters ... to Elizabeth Hitchener*—that sex-repressed schoolmistress who, for a short time, was the "soul-sister" of the great poet; but who was soon to be seen by him as that "ugly hermaphroditical beast of a woman," that "brown Demon" whose avaricious jaws snapped at a pension of £100.[3]

The letter from America was written to me by Mr. William H. McCarthy, of the Wrenn Library, University of Texas, and contained the following:

You select for inquiry one of the Shelleys we very much would like to own! Since the Carter and Pollard book, that Shelley item has struck me as having marks of being an overture to the forgeries themselves. We have proof sheets of the first edition of Shelley's *Letters to Elizabeth Hitchener*, heavily corrected throughout. These proofs are stamped with Clay's regular proof-sheet stamps of various dates in 1887 and 1888, but the title page has a New York imprint dated 1886. There was an ambiguity about the ownership of these letters, Elizabeth Hitchener having disappeared through a Continental marriage, leaving the MS in the possession of an attorney. He lost track of her and her heirs, and the trial New York imprint with the faked date were apparently planned to obviate trouble. The small edition was not run off, however, until 1890, and the imprint was given then as London. Trouble must have blown over by ... 1908. ... The entry for these proof sheets in the Wrenn Catalogue uses the title page of the 1890 edition, and says nothing about a projected New York imprint. These proofs were *a gift* from Mr. Wise to Mr. Wrenn.

[3] Her story is summarized in one of the admirable letters of Harriet, Shelley's unfortunate first wife, to whom biography now does justice as his best love. Harriet writes to Catherine Nugent, November 14th, 1812: "The lady I have often mentioned to you, of the name of Hitchener, has to our very great happiness left us. We were entirely deceived in her character as to her republicanism, and in short everything else which she pretended to be. We were not long in finding out our great disappointment in her. As to any noble disinterested views, it is utterly impossible for a selfish character to feel them. She built all her hopes on being able to separate me from my dearly loved Percy, and had the artfulness to say that Percy was really in love with her, and [that it] was only his being married that could keep her within bounds.—It was a long time ere we could possibly get her away, till at last Percy said he would give her £100 per annum. And now, thank God, she has left us never more to return."

The other communication is from Wise to a London bookseller and helps to complete the explanation of the *Hitchener Letters* mystery. Wise is writing, three years after his publication of the *Letters,* because the bookseller had copies for sale, guessed or knew that there was some difficulty about the publishing, and naturally asked questions. Wise explains that the possessor of the original letters was a Mr. Slack, who had allowed him to take copies of them upon his giving the undertaking that they would not be circulated among outsiders. Wise says he does not desire to incur the owner's displeasure, chiefly because he anticipates buying the originals at some time. He adds that he does not wish to seem to be going back on his undertaking of honor, and indicates that he does not wish publicity to be given to the publication—presumably by having it advertised for sale in a catalogue.

This letter exemplifies the liberties which Wise took with the truth in his dealings and correspondence. Actually what happened was that a Mr. H. J. Slack, of Forest Row, Sussex, had allowed William Michael Rossetti to copy these letters solely for future use in a Shelley compilation by Rossetti that was never published. Wise borrowed the transcript, and made his privately printed edition without the knowledge of Rossetti or Slack. Subsequently he seems to have feared trouble; and in the autumn of 1888 he attempted to buy the originals—Rossetti, now cognizant of the printing, suggesting to him to offer Slack an indemnity against all possible claimants for the use which had been made of the letters; for "I am quite persuaded there will be none such, and you will get off scathless." How the business ended is not clear from Rossetti's correspondence with Wise (Ashley Coll.). What is clear is that Wise printed Shelley's letters to Miss Hitchener secretly and without authority.

These facts about the origin of his volumes of the *Hitchener Letters* illustrate the surreptitiousness of his publishing methods. The Clay proof sheets in the Wrenn Library are important as showing his use of a false title-page date and faked imprint in 1887. Further, the *Hitchener Letters* were not the only ones in the Shelley Series to be so printed. Apparenly he was going to issue a similar volume of Shelley's *Letters to Robert Southey and Other Correspondents.* 1888. London: Privately Printed—described in the Wrenn Catalogue as "The Revised Proof of the First Edition, with corrections in the 'handwriting of the Editor, Mr. T. J. Wise. ... The volume was never completed"—a description passed by Wise, who edited the catalogue. When the Ashley Collection came to be removed to the British Museum, a set of page proofs on vellum of this item was found. Contrary to Wise's practice, even in the case of his suppressed publications, he made no mention of this projected "First Edition" in his own catalogues; probably because its false imprint would require explanation. For its title-page imprint reads: "1886. New York: Privately Printed. (Not for Sale)." To complete the exposure of this projected publication it has to be added (1) that the printing of this "New York" publication was done for him by Clays; and (2) that the Shelley Letters to Southey had already been published in 1881 by Professor Dowden in his Appendix to *The Correspondence of Robert Southey with Caroline Bowles.*

Wise's explanation in the *Ashley Catalogue* for the abrupt stoppage of the series of Shelley correspondence volumes (of the sixth and last selection in 1894, Vol. 2 never came out) is that "I had proposed to print the whole of the letters of Shelley arranged in volumes each of which was to contain the letters addressed to one particular correspondent. But the preparation by Mr. Roger Ingpen of Shelley's correspondence complete in one series rendered it unnecessary to continue my own work, and the project was relinquished accordingly." Unfortunately for that explanation, which leaves so much to be accounted for, the fact is that Ingpen's edition of the complete correspondence did not appear until

1909—twelve years later. If everything was straightforward, if there was no objection to his procedure, why so abruptly stop (even halfway through the last work) this production of correspondence of the highest importance in volumes that he could claim to be genuine first editions—unauthorized though they were?

These six Shelley publications had all to be bought by the British Museum Library. Not one was sent in accordance with the requirements of the Copyright Act or as a gift from a Shelley student, worker, or whatever the publisher may be called.

VI

To conclude the account of Wise's activities with the Shelley Society, that institution, which was popular enough in its early days to secure 400 members, got badly into debt. For this, the Society's stage production of *Hellas*, involving a loss of £90, was largely blamed. But it is now apparent, from private correspondence put into my hands, that the expenditure on those facsimile reprints was the greater cause. In the Society's first year, Wise's printing (over which he had entire control) at the works of Clay and Sons came to £190. In the next year, from January 10th, 1887, to January 17th, 1888, Clays' printing bill had gone up to £311 out of the Society's total expenditure of £412. Eventually, in the nineties, the Shelleyites found themselves in debt, mostly to their printers, to the extent of £800—and subscriptions falling off! Clays were patient: they looked to Wise, by whom they were much impressed. But there is a limit of credit to be given, even to literary societies backed by eminent and respectable gentlemen. An arrangement was made for the debt to be paid off at the rate of £100 per annum by private levies on a few of the leading members. Here, for example, are the chief contributors for two years to pay the piper for the facsimile-reprinting tune called by Wise:

1893	£	1894	£
W. M. Rossetti	13	W. M. Rossetti	14
Dr. Furnivall	10	H. Buxton Forman	18
H. Buxton Forman	13	R. A. Potts	18
R. A. Potts	13	T. J. Wise	18
T. J. Wise	13	[John] Todhunter	5
A. N. Other	3	Dr. Furnivall	10

Wise, in conversation, used to be fond of recalling that he put his hand in his pocket to pay for the Society's losses on the theatrical venture. But that he got some return for his own levied contribution (apart from the invaluable typographical experience at Clays) he himself partly discloses. In his catalogue there are certain Shelley publications whose presence called for some explanation. So he has this note: "When the Shelley Society issued under my superintendence its series of type-facsimile reprints of a number of the original editions of Shelley's works, I took advantage of the opportunity of having the type set for some of them [4] specially reimposed to suit a crown quarto page, and printed three copies of each upon fine vellum. Each was printed with a certificate signed by the printers Messrs. Richard Clay and Sons, Ltd." Further, his private bookseller's list of 1895, which will be dealt with later, contained under the heading "Shelleyana" no less than 19 pamphlets of papers read to the Society. These pamphlets, with two or three exceptions, were all run off for Wise from the type set for the Society's *Records*, after reimposition and provision of new preliminaries. Limited to small editions, of which the authors were sometimes (but not always) given a few complimentary copies, they were a publishing side line of Wise as a "Shelley Worker"—and not an unprofitable one either. And, as in the case of the *Pauline* facsimile reprint, "done for members of

---

[4] In all, nine books.

the Browning Society only," he was—as late as 1910—selling
to his agent, Mr. Herbert Gorfin, a bundle of Shelley Society
publications for £6.

It may be reasonably conjectured that Messrs. Rossetti, Furnivall, Potts, Todhunter, and Buxton Forman did not manage
to get out of a bad business in the same way.

CHAPTER 6

REVELATIONS OF THE CONTEMPORARY
DIARY OF MR. Y. Z.

I du believe in bein' this
Or thet, ez it may happen
One way or t'other hendiest is
To ketch the people nappin';

It ain't by princerples nor men
My preudunt course is steadied,—
I scent wich pays the best, an' then
Go into it baldheaded.

The Biglow Papers, by J. R. Lowell.[1]

I

ONE OF THE most debated questions—hitherto unanswered—in
connection with Thomas James Wise and his spurious nineteenth-century pamphlets is: When did the manufacture of
the forgeries begin? The authors of the *Enquiry into the Nature
of Certain Nineteenth Century Pamphlets* (which will be dealt
with later) observe: "The actual dates between which the
forger was engaged in production cannot, of course, be precisely determined. Kipling's *The White Man's Burden* shows
that he was at work as late as 1899." For the earliest indicated
date, they mention 1886, the year Wise "discovered" Dr.
W. C. Bennett's copies of Elizabeth Barrett Browning's *Sonnets* with the Reading: 1847 imprint. But when the *Enquiry*
was written, its authors did not know that subsequently Wise
was to retract his highly romantic story of how the things
came from Bennett—hence the date 1886 means nothing as
a guide here. They are on certain ground, however, in men-

[1] The American poet, when Minister in London for the United States,
was a member of the Browning Society.

64

tioning 1888, for we have seen the collector in August of that year bringing forward his spurious "first" edition of *The Runaway Slave* in order to entrap Browning. This year 1888 is also the earliest assigned (at the time this chapter is being written) by the British Museum Library's catalogue as the date of production of any of these forgeries.

There is one source from which light might have been thrown on the question of dates—indeed, on the whole story of this unparalleled manufacture of forgeries, the record of which is in the Appendix. That source, naturally, would be the printing house that did the forger's work. Unfortunately, the records of Richard Clay and Sons are no longer available. Mr. Cecil Clay, the present managing director of the firm, tells me that in 1911—consequent upon a decision by the Board of Directors—all the firm's old correspondence was destroyed. It is useless to lament the destruction of what might have been so revealing. But there is other evidence— circumstantial though it may be. It is an axiom in our Courts of Law that circumstantial evidence is often the most convincing. Many criminals are convicted on it.

In the case of some of these nineteenth-century literary forgeries there is contemporary evidence not only about the date of their manufacture, but about the forger.

II

In the course of gathering material for this study, I made the acquaintance of one whose father had been a well-known and highly esteemed member of the literary circles of the seventies, eighties, and nineties. There followed a delightful and memorable visit to the home of the son. Our initial talk naturally concerned Wise. Unexpectedly came the question to me: "Would you be surprised to learn that at the time the pamphlets were being fabricated his connection with them was known?"

Myself: "Hellup! That it was known Wise was actually producing the forgeries?"

My host: "Yes! There were evidently a few people who knew the source they came from."

Myself: "That news is indeed important. Is it hearsay, or is there evidence for it?"

My host did not reply for a few seconds. Then he rose ... went to a bookcase ... selected a small volume ... returned to his chair facing me ... opened the book at what seemed to be an already-marked place. These things were done with a silent deliberation that was impressive. At last: "This is my father's diary for the year 1888. See what he says there," said my host, handing me the open manuscript volume and indicating an entry. There I read under the date January 11th, 1888:

... Went to Shelley Society meeting. At this gathering Wise, Forman, Tegetmeier, Furnivall, Rossetti, &c were there, but not Dr. Salt, whom I had expected to see. Wise is still proceeding on his wild career of reprinting or pirating Browning, Shelley, Swinburne, &c.

It is unfortunate that for the time being the writer of this diary must remain under the anonymity of Mr. Y. Z. His identity would reveal with what authority it speaks. But after it had been shown to me without the least reservation or condition, and also after its owner had related circumstances which have assisted me in reaching other conclusions in regard to Wise, he provided a second surprise by stipulating that "in anything you say I do not wish my father's or my name mentioned at all." Notwithstanding the absence on my part of any promise as to the use of the material shown— material that was bound to influence me—I have come reluctantly to the conclusion that in the circumstances the request not to divulge names is one that in fairness ought to be complied with. But I hope that in due course the amiable and proud possessor of the diary will agree to this veil being lifted from a figure to shroud which there has been so re-markable a combination of design and accident.

This diary entry says more than is perhaps at first evident. Taking the date January 11th, 1888, in relation to the statement about "still proceeding on his wild career," the reference connotes that Wise's particularized activities covered an appreciable part, if not all, of the immediately preceding year, 1887—it may even have referred back to 1886. Next, the description "wild career" conveys not only the diarist's very proper condemnation of Wise's pursuits, but that they were already considerable in extent. He would not have used such sweeping terms in relation to two or three reprints or un-authorized printings. Next, we come to the objective words "reprinting or pirating." It is clear beyond a doubt—not only on the knowledge that the diarist proceeds to reveal, but on the fuller information we now possess—that he did not intend the expression "reprinting" to be interchangeable with "pirating." Diary entries such as this are often written hurriedly; the conjunction "or" in such a case is commonly used where "and" is really intended. What the diarist meant here—and shows indisputably that he meant—was "reprinting *and* pirating."

The proof is thus: The diarist, as a member of both the Shelley and Browning Societies, would know that Wise had done type-facsimile reprinting of both Shelley and Browning. These were activities open and aboveboard. But, as he never did any mere facsimile printing of Swinburne, the term "pirating" must refer at least to that author. The preceding chapter has shown that it did, in fact, also apply to Wise's publications of Shelley's *Poems and Sonnets,* and to some, if not all, of the volumes of his *Letters.* Lastly, the term "pirating" is ambiguous. Leaving aside the question of any unauthorized printings of Shelley, the diarist, at that early date, was perhaps at a loss how to describe the printings of Swinburne that he knew emanated from Wise—as the following pages show they did. So in his hurriedly written diary

entry he grouped the Swinburne things with the "piratings."
But they were worse than that.

III

Thanks to Mr. Y. Z. and his diary, the beginning of Wise's
"wild career" can be fixed as not later than 1887, and possibly 1886 (when he was 26 or 27), and the details can also
be amplified. In 1888, some months after the entry was written, there were advertised for sale in the secondhand-book
catalogue of Messrs. Matthew & Brooks, of Bradford, Yorks,
certain privately printed items of which the diarist, evidently
in wonderment, told Wise. That collector-dealer-publisher
was so moved to wrath that he swore. He damned as only
an Englishman damns. And the reason? That Matthew and
Brooks were asking prices too low for these books!
    It seems incredible that a book collector would make such
a complaint. But in this case Wise did not want to buy: he
wanted to sell. The explanation is that two of the three books
in the Matthew and Brooks catalogue were his own falsely
dated productions—namely Swinburne's *Cleopatra* (1866)
and his *Siena* (1868). Wise told the diarist that Mr. Brooks
had these pamphlets at the cost price of half a crown apiece,
(about half a dollar) which was why he could catalogue them
as cheaply at 3/6— damn him! He could have asked half a
guinea easily. And side by side with these he was asking six
guineas for D. G. Rossetti's pamphlet *Hand and Soul* (1869).
What a damn shame! To complete the explanation of Wise's
bitter anger, it has to be added that his *Siena* is now condemned as a forgery, and the *Cleopatra* classified as a suspected forgery. And as the diarist could refer to them as
early as January 11th, 1888, it follows (Wise having produced
no other Swinburne printings at that date) that both were
fabricated in 1887—if not 1886.

IV

Something needs to be said here about Wise's initial marketing of the forgeries.[2] The manufacture of them was only the first part of the business: there remained the more difficult part—the establishing of them and their sale: the reaping of the harvest. It has been mentioned in the opening chapter that he was almost solely responsible, through his bibliographies and catalogues, for establishing these spurious "first" editions, and making them the desiderata of the collecting world. Examples of the clever ways in which this was effected will transpire later. The reason for releasing a few copies of the pamphlets at cost price to provincial booksellers like Matthew and Brooks is doubtless that he realized the need for getting some copies into circulation as far removed from him as possible. It was not desirable that they should all emanate directly from him: a circuitous distribution would make them look more genuine. He himself would see to it that their values were written up. If he let a few copies go cheap, he could make his profit on the rest of the supply in his hands. By the autumn of 1888, the forgery ramp was at high pressure, and he was beginning to get his profits— mainly through his private book dealing and through indirect channels.

Instances of sales by indirect methods are provided by the British Museum Library's list of acquisitions of the now condemned pamphlets. On August 16th and October 23rd, 1888, the authorities bought Mrs. Browning's *The Runaway Slave* and George Eliot's *Brother and Sister* for five and three guineas respectively from one E. Schlengemann, a fellow employee of Wise's in Hermann Rubeck's firm. In the following year the Museum bought copies of the Swinburne *Cleopatra* (catalogued by Mr. Brooks at 3/6—damn him!) for £5.5., two Ruskin pamphlets for £2.2. each, and the Matthew Arnold *St. Brandon,* also for two guineas. The vendor in these latter

2 E.g., Chapter 9, Sections IV and VI.

cases was Hermann's son, Otto P. Rubeck, with whom we shall find Wise entering into an important partnership in the city.

In between the selling of these copies to the British Museum, Wise presented three of his spurious Swinburne printings to that institution. It may be reasonably assumed that the officials of our Record Office of Literature never dreamed in their worst attacks of private indigestion that the generous donor was the fabricator of both his gifts and those other pamphlets on which they had been innocently spending the nation's money. It is equally feasible that this consideration was not absent from the mind of the astute young builder of the Ashley Library. But it is an ironical thought, in view of the nation's ultimate purchase of that Library, that it was partly built out of the profits of these forgeries. If he got nothing on the swings when he released a few of the pamphlets at the cost price of half a crown each, he made up on the roundabouts when the same worthless frauds immediately brought him from two to five guineas each. He was to make even better prices than these—that is, when his gigantic bibliographical and cataloguing publicity schemes got working. Some of the pamphlets were to acquire values—fictitious as themselves—of up to £100 each in some cases.

Thus in the eighties did the young man "scent wich paid the best, and go into it baldheaded." A posthumous acknowledgment is due to our Mr. Y. Z., who would surely not regret that his Diary had been the means of throwing light on the mystery of Thomas James Wise and his nineteenth-century forgeries.

CHAPTER 7

WOMEN, WINE, & FRIENDS: THE ROLES OF BUXTON FORMAN AND EDMUND GOSSE

Why should you grudge me lyre and laurel,
O toothless mouth, O soundless maw?
I never grudged you bell and coral,
I never grudged you troughs and straw.
Algernon Charles Swinburne.

I

THESE WERE hectic days for Wise in the eighties when he was forging ahead, mastering trade and trader of essential oils, making his type-facsimiles, printing those mysterious little pamphlets, attending meetings of the literary societies (a little cynical, it may be hazarded, about their unsophisticated devotees). It was a life of driving work, ceaseless scheming, severe concentration. His script in those days had just the same characteristics as in his late years—scrawling, sprawling script, showing hand and pen hopelessly unable to keep pace with his ideas and the urge to get things done. He was the human dynamo working at top speed. Did the old-young man never relax? Oh yes! There were times when the bookworm turned. He had his off days—or nights. There was in him a dash of the Rabelaisian—a dash that reveals itself in his books.

He liked going to the theater, especially to music halls of the type whose passing is now lamented: those with the open bars running alongside the stalls, where the whiskered Victorian beaux could sip champagne or sherry and keep an eye on the billowing petticoats of the chorus at the same time. On such occasions young Wise left his bibliographical and other cloaks in the Baptist home at Holloway, and went up West. One night, in '88, he joined a party of officers from the P. and O. *Verona*. The program began at the Alhambra; where it ended is not recorded. But he did tell an intimate friend that he had his gold tiepin—a very posh pin, heart-shaped, and set with a diamond—pinched by some something girl. And he added with undisguised relief that he got into no trouble whatever. He was not always so fortunate, however, in his escapes from the verse and letters of immortal poets and the inks and types of mortal printers. After one such occasion he insisted on showing the fevered instrument of mischance to his office colleagues, much to their embarrassment—males though they were.

Thomas James Wise was never a bibliophilic recluse. No Dryasdust was he—as doubtless many a guest realized when, triumphant at last in his celebrity and wealth, he would produce the whisky decanter and (with a merry twinkle of his keen eyes) some of the "naughty" manuscripts he had acquired.

II

We have seen how Wise's membership of the Browning and Shelley Societies introduced him into some of the literary circles of his day. This led to a few lifelong associations with men of letters, who put their knowledge at the disposal of the reputedly rich collector always so generous with his little privately printed first editions. For the most part, his relations with men like Furnivall, Stopford Brooke, Dykes Campbell, and Edmund Gosse depended on the communion of book-collecting interests rather than on friendship. Such visits as he paid at this time were usually made in the evenings when the recipients had dined.

It was in 1885 apparently that there began the long and fruitful association with Henry Buxton Forman (1842-1917), a Controller in the General Post Office, where he was sometime Second Secretary. He was also a most successful book collector; and as a student and editor of Keats and Shelley he did useful work. Wise, in conversation, used to give the impression that it was himself who was the pioneer in Shelley collecting and bibliography. The truth is that Harry (as he preferred to be called) Buxton Forman was the complete Shelley expert when Wise was a groping novice in the same line. But Tommy saw to it that his friend was denied the honors. In 1886 there was published *The Shelley Library An Essay in Bibliography* by Forman, a book of 128 pages crammed with the most valuable and surprising information. Nothing like it had been done: it is the very fountainhead of Shelley bibliography. Thereafter the collecting and bibliographizing of that poet was comparatively easy. Nevertheless, the reader will look in vain throughout Wise's books for one solitary tribute to this work of his old friend to which he was so greatly indebted. Instead, there is an endeavor to divert attention from it. Wise had to catalogue his copy, of course; but he adds: "No further portion of this projected work was produced"—a note well calculated to put off anyone interested. But that it is deliberately misleading by the use of the word "projected" is obvious from the work itself; for Forman makes it clear that this Part 1 deals with Shelley's first editions and their reproductions; the second part, which for some reason he never completed, was to be devoted to minor and miscellaneous matter. Even if it was an "essay" and had the faults of most pioneer efforts, it was a source book; it had considerable merits; and it was extremely useful to Wise. His treatment of it was shabby in a bibliographer, and mean in a friend.

Much the same thing happened regarding the bibliography of Mrs. Browning. Here again, Forman was the pioneer and allowed his material—*Elizabeth Barrett Browning and her Scarcer Books* (1896)—to be printed in the *Literary Anecdotes* (1895-6), produced by Wise and Sir W. Robertson Nicoll, editor of the *British Weekly*—surely one of the most curious combinations ever seen in literary harness; though

Nicoll was very much the sleeping partner in the affair. Publisher Wise made his usual off-print edition of the E. B. Browning bibliography; but he did not send a copy to the British Museum—the very first place to which such a book ought to have gone.

Apart from obligation as to a pioneer, Wise was under a private indebtedness. Harry Buxton Forman was used in the furtherance of Wise's schemes to boost his spurious first editions. There were, indeed, other contemporary bookmen similarly used by Wise—men like J. H. Slater and Colonel W. F. Prideaux, whose reputations were, as they are now, above suspicion. Buxton Forman, however, was the most useful. He it was who first began the business of establishing the faked *Runaway Slave*. It seems to have escaped notice that as early as 1891, in the introduction Forman contributed to Wise's type-facsimile of Mrs. Browning's *Battle of Marathon*, he went out of his way to incorporate material purporting to authenticate the fraud, material that could only have been supplied by Thomas James Wise.[1]

III

Ever since the exposure of the nineteenth-century pamphlets the view that there must have been someone else involved with Wise in the forgeries has been persistently put forward in private discussion. The man whose name has been most frequently joined with Wise's in consideration of the affair is Harry Buxton Forman. Whatever suggestion has been implied by the conjunction of the two names probably derived its force, if not its origin, from the astonishing correspondence in *The Times* Literary Supplement to be

---

[1] Says Forman: "It [the first edition of *The Battle of Marathon*] is probably even rarer than the separate issue of *The Runaway Slave* ... which was also unknown to Mr. Browning until a year or two before he died—a circumstance, however, which he readily explained." But Browning did not explain: what he did was to theorize about the origin of the pamphlet which he was misled into pronouncing as genuine. Forman proceeds to quote the letter from Browning to Wise—which has been given here (see page 33).

HARRY BUXTON FORMAN

"So far, therefore, the only explanation made by Mr. Wise is to
throw back the provenance of the pamphlets on to Mr. Buxton
Forman. Does he suggest that Mr. Buxton Forman was the
forger?"—Lord Esher's challenge.

referred to in Chapters 20 and 21. But it must be said in fairness to Forman that not a tittle of evidence has ever been advanced to show or suggest his having played a part in the production of the frauds. The diarist quoted in the previous chapter names Wise, and Wise only, as the person engaged in the "wild career." Mr. Y. Z. was a well-informed man, and had he possessed knowledge of anyone else being involved, it would surely not have been withheld from the secrecy of his diary. Whether Forman knew, or came to know, of Wise's "wild career" is perhaps a more arguable point. New information which has been made available to me suggests, but does not prove, that he did know.

I have seen, by the kindness of an American collector, Mr. John Kelly, a letter from Wise to Forman dated December 7th, 1916, which evidently accompanied a presentation copy from Wise of his *Bibliography of Wordsworth* published that year. He is concerned to give Forman (then aged 73) assurances as to the note on page 167 in the *Bibliography*, referring to the Ashley Library copy of the Wordsworth verses *To the Queen* (1846) that has been dealt with in Chapter 4. The note is as follows:

These verses were written by Wordsworth upon a copy of his Poems presented by him to the Queen and were first printed in the present slender *brochure,* of which it was at one time believed that only two examples had survived. But a few years ago a tiny "remainder," consisting of some half-dozen copies, was unearthed, but even with these the pamphlet remains one of the most uncommon of the First Editions of Wordsworth.

The extraordinary casualness and lack of detail in this note is explained by the fact that the pamphlet is one of Wise's forgeries. The object of his letter to Forman is to assure him that what is said in the note about the examples of the pamphlet in existence is right; and to tell him that the majority of copies that were in the "remainder" they had shared was destroyed. The material passage is ambiguous and guarded. Whatever the reason for the assurances, they do not prove that Forman had anything to do with the production of the forgery. But they do reveal, according to Wise, that (1) Forman shared the spurious pamphlets; and (2) he knew the pamphlet was made artificially rare. His copy of the fraud, at the sale of his library in 1920 in New York, sold for $165— say £33.

IV

"Three hundred and sixty-five days were included in the year 1886. One of these days was a red-letter day for me . . . it was with a thrill of delight that I was one day informed by Miss Mathilde Blind that she had asked and obtained permission to bring me to The Pines"—says Wise,[2] telling of his meeting with Algernon Charles Swinburne. Judging from the poet's brief correspondence with Wise, 1888 would appear to have been the year of his red-letter day, and not 1886. With the exception of two notes of thanks for gifts in 1886,[3] the correspondence was confined to the period 1888 to 1896, during which, Wise relates, he received from Swinburne "some twelve or fourteen letters of interest and importance"; but of these only seven letters and notes were found "after diligent and protracted search." Wise was a careful man: it is incredible that he could not put his hand on all he received. The significance of the alleged missing letters will be seen in Chapter 13, where it is shown that Watts-Dunton was threatened with the production of one of them.

Whenever it was, the meeting with the poet was a curious affair, from what may be read between the lines of the visitor's account. To see Swinburne's original editions of Shelley "was the professed object of my visit to Putney. In about half an hour from the moment I had been ushered into Swinburne's study the door slowly opened; Watts-Dunton stole silently into the room and gently shepherded me away."

The gently shepherded visitor considered that he must

[2] In *A Swinburne Library* (1925).
[3] One printed by Wise; and the other left unprinted.

have found favor in the poet's sight because an appointment
was made for the following Sunday for him to see some first
editions of Elizabethan plays. But Wise, for once, was late.
"Watts-Dunton himself admitted me. He was obviously nerv-
ous, and quietly reproved me for my lack of punctuality,"
saying that Swinburne had been expecting him for the last
half-hour, and was "quite excited by your non-arrival." Very
excited he was, according to the account. But Wise has nothing to say about such treasures as an English black-letter book
(not in the British Museum or Bodleian!) that Swinburne
proudly displayed, and that, one would expect, would have
been the subject of reminiscence.

The first two printed letters of 1888 from the poet were
concerned with the 1868 pamphlet of his *Cleopatra*. Working precisely the same stunt tried with Browning, Wise had
written telling Swinburne about his "discovery" of a copy of
this rare edition of *Cleopatra*. The poet cried to Heaven in
wonderment at Wise "wasting good money" on a "trumpery
ephemeral," of the printing of which in that form the author
knew nothing. "Seven guineas!" exclaimed the poet. It would
have been "dear at as many shillings." He thought it a shame
to deprive Wise of his copy. But that it could easily be spared
(though that fact the innocent author never guessed) may
be fairly argued, since it is now known that Wise had a stock
of copies which he sold in subsequent years. This pamphlet is
the suspected forgery discussed in the last chapter.

It was after the subject of book collecting had been introduced in the two above-mentioned letters that Swinburne
wrote in May, 1888, about his Shelleys and Elizabethans;
which fact suggests the origin of Wise's "intercourse with the
circle at The Pines." The association, however, was obviously
never a close one in the time of Swinburne, notwithstanding
his polite interest as a "bit of a bibliomaniac" himself.

But we shall not tarry longer in this remarkable year of 365
days, because the amazing sequel to Miss Blind's introduction
of Wise to The Pines belongs to the year 1909—which also

had 365 days, including some brilliantly red-lettered ones for the collector-dealer. But these require a chapter to themselves.

V

To the late Sir Edmund Gosse is attributed the bon mot "I am sure that on the Day of Judgment Wise will tell the good Lord that Genesis is not the true first edition." Gosse, the happy essayist and richly informed literary critic, formerly Librarian of the House of Lords, was—like so many of his kind—an ardent book collector. He came to have what now seems a pathetic confidence in and esteem for Thomas James Wise as a bibliographer and collector; and he died before the exposure of those Ashley Library rarities. Those of us who knew the proud and sensitive critic can well imagine his horror and dismay if he had heard a confession to the good Lord that certain nineteenth-century pamphlets also are not true first editions.

Wise got to know Gosse in the late eighties. Miss Sylvia Gosse, Sir Edmund's artist daughter, sends me the following drypoint reminiscence: "He used to come and see father at 29 Delamere Terrace—our home then—*after* dinner. As a small child, in my bedroom, I heard them through the ceiling. They would mumble, mumble, mumble into the night. Mr. Wise was in the wholesale and importing chemist world, and therefore only free in the evenings and week ends to chase the Arts."

The result of Gosse's confidence was of incalculable value to Wise in his bibliographies and catalogues. To the critical commentary in Wise's books Gosse was by far the most generous and valuable contributor. For example, the admirable prefaces to Wise's private printings of Swinburne and Borrow manuscripts, and also many anonymous notes in the *Ashley Library Catalogue* displaying intimate knowledge of the Elizabethan dramatists, poetical understanding, and critical acumen, are the work of Gosse. It is true that in two or three of his introductions, the cataloguer pays tribute to helpers like Sir Edmund Gosse and Sir John Murray—although there were others, like Furnivall, Forman, Aitken, and Herne Shepherd, who were passed over. Only those who have had the opportunity of learning the sources of his information, and seeing the original documents (as I have), can fully appreciate how much of the best in the Ashley books originated with Wise, and how much otherwise. More frankness regarding the sources of his information would have added interest to his commentaries, and not left him open to the criticism of allowing the scholarship of others so often to appear as his own. He could do enough himself for merit.

Gosse was forever pricking bubbles in Wise's editing, and sending corrections. On July 6th, 1909, the critic warns him: "But I hope you will forgive me if I urge you to collate the text with the greatest care. At present it is full of what can hardly but be errors of transcription. I send you my suggestions . . ."

And here is an instance of how Gosse, from his booklore, could direct the bibliographer: "Who wrote *The Meretriciad?* I should think that he was, very likely, also the author of *Cooper's Well.* . . . I think you will probably find, if you look closely into the memoirs of the time, that Miss Cooper was a fashionable prostitute in 1767, and this would give point to the title, which is otherwise meaningless . . ." [Discussing the possibility of John Hall Stevenson's authorship] "but I think not, for he had enjoyed a college education, and would hardly have been guilty of several false quantities— *Priapus* and *Illium,* etc."

VI

There was a grave occasion, however, when Gosse—fearfully perturbed—tried to restrain Wise. Among his "naughty" manuscripts is one entitled "Algernon's Flogging" that he chose to assert was "autobiographical." This MS, which certainly appears to be in Swinburne's script, is inserted in a Holywell Street type of publication entitled *The Whippingham Papers. A Collection of Contributions in Prose and Verse, chiefly by the Author of the "Romance of Chastisement."* (London: 1888). "Although Swinburne's name does not occur anywhere in the volume, a large portion of the contents, both prose and verse, was written by him," says Wise—who does not add, as he might well have done, that the verse (both that in the manuscript and in print) is puerile and absurd, and could hardly be other than the aberrations of a sick man. On receiving a proof containing the entry of this sorry trash, Gosse at once wrote to Wise:

Now comes the question of N. 226. You must take the responsibility of it. But I should not be honest if I did not tell you that I am greatly distressed. What does it matter whether any dirty fellow should "pounce upon" the W. Papers and hold them up as "a rarity unknown to Wise and Gosse"? Any little vanity which we might possibly feel seems to me nothing beside the dishonour done to a great name.

However, you have printed this, and I know you too well to expect you to cancel the entry altogether. But I do entreat you to modify it. It is absolutely needless to dwell on the details, and gloat over the thing. It must be sufficient to quote the nasty title, without exciting prurient interest by quoting the sub-titles and first lines of the four sections. I *entreat* you not to do this. I think it will be a cruel offence against Swinburne's memory to do it. And to what purpose? Merely to gratify the last pedantry of bibliography. It is surely enough, since you were so anxious to be "complete," to mention the publication. That will preserve you from the charge of not knowing its existence, an ignorance which might (however) be well considered honourable. But to print these titles and first lines is to give away the whole secret, which I have done my very best to hide. You might just as well publish the whole hideous rubbish in full as print these titles and lines. They expose the whole disgrace.

I entreat you not to be so cruel to Swinburne's memory.

Wise could hardly ignore this forceful and moving appeal. He suppressed the subtitles and quotations in his 1920 *Bibliography of Swinburne,* tucking away the entry in the appendix of "Contributions to Periodical Literature, etc." But in his later and bigger catalogues it was promoted to a place among the *Editiones Principes* of Algernon Charles Swinburne, with enlarged notes.

*   *   *   *

It was in a philosophical mood that Gosse wrote to Wise in February, 1901: "As life goes on, it seems more and more to run in a rut, and the adventurous grows more difficult to grasp. Friendship and letter-writing are really adventures...." How adventurous will be revealed in Chapter 13.

CHAPTER 8

MARRIAGE, SECRET PUBLISHING, AND RUSKIN RUSES

He was reputed one of the wise men, that
made answer to the question when a man
should marry? "A young man not yet; an
elder man not at all."
　　　　　　　　　Bacon: *Of Marriage.*

I

In 1890, the 30-year-old cashier, book collector, and publisher found time from these absorbing avocations to make two important moves: the first, into matrimony; the second, consequently, into a new house—52 Ashley Road, Crouch Hill, North London. The former was not to be so distinguished as the latter, which gave its name to his collection—the Ashley Library.

His first bride was Miss Selina Fanny Smith, aged 22, daughter of Frederick Smith, a salesman. Thomas James and Selina Fanny were married on July 12th, 1890, in the Parish Church of Kentish Town, Wise describing himself as a commercial clerk and giving his age as 31 (he was actually 30). It is an instance additional to those given of his inaccuracy in such details.

Shortly before the marriage, Wise had left the paternal home in Holloway and made a temporary abode at 33 Leighton Grove, N., Miss Smith's home being 174 Leighton Road. After the marriage, however, they moved into 52 Ashley Road, which leads from Hornsey Rise to Crouch Hill. What with his improved position at Rubeck's, and the money he was making out of his book deals and those rare little pamphlets, Tommy was doing well. The chosen home for the blossoming library and the blooming Selina reflected his new status and confidence. No. 52, standing in a good-sized pair of grass plots with privet hedging, and wearing a showy gable—itself like a respectable cashier in white spats and shining topper—was an improvement on the home in grim Holloway.

No doubt Selina, who was little and lively, thought it was a good move also. Such a sleek, well-dressed young husband, so busy in the City, and this nice home with all these books— oh yes! she had done well. Perhaps secretly she had her doubts about all those books, not having much inclination their way. But it was all very imposing; and when you are newly married and settling down, there is plenty to occupy the time—at first. There, for the moment, we must leave Selina to herself . . . as Thomas soon did; because he was now busier than ever. He was no longer living cheaply at his parents' home. There was this establishment to keep up, and there were all those private enterprises of his.

II

The production of the spurious pamphlets that we have seen initiated in 1886 or 1887 was certainly continuing at this time, although there is a lack of evidence by which most of their dates can be precisely assigned. Also the rare-book selling business was developing as his private list of clients grew—a list augmented by Browning Society and Shelley Society contacts. But it is the third phase of his private activities with which this chapter is concerned: his publishing business. For at all times from the middle eighties Thomas James Wise was a publisher—under the usual cloak of anonymity, of course; as he was a bookseller.

It was publishing in a small way, maybe; but publishing of a particularly ingenious and novel kind. The method generally was this: He would get hold of a series of an author's letters or manuscript of verse or prose; print the material neatly but inexpensively; serve up as first editions purportedly limited to a small number of copies; and sell hot. His editing, unless he derived help from others, was often nominal: where there was some effort at proper presentation and annotation the work was poor and inadequate. For example, Charles Augustus Howell was one of the recipients of Rabelaisian letters from Swinburne's "festive" pen. When some of these got into the hands of a dealer, the poet (through the offices of Richard Herne Shepherd) was glad to buy back the indiscretions; and after his death Wise seized the chance of printing such a festivity. Some of these, he says elsewhere in relating the episode, were included "with necessary omissions" in his privately printed *Letters from . . . Swinburne to Richard Monckton Milnes and Other Correspondents* (1915). But there is a complete absence in the book of marks indicating that Swinburne's letters have been castrated.

At first, as we have seen in the case of the Shelley first editions issued by Wise, original manuscripts were borrowed, publication being sometimes made without authority. Later, however, when he had more capital, he mostly printed only such material as he bought. There is little doubt that the proceeds from the sale of these small books and pamphlets often covered the cost of acquiring the original MSS, plus the comparatively insignificant printing charges. If Buxton Forman could buy his Byron rarity for £70 and pay for it out of the sale of a mere facsimile reprint, Wise went one better (and a big one!) in being able to produce first editions of the manuscripts they were to pay for. It was buying your cake, eating it, selling it at a profit, and yet keeping it in the pantry all the time. Thus another way in which the Ashley Library grew is illustrated. Providing that no copyrights were being infringed, and providing also that the subscribers to these editions were always getting what these publications were represented to be, the enterprise was legitimate enough, notwithstanding the secrecy.

While Wise throughout his career always had something or other in course of production at his printers, there were—apart from the printing of the spurious nineteenth-century pamphlets and his own large compilations—five periods of publishing of certain authors. They were:

> Shelley, from 1886 to 1897;
> Ruskin, from 1890 to 1897;
> Swinburne, from 1909 to 1918;
> Borrow, 1913 and 1914;
> Conrad, 1919 and 1920.

Between the earliest of these dates and 1929 he also published privately printed first editions of Matthew Arnold, J. M. Barrie, the Brontës, the Brownings, S. T. Coleridge, Charles Dickens, Edward Fitzgerald, George Gissing, Thomas Hardy, Walter Savage Landor, D. G. Rossetti, E. J. Trelawny, William Wordsworth, and lesser authors. Although not all the publications are important, the material on the whole includes much of literary and biographical value. The list (it is given in full in the Appendix) is one of which Wise was proud. On the face, it is a list on which he could well pride himself. The pity is that a record of useful publishing should have been besmirched by piracies and other objectionable features.

In all, so far as I have been able to trace, Wise published privately 250 separate works, exclusive of his own bibliographies and catalogues, and exclusive also of the nineteenth-century pamphlets condemned or suspected that are detailed in Part IV of the Appendix. Many of the 250 publications are from 20 to 50 pages, but others are considerably bigger in content. The following is an analysis:

Privately printed publications by Wise 250
Examined 250
Bearing no printer's imprint 183
With Clay and Son's imprint 58
With other printers' imprints 9
Bearing no identification with Wise as publisher .. 62[1]
Not delivered to the British Museum Library 46

III

Wise represented—both in talk and in his books—that these private publications were done for the purpose of preserving the manuscript material in print, and thereby making it available to students. Very laudable and usual are such purposes; but in some cases the material was already in print, and the greater part of it was fairly certain to be printed sooner or later. However, let us take the avowed purposes without these reservations.

The very first place in which a person printing such material for preservation is anxious to see it deposited is the British Museum Library. Nor is this a voluntary matter. The Copyright Act requires, under penalty for non-compliance, that a free copy of every work printed shall be delivered to the British Museum Library and also to each of five other libraries.[2] Yet here we have a bibliographer with the knowledge and reputation of Thomas James Wise, whose privately printed books were alleged to be done as records and for students, failing in 46 instances to send a copy to the British Museum—which at various dates, usually long after production, had to buy 23 of the books (several from Wise himself), and never possessed the remainder until 1937, when the Ashley Library was bought for the nation. Of those of his publications that were sent to the British Museum, a

---

[1] This figure includes three items which bear statements that they were "edited" by Wise, the ten printed with Conrad's imprint, and the nine with Watts-Dunton's imprint, because they were produced by Wise (by arrangement in these last two cases), he retaining the bulk of the editions.

[2] Those of Oxford and Cambridge Universities, and the National Libraries of Scotland, Ireland, and Wales.

small proportion was presented by the Shelley Society and other donors such as Dr. Furnivall and Harry Buxton Forman.

The absence of any identification with Wise as publisher in 62 of the works, regarded in conjunction with his pirating, suggests an obvious reason—at least in some cases—for his not using either his imprint or the more usual Ashley Library book device, which is a feature of his publications after 1894—except where it was suppressed (see illustration). The absence of a printer's imprint in such a large proportion of the works is an even more serious matter. Here was a long-sustained course of illegality, for the law is that:

> Every printed paper or book which at the time it is printed is meant to be published or dispersed must have upon the front of such paper, if it be printed upon one side only, or upon the first and last leaf if it consists of more than one leaf, the name and address of the printer.
>
> 32 and 33 Vict. c 24 [3]

The 183 publications issued by Wise without a printer's imprint are most of them identifiable typographically with Clays; and there is no reason for doubting that the omission was procured by him. Clays had innocently printed for him the spurious nineteenth-century pamphlets, and certain of them were also identifiable with some of these 250 privately printed first editions, the majority of which bore the Ashley Library book device. He may have deemed it undesirable, as he had been in charge of the Browning and Shelley Societies' printing done at Clays, to have such a series of uniform volumes like his Shelley and Ruskin letters labeled by the same printers. As for his piracies, the less said about their printing origin the less risk of detection.[4]

[3] There are a few exceptions, such as Parliamentary Papers, Bank of England Notes, certain legal and financial documents, and sale catalogues.
[4] When I discussed Wise's practice with Mr. Cecil Clay, he said that his firm would always include its imprint on a work unless it was a printing where omission was permissible. They did not know how the imprints came to be left off Wise's publications. That customer's instructions were always

The fact is that, however much he might claim to be doing disinterested service to literature, the publishing of these things was first and always a commercial proposition. If the profits were small, the returns were quick, the labor light, and the risk of loss almost negligible. For him it was good business although not always legitimate business. When he declared—as he so often did after the World War—"this boom in modern first editions is preposterous," he was silent about the extent to which he had so ingeniously played a hand in it.

Apart from the sale of these private printings to his clients, he reserved some as "gifts" to authors, to obtain in return interesting autograph letters and services. Browning, Swinburne, and Sir Edmund Gosse have been mentioned as illustrative cases. The last named was a particularly favored recipient of the first editions from Wise: what abundant value he received for them is only now demonstrable. The profits these privately printed editions brought their publisher will almost certainly never be known. Probably they varied considerably. But that they must have been appreciable is indicated by the reminiscence of Mr. Herbert Gorfin. He relates that in 1913 on the publication of the long series of George Borrow first edition pamphlets, he sold to an Oxford Street bookseller ten of them for £80 on behalf of Wise, who accompanied him, and who waited in a neighboring café for the proceeds of the transaction.

I have also been shown a list in the handwriting of Wise giving the prices at which he suggested five of his privately printed Swinburne pamphlets should be catalogued for sale. They were *Queen Fredegond*, £30; *The Worm of Spindlestonheugh*, £25; *Letters on the Elizabethan Dramatists*, £18.18.; *Border Ballads*, £25; *Liberty and Loyalty*, £21. This was perhaps a case of forcing his market. But these figures—for pamphlets that at most could hardly have cost

taken by a representative in the London office of the firm; and presumably the omissions were due to a request by Mr. Wise which unfortunately went unnoticed and unquestioned.

10/- apiece to print—show what prices he was aiming at, and probably asked from his private customers, who were invariably men of wealth.

IV

When Wise in his catalogues described books that did not meet with his approval, he was severe in his criticisms. "This pamphlet is one of the most impudent examples of exploitation I have yet encountered," is an example. "Extortionate," "not a legitimate first edition," "this unsightly scrap" are other instances of his outspoken disapprobation. Yet irrespective of his nineteenth-century forgeries, his privately printed publications include some that come within the same terms of censure. As late as 1930 he produced a little volume, *Autobiographical Notes with Comments upon Tennyson and Huxley,* by George Gissing, consisting of three long letters to Edward Clodd. But these three letters had already been included by Wise among the thirteen which he had privately printed in 1914 under the title *Letters to Edward Clodd.* The three letters of the 1930 reprint are the longest in the 1914 edition, and the versions are practically identical; [5] nor can the duplication be justified by the autobiographical grouping. Yet Wise catalogued both as first editions, and presumably sold them as such.[6]

Another example of his loose publishing methods is the private printing of George Borrow's *Letters to his Mother Ann Borrow & Other Correspondents* (1913). The reader will be surprised to find that the little book consists of one letter of twelve lines to Borrow's mother, and the remainder (14) to

[5] The only differences are a few literals arising from faulty transcription, the omission of a four-line paragraph, and a postscript.

[6] A comparable instance is that of his privately printed edition of Coleridge's *Two Addresses on Sir Robert Peel's Bill.* Edited with an introduction by Edmund Gosse, C.B. (1913). This is a reprint of the folio brochures of the *Addresses* that Coleridge caused to be separately printed in 1818. Merely because Wise printed them together in different format in 1913 (from the "unique" original printings in the Ashley Library), he calls his publication a first edition—and, again, presumably sold it as such.

his wife Mary, with the exception of two to other correspondents. But Wise had already produced a selection of
Borrow's *Letters to his Wife*—hence the other misleading
title.

This manufacturing of first editions was not without its
alarums and excursions. On one occasion, when he was older
and wiser, Thomas James came into possession of a series of
letters from Swinburne to Pauline, Lady Trevelyan—an ac-
complished lady whom for her sagacious encouragement and
corrective advice Swinburne had cause to revere. Here was
something for Wise's market . . . away went the transcripts
to the printers . . . and back came the proofs. But Wise was
afraid to take this trip under the pirate's flag; so he asked
Gosse to forward the proofs to Sir George Trevelyan for his
permission. Sir George came down on the project in no uncertain manner, and without bouquets either. He insisted
that the letters must first appear in public form "in some
work of authority"; and Gosse told Wise that the inevitable
must be bowed to, and the pamphlet suppressed—which was
done, save for the usual few copies of the proofs. There was
apparently much concern about a long paragraph in one of
the letters. It referred to some "venomous backbiter" to
whom was attributed the story of a mutual acquaintance having boasted of murdering his own illegitimate children. Wise,
in his *Ashley Library Catalogue* (Vol. VII, p. 44), points out
that the long paragraph of scandal was omitted when the
correspondence was officially published. But the result was
that he had made another rarity for the Ashley Library, and
the unsuppressed version available for the general public to
read in his proof copy at the British Museum—if there is any
satisfaction to be gained from the absurd scandalous talk. A
curious position!

This was not the only Wise pamphlet to be suppressed.
Another was *The Early Letters from Algernon Charles Swinburne to John Nichol* (1917). The publisher's MS note in one
of the preserved proofs in the British Museum reads: "A

lady, part proprietor of the holographs of the letters printed in the following pages, whose name it is wisest not to expose in writing, desires so many excisions from the text that the letters if so dealt with would be worthless as documents. It has therefore been decided to withdraw the pamphlet from the press."

V

A surprising feature of Wise's first-edition publication is their certificates as to copies printed. In the case of limited editions the object of such certificates is to record in the work itself the actual number of copies printed, and—when published for sale, as were those by Wise—to provide a guarantee for the subscriber, who is usually charged a higher price by reason of the restriction on copies. Wise's publications generally bear statements that the "edition of this book is limited to a few copies," or (more usually) variations of "Of this book Thirty copies only have been printed." The numbers vary up to about 50 copies. Wise's catalogue descriptions of his own publications frequently give figures different from those in his certificates. For instance, the number of copies of Shelley's *Letters to Elizabeth Hitchener* is certified to be 29 (25 on handmade paper, and 4 on vellum) while in the *Ashley Library Catalogue* the number is given as 34 (30 and 4 respectively). Such differences are not very much even considering the proportions; but that they should be made by a bibliographer about his own books is shocking.

But, discrepancies apart, what number, in the case of a certificate of "a few copies," constitutes "a few"; and who is the arbiter? And where a number only is specified, what guarantee is there that it was not exceeded, bearing in mind the unfortunate fact that other circumstances in Wise's publishing preclude trust in his honesty? A rare-book expert, through whose hands many of these limited first editions have passed, surprised me during my researches with the question:

"How many copies do you think Wise printed and sold of his private editions certified to be limited to thirty copies?"

Myself: "Do you suggest that he overprinted the numbers stated in the certificates?"

Expert: "All I know is that some of these books have been appearing with enough regularity to suggest that there were nearer 130 copies."

What that expert says is surmise, and not evidence, and should be so regarded. A copy may circulate and appear in the market more than once. It would take many years and a careful census to get at the truth of this matter. Some independent corroboration of the expert's experience is, however, supplied by Mr. Herbert Gorfin, who sold many of the publications. He gave me his view that in the case of the earlier publications Wise printed more copies than he certificated; but he thought that the stated numbers of the later first editions, like those of Swinburne, Borrow, and Conrad, were pretty closely adhered to. It is possible that the pamphlet Charlotte Brontë's *Adventures of Ernest Alembert* (1896) would be illustrative. The printing is stated by Wise to have been limited to 30 copies. There must surely have been plenty of subscribers for such a small number of a purported Charlotte Brontë first edition.[7] Yet we find Wise still selling the edition in 1910—disposing of a bundle of fifteen copies for £6.19.0. fourteen years after the production of "30 copies only"!

There is one form of certificate of limitation that fulfills its object: it is the one that not only specifies the total of copies printed, but enumerates each copy, and is signed by the publisher or printer. Wise, with his bibliographical experience, ought never to have permitted himself such looseness in regard to his certificates. That he did so is in keeping with his publishing principles.

---

[7] It was actually an off-print from *Literary Anecdotes of the Nineteenth Century* (1895-6), edited by Wise and Robertson Nicoll, in which it first appeared.

VI

In spite of his success in making acquaintance with authors, and of producing their letters and fragments with or without permission, Thomas James Wise had one great disappointment in his active and varied career. He never could get in with John Ruskin. Try as he might, write letters, seek introductions, that proud, sad, disillusioned idealist would have nothing of him, and never wrote a single letter so far as I can ascertain; on the one or two occasions that it was necessary to reply to the collector-dealer-publisher, he did so through a third person. This was all the more grievous to Thomas James because for a long time Ruskin was a great shining orb in the book-collecting constellation. Wise paid him homage (in collaboration with James P. Smart) with a monumental *Ruskin Bibliography* (1893). All to no purpose: it did not bring him grace. But he was wholly undaunted. There was a rhinocerotic quality in his psychological skin. Sesame and Lilies open or closed, he would find something for Clays to print—something of which to make Ruskin rarities. Result: six pamphlet forgeries, two suspected forgeries,[8] and eleven privately printed first editions, some, if not all, under very doubtful authority.

The first five of the privately printed editions were issued by Wise under his cloak of anonymity, although in the fifth he gave his name as editor. After that one—in 1893—there seems to have arisen a cloud of suspicion: apparently lenders of original material required assurances as to Wise's rights, and there was some objection to the paucity of acknowledgment. For example, the Reverend J. P. Faunthorpe was really obstinate, insisting upon having a declaration from Wise that no copyright was being infringed, and that he was printing Ruskin's letters to him with the author's knowledge and approval. Another lender was Mr. Charles Fairfax Murray, who

---

8 For details, see Chapter 11, "The Writing on the Wall," in which the story of their first exposure is told; and also the Appendix.

supplied his own annotations, but who insisted on a proper printed acknowledgment, and on having his footnotes initialed. In the case of ten of the Ruskin private printings the subscribers had to be content with the assurance of the editions being limited to "a few copies only." It was only with the eleventh—the *Letters to Frederick J. Furnivall*—that the certificates specified 30 copies as the limitation. Furnivall was just the man to insist on a little detail like that—the meticulous old nuisance, as perhaps Wise thought.

Now that people were worrying themselves and him about copyrights, it meant submission of material to authors. The character of Ruskin's acquiescence will emerge. But coincident with the stricter attitude of lenders, we find Ruskin in the intervals of his mental afflictions giving closer attention to those proofs that were submitted to him. In one set he made two suppressions: the first of a passage which referred to his forbidding study of "the act of Copulation, and the process of Generation in the Womb"; the other, of a saying of his that when there was the least chance of getting a kiss he felt "all scrubbing brush" about his lips owing to cutting his mustache. When such suppressions were made, the lenders of the original letters doubtless congratulated themselves on their caution, even if it was not so agreeable to the publisher. He, however, usually had his way in the end. Years later, when he came to compile his catalogues, the censorship imposed as an understood condition of publication was evaded by his custom of quoting the suppressed passages in annotations.

VII

The most revealing example of Wise's methods is supplied by the careful Dr. Furnivall in regard to one of these Ruskin editions entitled *Two Letters concerning "Notes on the Construction of Sheepfolds"* (1890)—a pamphlet, by the bye, which has nothing to do with agricultural architecture. However anonymously it might be published, Furnivall was having no hanky-panky about the facts, which he boldly gave away in his "Forewords" as follows:

Of late years Mr. Wise has most kindly given me, who could not afford to buy them, many of his privately-printed rarities. Thinking what I could do in return for these benefits, I askt Mr. Wise if he'd like to print privately my copies of the *Sheepfold* correspondence between Maurice and Ruskin in 1851. He said Yes, but ultimately determined to print only Ruskin's two letters, as Maurice's theology had no interest for him. He has also just shown me Ruskin's letter from Brantwood, "29th May 1889," to some correspondent, part of which has already appeared in print: —"... You may print this ... where and whenever you like; *as anybody else may, whatever I write, at any time, or say*—if only they don't *leave out* the bits they don't like!" Under this authority the present print appears.

Six years after the candid and cautious Furnivall made the above explanations, which have several points of interest in this study, Wise in the second volume of *Literary Anecdotes* (1896) gave pride of place to a contribution by himself on this *Sheepfolds* correspondence. The contribution [9] reveals Wise's little way with the public. It begins:

In October, 1890, Dr. F. J. Furnivall caused to be issued for private circulation a tiny volume which contained within its thirty pages matter of greater interest and higher importance than is to be found in any of the many pretentious volumes of *Ruskiniana* which have made their appearance during the last decade.

The tiny volume referred to is the *Sheepfolds* pamphlet described above that was printed by Clay, and published and sold by Wise, and for which Ruskin's original letters had been made available to him by Furnivall as carefully recorded in the latter's "Forewords." The distortion of facts about the responsibility for publishing is repeated by Wise a few pages later: "It is to be regretted that, for quite sufficient reasons, Dr. Furnivall printed Mr. Ruskin's letters only, contenting

---

[9] It is not signed by Wise, but internal evidence and the attendant circumstances go to show beyond question that it was by him. There was precious little of Wise in the contribution, which was a scissors and paste affair, quoting from Furnivall and giving Maurice's part of the correspondence in addition to reprinting Ruskin's two letters.

himself with quoting three short passages from those of Maurice." For "Dr. Furnivall" the reader needs to substitute "Thomas J. Wise" in these last two quotations [10]—and then marvel at the latter's impudence. First of all he obtains his materials from Furnivall (who obviously would have preferred to have Maurice's letters included in the private printing). Then, on the somewhat loose authority of the 70-year-old and mentally unbalanced Ruskin's remark that anybody could print whatever he wrote, Wise prints that material in one of his first editions, suppressing his connection with it. Finally he puts the responsibility for the publishing on to Furnivall.[11] But why all this Machiavellian maneuvering? Why the deception? The answer is MONEY. And that answer is unintentionally supplied by Wise himself in the first page of *Literary Anecdotes*. After saying that Furnivall had caused the "tiny volume" to be printed, Wise sets out the title page of that volume—*Two Letters concerning . . . Sheepfolds*—appending the footnote:

"Naturally this little volume has become of considerable scarcity, and upon more than one occasion a copy has realized some five or six guineas."

So here we have Wise boosting the price of the tiny pamphlet he had surreptitiously published and then foisted on Furnivall. How it came about that Dr. Furnivall, a man of fearless and independent character, allowed to pass Wise's willful distortion of the facts in a work of importance like the *Literary Anecdotes*, is difficult to understand. The distortion, however, may not have been seen, for Furnivall was 71 years old when Wise wrote that paper in *Literary Anecdotes*, forgetting what the doctor had written in the "Forewords" to the tiny volume, or else trusting that it would be overlooked.

---

[10] I found during my researches that, in defiance of one of the most sacred rules of the British Museum Library, an anonymous reader had already done this in its copy of *Literary Anecdotes*. The unknown had written in ink in a minute hand above the two citations of Furnivall's name—"t.i. T. J. Wise." The "t.i" is presumably a contraction for "that is."

[11] The Dictionary of National Biography in its article on Furnivall has been led into error by accepting Wise's willful misstatements as to the origin of the pamphlet—quoting his *Literary Anecdotes* as its authority.

CHAPTER 9

THREE MEN AND A BOY

Thy bounteous hand with worldly bliss
Has made my cup run o'er,
And in a kind and faithful friend
Has doubled all my store.
Joseph Addison, *Spectator*, 453.

I

EVERYTHING went well for our benedick from the time he settled in his new home: everything, even the partnership with Selina—at first. The enterprising bookseller and private publisher was soon making partnerships of another kind— two of them being furthered by, if not due to, his choice of Ashley Road for residence. For, after his move to No. 52, 1891 and 1892 proved to be the wonder years for Wise. In these two years were begun four friendships of outstanding importance to him. Three of them were with men all his seniors. In the order of event they were: first, with Clement King Shorter, aged 35, editor of the *Illustrated London News*—who was a neighbor, and who is credited with having suggested to Wise the naming of his Library after Ashley Road. The second was with William Robertson Nicoll, aged 41, editor of the *Bookman,* and also a neighbor—he was not yet knighted. The third was with John Henry Wrenn, a 50-year-old Chicago banker, then about to begin collecting books in the grand manner of American millionaires.

The fourth friendship was with a bright happy lad of fourteen, just beginning as office boy at Rubecks—Herbert Gorfin. As in the three other cases, the friendship that was fostered with this smiling, perky youngster was turned by

Rubeck's cashier to full advantage for himself. But it had
a remarkable sequel.

II

Clement King Shorter for a time managed, with that by
no means uncommon facility of Civil Servants, to combine
a job at Somerset House with journalism, for which he had
a flair. Obtaining an editorship, he became something of a
figure through a weekly literary causerie which was sometimes refreshingly individual, but which was not conspicuous
for the soundness of either its judgment or its style. *Punch*
satirized him as the "Wee Cham of Literature." He was philosophical about his literary limitations, however; and it was
as well, for not even his friends spared him their wit or their
criticism. Like Wise, he was not a man to be easily abashed;
he was of the determined, thrustful sort, although along more
conventional lines. Also, he was an ardent collector of books
and manuscripts.

Dr. J. M. Bulloch, who knew Shorter intimately for many
years and who edited his autobiographical fragment, described
him to me as "a man who was always making other men do
what they did not want to do," and "a pusher." It was Mrs.
Florence Hardy who gave me an enlargement of Bulloch's
miniature. Shorter once visited Thomas Hardy, and begged
to see the manuscripts of any of his works. Obligingly, the
author produced some bundles out of a drawer. Shorter
seized them, urged that they ought to be bound to preserve
them safely, and finally insisted upon taking them away with
him for that purpose, to save the owner trouble. Hardy appreciated that the MSS would be better in bindings; but,
somehow, the way the service was proffered irritated him.
However, his evident reluctance to be under an obligation to
Shorter was weakened by a courteous desire not to hurt his
guest's feelings—whose toughness he little knew. But Shorter
was overwhelming; and in the end he departed from Max

Gate hugging the precious manuscripts. In due course he had them bound, and they were returned to Hardy—all except one that Shorter asked to be allowed to keep, suggesting that it might set off the binder's bill, which he had already settled.

These are illustrations, it is true, of the character of Clement Shorter, but they have a reflective interest.[1] He was Wise's boon companion. In each other's merry company they would relieve themselves from the tiresome poses that other contacts required: they could hail each other beneath their veneers. If few men are heroes to their valets, not many more are gods to their bosom pals.

Another flair of Shorter's was for acquiring autograph material. Many a mutually advantageous deal there was between him and Wise. He once made a sensational haul of Brontë MSS for which he had financial backing from Wise, who was not only the wealthier of the two but the bolder and more confident speculator. In 1895 Shorter "became possessed," to use his own words, of a packet of letters written by Charlotte Brontë. Of course he wanted to publish them; for to a small extent he copied Wise in private printing, but he was more scrupulous in the matter of certificates. To secure the copyright, and also to buy any other relics of the Brontës, he determined to seek the Reverend Arthur Bell Nicholls, one time curate of Haworth, whom Charlotte married in 1854 for a happy union of a few months. Nicholls was traced to Banager, King's County, Ireland, where he was farming, having left the Church. He had married a woman who remembered Charlotte on her honeymoon, and who talked freely and kindly of her illustrious predecessor in the affections of Nicholls.

Shorter, accompanied by Robertson Nicoll, crossed the sea, found the "genial little" Nicholls at the "precise psychological

---

[1] There is another which, although unconnected with Wise, deserves rescuing from Shorter's fragment of *Autobiography* (1927). Shorter, writing about his first wife, Dora Sigerson, tells of the night before she died: "I recall that she wanted Pepys's *Diary* read to her, and I hesitated for fear of shocking the nurse. We were both amused at the time at the idea."

moment" when he was ready to talk, not only about Charlotte, but about business. Apparently the ex-curate was not doing better than most farmers at the time, and was glad to see the cash that Clement held out for a brown-paper parcel full of MSS and letters by the Brontë sisters, including those tiny MS books of tales that were the girls' first amazing efforts in authorship. These relics had lain by for 40 years. According to Shorter, Charlotte's husband intended to burn them all; but perhaps this was embroidery to lend romance to the tale of the "find."

Wise bought the bulk of the manuscripts, Shorter retaining what copyright there was in them. Subsequently Wise acquired other material from Nicholls through the agency of Harry Buxton Forman as a result of the contact thus established. The inevitable first editions were privately printed to pay for the outlay on the originals. It must be noted, however, that Shorter's own contribution to Brontë literature as a consequence of his "find," was by far the more considerable and appreciated, notwithstanding he passed over the Angrian cycle of MSS as worthless. Wise's few printings are set out in the Appendix and need not detain us here. A sequel to his haul of Haworth relics—the story of his printing of Charlotte's love letters to Professor Héger, and of *The Times*'s heavy hand on Shorter—will be related in its chronological place.

III

While the two men worked in the very closest harmony and co-operation, Wise was much given to chaffing his friend, and even to scoring off him—as he did off others. When he made his astonishing coup at The Pines in 1909, Shorter was allowed to have a little finger in the pie. Among other things, he was lent the MSS of some unpublished fragments, including poems rejected by Swinburne when sending his *Songs before Sunrise* to press; and these fragments were duly produced by C. K. S. in a crude pamphlet of 25 copies. But he

THOMAS HARDY (left) AND EDMUND GOSSE (right)

was more Mrs. Grundyish than Wise, and considered that some bowdlerizing was necessary. For instance, when transcribing "Moonrise by the Sea," says Wise, pulling his friend's leg, "Mr. Shorter unfortunately overlooked a line included in the MS. . . . In place of the second line we should therefore read:

> *The small dark body's Lesbian loveliness*
> *That held the fire eternal."*

The development of the friendship between Wise and Gosse, with its promise of usefulness to the former, led to an awkward situation which was long handled with masterly skill. Shorter disliked Gosse, an attitude even more thoroughly reciprocated. C. K. S. characteristically vented his prejudice through his weekly causerie, once observing: "Personally I do not like either Mr. Gosse or Sir Sidney Colvin"— an outburst which prompted some sarcastic lines in *Punch* from E. V. Lucas, of which these touch our subject:

> *Alas, alack, for Sidney C!*
> *Alack, alas, for Edmund G!*
> *On both must History's verdict be*
> *That Shorter did not like them.*
>
> *In vain poor Edmund's enterprise*
> *In baring Putney to the skies,*
> *And linking up with T. J. Wise,*
> *For Shorter doesn't like him.*

Gosse wrote (Apr. 4, '14) to Wise, on the occasion of another of the weekly causerie attacks: "Will you explain to me why I have suddenly received over my head and shoulders this bucketful of Mr. Clement Shorter's bedroom slops?" The friend-of-the-enemy replied soothingly in terms that are implied in Gosse's acknowledgment of Wise's "excellent advice" about the "irresponsible little journalist."

"Tommy" and "Clem," as they called each other affectionately, were wont to spend a day together every week, visiting bookshops and hatching their schemes. Just after the World

War, I often met them slowly making their way from Hodgson's, the book auctioneer's, up the Strand, and into West End booksellers'—laughing and confiding like two lovers. Except that "Clem" was hairy and "Tommy" was almost hairless, they were two for a pair in their chubbiness, joviality, and shrewdness. Seeing them, I was invariably reminded of a poem entitled "Twin Souls" from Wise's *Verses* previously quoted—his solitary effort in print as a poetaster. Here is the first verse:

> *Calm and bright*
> *In the fading light*
> *Two hearts together singing!*
> *Sweet and fair,*
> *In the summer's air,*
> *Two forms together clinging.*

How they did enjoy their days out, this clinging pair of bookmen! And there was that weekly lunch, of which Wise told me that the arrangement between them was that one week Shorter should settle the joint bill, and the next week Wise should pay—and so on, alternately. Now Clement was ingenious in drawing famous authors into correspondence with him. How this affected the sweet feasts of the twins is best told in Wise's own words: "On the days that it was Shorter's turn to pay, he would tell the waiter to make out the bill 'all on one.' Then, while this was being done, he would take out his wallet from an inside pocket, carefully select a letter he had received from Thomas Hardy, or George Meredith, or some other author, and—holding it high between finger and thumb—slowly advance it to me, saying: 'Well, Tommy; if you settle the bill and I give you this, we shall be quits—eh?' This," added Wise, "became a regular thing; and so I nearly always found the cash for our luncheons."

IV

Leaving the bosom pals at their trading in friendships' tokens and the innocent missives of unsuspecting authors, we come to the other neighbor, the editor of the *Bookman*. Robertson Nicoll in person does not figure much in this study of Wise's career. But his *Bookman* does. For in 1892 Wise began a journalistic association with that monthly that was not only witness to his shrewdness, but calculated to be of great value to him—alike in his legitimate publishing and in the other sort.

There was no use in producing spurious pamphlets by nineteenth-century authors, and also piracies, if they were not established as collectors' items, and their commercial values correspondingly forced up. We have seen one way in which Wise put them into circulation, by selling a few cheaply to provincial booksellers; the majority, of course, would be reserved for his private clients at profitable prices moving upward with whatever "market" quotations he could manipulate. But it was publicity that was now wanted for the things. The *Bookman* provided just such an opening as was needed. It is almost unnecessary to add that Robertson Nicoll, as also the proprietors, Messrs. Hodder & Stoughton, would be unaware that the *Bookman,* emanating from the same highly respectable office as that popular religious newspaper, the *British Weekly,* was being utilized to boost the values of publications that were to be proved forgeries. Had they known, oh! the groans in that peaceful square off Warwick Lane!

Wise began in 1892 with a few notes of general interest on book collecting. Then, in 1893, Robertson Nicoll proudly announced that Mr. Thomas J. Wise, the "well-known collector and bibliographer," had undertaken the "editorship" of their "Recent Book Prices" reports, and that he would add, "out of the fullness of his knowledge and experience," comments "particularly valuable to bookbuyers and booksellers." The description, "well-known bibliographer," was a little premature—perhaps divinely inspired intelligence from the heavenly correspondent of the *British Weekly*. Wise had not then published a single bibliography; that of Ruskin (done in collaboration with Smart) appeared later in the year;[2] nevertheless, it was intelligent anticipation, and no one could quarrel with the compliment to the fullness of Wise's knowledge and experience of prices. No one!

In this year the *Bookman* contained long puffs of one of Wise's Ruskin forgeries, and of three of his volumes of privately printed Ruskin letters. In 1894, however, the publicizing had a twofold object. Earlier in that year there had been some lively controversy in various periodicals over the new craze for collecting the first editions of modern authors —even living ones! Mr. William Roberts, long recognized as an authoritative writer on the subject, was unpleasantly outspoken. Of the "First Edition Mania" he wrote: "Time was when the craze existed in a perfectly rational form, and when the first editions in demand were books of importance and books with both histories and reputations, whilst their collectors were scholars and men of judgment. Now, every little volume of drivelling verse becomes an object of more or less hazardous speculation, and the book market itself a stock exchange in miniature." Roberts was still more pointed with references to "rubbishy tracts by living authors," and "operators working the market," and *"too-zealous persons who feed their own vanity by hanging on to the coat-tails of eminent men and claim the title of public benefactor by 'resurrecting' from a well-merited obscurity some worthless tract or obsolete and ephemeral magazine article, and trumpeting it about as a masterpiece."*[3]

All of which shows the suspicion that was abroad concern-

---

[2] The *Bookman* for January had an effusive paragraph heralding the coming Ruskin bibliography by Mr. Thomas J. Wise, whose co-author—Smart— was not even mentioned.

[3] The italicizing is mine. The article appeared in the *Fortnightly Review* for March, 1894.

ing the artificial manufacturing of first editions—although the time had not arrived for exposure of the full extent of the evil, the faking of rarities then being unloaded upon the public. Roberts's sweeping criticism laid him open to counter-attack.[4] And Wise, the very leader in the new fashion, joined issue in his April article. It is instructive that he is more concerned with prices than principles. Out of twelve selected cases discussed, ten are treated from the point of view of cash values; and, in refutation of the criticisms about worthless ephemera, he blandly instanced Browning's *Cleon, The Statue and the Bust,* and *Gold Hair,* as being worth ten or twelve guineas each—the first two his own forged productions, the third, one of his suspected pieces; the cost of printing which, we can estimate from his own figure of half a crown for similar things. The remainder of his reply to Roberts was an effort to support what had been rightly conjectured was the falling market in Ruskin first editions.

In his next *Bookman* article (May, 1894) he gave publicity to some of the first-edition productions of writings by Matthew Arnold, George Eliot, William Morris, Ruskin, Rossetti, Swinburne, and Tennyson that he issued, and that are now condemned as forgeries or suspected forgeries. That he could quote a sale price in 1892 of £42 for his 16-page spurious Ruskin, *The Scythian Guest,* indicates both his pride in and the success of the dark enterprise.

There were other channels used for disseminating the news of these nineteenth-century "rarities" and their prices—Harry Buxton Forman's introduction has been mentioned, for one example. Worthy of employment in a better cause was Wise's skill in priming various writers with exactly the information he wanted brought out, in order that he could quote them as independent expert opinion about these precious "first

---

[4] Roberts was then representative of the traditional type of book collecting, with its heavily bound fat quartos and tall folios. The resentment against the new tendencies of the eighties and nineties went too far. The collecting of contemporary authors always offers its fair field. Nevertheless, in the immediate object of his attack Roberts was sound enough.

editions" he was so zealous to champion. Equally diplomatic was the quieting, if not winning over, of some who were critical, and even suspicious.

V

Wise's acquaintance with John H. Wrenn began in the summer of 1892; and it quickly ripened into friendship under the influence of the American's admiration for the other's book knowledge. Every year thereafter, Wrenn's annual visit to Europe included a Continental trip, on which he used to take Wise and his wife. Wrenn paid all the expenses; but, objecting to the bother of the constant tipping, he stipulated that Wise should settle with the politely insistent seekers for gratuities on leaving the various hotels visited. Back home, the gratified guest was wont to describe enthusiastically the royal time he had enjoyed with the generous millionaire. "But mind you," he would add, "it wasn't cheap—having to pay all those tips!"

Under Wise's encouragement and guidance the Chicago banker began building up a library in the magnificent tradition of old American book collectors like General Rush Hawkins, John Boyd Thacher, and Hoe, while he had such contemporary rivals as Henry E. Huntington, J. P. Morgan, and F. R. Halsey. It would be gilding the lily to praise these able and generous men now for what they have done for American culture by forming noble libraries from Britain's rare books representative of her literature, and leaving them for the people of the United States. They form a happy and unrivaled bond between the two countries.

There has been a tendency among the less-informed public opinion in Britain to deplore the passing of so many of our literary and artistic treasures across the Atlantic, the belief being that we were denuding our libraries. Never was there a greater error or more shortsighted view. For the most part we could amply spare the rarities that America paid us the compliment of coveting: with a few exceptions they are well represented in our national collections—not to speak of our private libraries, which, notwithstanding the dispersals of the last few decades, still make a handsome showing.[5] And if those ardent American bookmen had a big and natural appetite for the good things from the Old Country, they did not begrudge paying handsomely for the feast.

With growing competition, the grand hobby became more exciting—sometimes unpleasantly exciting, alas! as rogues and opportunists on both sides of the Atlantic saw their chance of illicit reapings from the harvest. American collectors, shrewd and keen though they might be, were not always, and could hardly be, completely informed in the often tortuous mazes of the original editions of old English writers. Naturally, they placed much trust in British booksellers of repute, and in other advisers presumed to be independent of commercial interests. Of the latter class Wise came to be regarded as the chief figure. It is doubtful whether any English bookman, supposedly unprofessional, has ever attained quite the same eminence and wide reputation, alike for his knowledge and for his boasted intolerance of anything second-rate, shoddy, or spurious. For over twenty years he was helping Wrenn to build his library. During those years, the American, with his almost childlike affection for and curiosity about the books he was amassing, must have prided himself in having such a high and distinguished mentor. Wrenn died before the exposure of the nineteenth-century forgeries, and so was spared a terrible disillusionment.

Wise related his connection with the Wrenn Library in his introduction to its five-volume catalogue (1920) which he edited.[6] The material part reads:

[5] To take, for example, the class of early printed books. It is probable that there are now in America few short of 7,000 fifteenth-century works. This is about half the total in Britain's public libraries, besides which there are many copies in private ownership.
[6] It is further demonstration of Wise's limitations as an editor and cataloguer that it has been found necessary to recatalogue the Wrenn Library—a work now being done by Mr. W. H. McCarthy, the assistant Librarian of Texas University, who is adding a sixth volume containing corrections of all the bad entries in the original work.

... For two decades we worked together. To prevent needless competition and to avoid any possible cause of friction, we agreed that each should have the first claim to the books of certain authors as they came into the market. For example, whilst I had "first call" on Shelley, Dryden, Prior, and the early quarto plays, Wrenn had "first call" on Pope, Wither, and other authors. To carry out this arrangement, Wrenn looked after my interest in America, whilst I attended to his interest here. As a result, *a few by no means unimportant* items came back to me from the United States, whilst quite a substantial proportion of the books now safely and finally housed at Austin were purchased by me in this country.

This is a very carefully concocted statement: Wise could hardly help acknowledging his considerable part in the forming of the Library. It is intended to convey the picture of two wealthy book collectors combining in a friendly alliance not to compete in their hobby, and to help each other in their respective countries. A very pleasant picture too! But it is misleading—as such of Wise's explanations often are misleading. The arrangement actually in effect was that Thomas James Wise, the private rare-book dealer, was selling to Wrenn—undoubtedly the best of his several rich clients, who included Lord Brotherton, Sir Algernon Methuen, Colonel W. F. Prideaux, John Morgan of Aberdeen, R. A. Potts, and G. A. Aitken; and in the United States: William Harris Arnold, Judge Klein, E. K. Butler of Jamaica Plain, and Harry Elkins Widener, in addition to Edwin N. Lapham, Henry W. Poor, and others who were supplied with the forgeries, some probably through an agent. The extent to which Wrenn, the banker, was the agent of Wise in America may be dismissed as almost negligible.

However friendly was the relationship between the two men (collectors are usually on good terms with their trusted booksellers), and however zealously Wise played his part— subservient or not to his own interests as a collector in several of the American's special "fields" [7]—the fact is that from his

[7] The "other authors" Wrenn collected included Swinburne, Shelley, and Tennyson—all of whom, in addition to Pope, Wise specialized in.

transactions with Wrenn he profited greatly. It is related by his assistant, Mr. Gorfin, that on one occasion, when they were busy dispatching books to America, Wise, in a burst of confidence, said: "Wrenn is worth a thousand pounds a year to me."

This figure is not difficult to accept. The Wrenn Library comprises some 6,000 items. It entailed an average yearly rate of acquisition of about 300 books and manuscripts, the individual prices of which would vary between £5 and £500. Of these, Wise says himself he bought a substantial proportion for the Library. The dealings would, of course, include the sales to Wrenn of Wise's privately printed books, and also his nineteenth-century forgeries (about 60, including duplicates). As to the latter, the Keeper of the Wrenn Collection, which is now housed in the Library of the University of Texas, estimates the approximate total cost to Wrenn of the forged and suspect pamphlets alone as between $5,000 and $6,000.

Whether Wrenn knew or guessed the true character of his friend's "arrangement" it is idle to speculate. The provenance of the proof sheets of Mrs. Browning's *The Runaway Slave*, now condemned as a forgery, is given in a note in Wrenn's hand as "Underwood. 4/10/1908." But the Wrenn Librarian has traced the sale of these proofs through Wise, who stated in editing the Wrenn Catalogue (1920) that the Swinburne *Cleopatra* pamphlet, now condemned as a suspected forgery, was bought by the American collector from "the late Dr. Underwood." If there was "no sich a person" as Dr. Underwood, the choice of pseudonym is an amusing cynicism.[8]

If, again, Wise made £1000 a year out of Wrenn alone, as seems likely enough, it is now evident that a substantial part of his fortune accrued from rare-book dealing—remembering that the "arrangement" with his American friend lasted for twenty years. The remarkable thing is that throughout his

[8] There is no "Dr. Underwood" in the official indices of obituaries in *The Times* between 1908 and 1920.

life he so successfully veiled these activities from most of his
acquaintances and from the general public. As I write these
words, again that scene in the Ashley Library comes back,
when he declared to me with such angry vehemence: "I am
NOT a bookseller."

VI

Another of Wise's American collector-clients was William
Harris Arnold. The contact was made in 1896. It was timely;
for most, if not all, the spurious Tennyson pamphlets were
printed apparently in the five preceding years. The first editions of that poet were collected by Arnold, who bought the
forged rarities avidly. As the Appendix shows, there were
more of them than of any other author. What touching confidence Wise was able to establish through his reputation and
tact is evidenced by the American, who has recorded in his
Ventures of Book Collecting:

Through the kind offices of my new, but now dear old, friend,
the distinguished collector and bibliographer, Thomas J. Wise,
...I obtained one Tennyson rarity after another, most of which
at the time were unknown to American collectors.

It is clear, in this case also, that Arnold did not recognize
Wise as a bookseller. The dealings were all "kind offices."
He prints an excitedly flattering letter from Wise, who applies to his private client the proverb "whom the gods love
die young" because of his good fortune in two new Tennyson
"finds," forecasting the early demise of his correspondent
if the saying were true. As a fact, Arnold died in January,
1923, at the age of 68, a few months before his book was
published. Once more there is the remarkable coincidence
of a trustful, almost reverential, client who did not live to
know the nature of some of the things he had so eagerly
bought through the "kind offices" of friendship, or the character of the man who was so quick to plant them on him.
Wise contributed the foreword to Arnold's posthumous book,

from which this gem shall point the tale: "For me it must suffice to tell in ever so small a whisper that, whilst living, his society encouraged me, and that I hold his memory dear."

Here is a short list of some of Wise's nineteenth-century pamphlets that were sold at the dispersal of Arnold's library. The details are a revelation of what was paid by the American bookman for pamphlets whose production cost (as we have seen Wise admitting) averaged about half a crown; and also of what profit they realized before the exposure of them. "C" within parenthesis after the title means that this pamphlet is now condemned as a forgery, "S" that it is classified as a suspected forgery. The word "Collector" or "Bookseller" is Arnold's indication of the source from which he got the pamphlet; the collector is undoubtedly Thomas James Wise. In the case of the three items indicated as exchanges, the cost prices against them are presumably nominal.

			Cost	Sold for
E. B. Browning's	Sonnets (Reading) (C) Collector		$115	$440
" " "	Runaway Slave ....(C) Collector		30	25
R. Browning's	Cleon ....(C) Collector (exchange)		10	80
" "	The Statue and			
	the Bust ....(C) Collector "		10	91
" "	Gold Hair ....(S) Collector "		13.60	68
A. Tennyson's	Falcon ....(S) Bookseller		350	410
" "	The Promise of May (S) Collector		330	430
" "	Lucretius ....(C) Bookseller		25	32.50

The sale catalogue of Arnold's library describes the copy of the "Reading: 1847" edition of the Sonnets as presented by Miss Mitford to Charles Kingsley. As the thing is a forgery produced at a date subsequent to 1886, Miss Mitford (died 1855) could not have presented it, and therefore any presentation inscription must also be a forgery. I have not seen the copy; but it will be noted that it came to Arnold from his "collector friend."

VII

Young Herbert Gorfin, the bright intelligent boy at Rubeck's—the essential-oil merchant—soon commended himself to Mister Thomas James Wise, who, the boy found, ruled the office outside the closed door of Hermann Rubeck's inner room. His voice, indeed, was not infrequently heard from within that sanctum; if it was not in altercation with the proprietor (as the junior opined), then their business involved pretty vigorous discussion. Anyhow, back in the outer office, its ruler took an interest in the boy, who showed a proper disposition to get on in the world. Before long, he was permitted to wrap up some parcels of books for the cashier: some of those parcels were mailed to America. Thus, in due course, the keen youth got to know that his immediate Lord-and-Master-of-the-Outer-Office was a dealer in rare books. This greatly interested Gorfin, who was fond of books. He liked handling those curious little volumes that Mister Wise treated so reverently, and seemed to know so much about.

There was one occasion each summer which Herbert came to anticipate with GREAT EXPECTATIONS. It was when Mister Wise brought with him, for a short call at the office, a small-built, kindly-looking American, who was told that this was the youth who packed his books. With a few words of praise for the care with which the parceling was done, the gentleman from Chicago (Yes! John H. Wrenn) would dip a finger and thumb into a capacious top pocket of his waistcoat, extract two sovereigns, and present them to the awed youngster as encouragement for his attention. The dip into that waistcoat treasure chest, so gratifying to the industrious apprentice, was never overlooked by Wrenn.

But the joke of the pleasing little annual ceremony was that the master himself actually did more of the parceling than did his pupil. For Wise would pack a parcel as deftly as he could collate a book. He never lost the true shopman's pride in delivering the goods. Even when he had retired on his comfortable fortune, and when he was producing the imposing catalogues and bibliographies of his fine Library, the recipients were able to observe that they had evidently been packed and addressed in his sprawling hurried script by the author.

Here, for the time being, we must leave Herbert, the bright promising youth, who is next to prove so useful to Wise—and then so devastating to his reputation.

As we are in the nineties, two of his essays in literary work should be recorded here. In 1894 he edited the edition of Spenser's *Faerie Queene*, concentrating chiefly on the bibliography of the work. The edition, which was lavishly illustrated by Walter Crane and produced by George Allen, was a failure, more than half the copies being sold as remainders. Wise's remuneration was 100 guineas; while Crane received nearly £1,500. In the following year Wise also edited a new edition of Ruskin's *Harbours of England* (George Allen) for a fee of 15 guineas.

CHAPTER 10

"RUSKIN'S ROMANCE" AND THE ARCHIVIST'S DISILLUSION

It is a strange story, and the world knows little about it, and some men have condemned him, as some women have censured her. But the two men and that one woman who know best have been happy and contented with the change that John Ruskin's pure unselfishness brought into their lives. And so the world should not complain.

Ruskin's Romance: 1889 (see page 120).

I

WISE WAS NOW very actively associated with a venture which seems to have escaped notice in connection with his career. This was the inauguration in 1893 of The Society of Archivists and Autograph Collectors, of which he was apparently the chief promoter. The Society's design was stated to be the publication of a *Reference Catalogue of British and Foreign Manuscripts.* This catalogue was composed of separately issued monographs on the scripts of various authors, each part being contributed by a specialist "giving hints for guidance in the detection of forgeries."

Between 1893 and 1898, seven parts of the catalogue were published, the authors and their autographs dealt with being (1) Charlotte Brontë, (2) Robert Burns, (3) Charles Dickens, (4) John Keats, (5) Alexander Pope, (6) Matthew Prior, and (7) Lord Byron. Of these, Wise contributed those on Charlotte Brontë and Charles Dickens, in addition to "editing" the other parts.[1] In his prefatory note to the first monograph,

---

[1] Strangely enough, it seems that two more parts were published by the Society, which are not listed in the British Museum but are to be found in the New York Public Library. In these, Wise's name has entirely disappeared, although the other Society members are listed. The two parts are:

(8) *Ludwig van Beethoven*, edited by H. Saxe Wyndham. London. 1899.

(9) *Her Majesty The Queen*, edited by H. Saxe Wyndham London. 1900. One hunded copies of each were printed.

he said: "It must, I suppose, be considered matter for congratulation that no forged or spurious letters of Charlotte Brontë are known; none, at all events, have [sic] ever occurred for sale." Against this he subsequently wrote in the British Museum's copy (in defiance of the Library's rule): "This statement is now, unfortunately, incorrect!" No doubt it was. But if all the errors made by authors were to be amended in the Museum's books, what a mess many of them would be in!

These archivistic activities of Thomas James Wise are not surprising when we consider his interest in autograph material, and how largely manuscripts figured in his dealing and collecting. He once said that he had made some study of the chemical constituents of ink. It will be seen that five of the seven authors chosen as subjects for monographs were authors in whom he specialized as a collector. But it is a strange circumstance that in the various books he compiled he is silent about the Society, and that he did not include its monographs—not even his own—in his Ashley Library catalogues.

II

Every young husband and wife in the Victorian days had experience of those embarrassingly solicitous friends who had the curiosity to inquire of one or the other (but never of both together): "When may we expect...?" In these days the Unfinished Sympathy is not so popular. Thomas Wise used to turn off such inquiries with the remark: "Children! I can't afford children. They cost a thousand pounds each; and what a lot of books I can buy for that!" Presumably this was his idea of a joke. All the same, Selina had her own ideas about hobbies; she was eying the increasing bookshelves at 52 Ashley Road still more dubiously.

Occasional visitors there found the young wife rather attractive, with her unexpected turns of speech, her quaint ways, and her natural gifts: as a singer she had a pleasing voice. Once, when a guest was sharing the evening meal, Wise remarked with considerable brusqueness—as though Selina had omitted the pagination in a book collation—that there was no cheese upon the table. Whereupon she left the room, and was heard calling down into the kitchen: "Mary! Bring up the cheese pot." Thomas's petulance having increased, the amused guest asked about the unfamiliar term; and it was explained that "cheese pot" was the name for that kind of receptacle in Selina's native county. "But the hurried appearance of the pot in no way mollified my host," added the narrator; whose impression it was that however increasingly prosperous its master, the Ashley Road menage was under a cloud. This was also the impression, a few months later, of Mr. William Roberts, who had written that unpleasantly outspoken article in the *Fortnightly Review*,[2] but who soon after received a cordial invitation to call and see the collector's books. This little way with awkward critics illustrates what has been said here about Wise's diplomacy.

III

How busy he was in the eighties has been shown; but he appears to have been even busier in the "Naughty Nineties": 1899 is the last attributed date of one of his "wrong" things (the Kipling piracy of *The White Man's Burden*,—his "wild career" continuing from the age of 27 to 40. In addition, there was a continuous stream of his privately printed first editions, including several piracies. One of these first editions was Swinburne's poem, *Grace Darling* (1893)—a poem which appeared in friend Shorter's *Illustrated London News* of June that year. Wise in his *Swinburne Bibliography* proudly describes it as "one of the most interesting volumes in the Ashley Library Series of Privately Printed Books." If it is true, as he says, that he printed the poem at Swinburne's

2 See page 104.

expressed wish,[3] it is curious that the 20-page pamphlet bears no mark of identification with Wise or his Library, that it was not described in his 1905-8 *Ashley Library Catalogue,* and that the British Museum had to buy its copy—in this case from the publisher himself at 10/6. The inferences from various circumstances are that *Grace Darling* and also Swinburne's *Ballad of Bulgarie,* privately printed in the same year by Wise, a copy being sent anonymously to the British Museum Library, are piracies. In fact, Wise himself in his *Bibliography* (Vol. 1, p. 450) admits that the *Ballad* was produced without Swinburne's consent.[4]

Similarly, his production of J. M. Barrie's poem, *Scotland's Lament* (1895), is almost certainly a piracy, and one which had a surprising and amusing sequel. This ode on the death of Robert Louis Stevenson appeared in January, 1895, in the *Bookman,* conducted by Robertson Nicoll, from whom Wise bought the manuscript. From this he promptly printed, in a more correct text than the *Bookman*'s, his usual edition purporting this time to be limited to twelve copies. But he kept very quiet about it, sending no copy to the British Museum and omitting this desirable item from his 1895-8 catalogue.

Now comes the comedy. In 1918 his twin soul, Clement Shorter, made a great discovery. He found out about this ode to R. L. S. and where it appeared serially. He then rushed out one of his editions for private distribution, limited to 20 copies. He was only 23 years too late! Doubtless Thomas James grinned as he wrote "First Edition" against the entry of his own pamphlet in his great catalogue of 1922-36. Nevertheless Shorter could at least say that he had obtained Barrie's authority for the printing.

When Mr. Herbert Garland was completing his Bibliography of Sir J. M. Barrie (*The Bookman's Journal:* 1928),

---

[3] A statement not repeated by Wise in his subsequent *Ashley Library Catalogue* (1922-36) and his *Swinburne Library* (1925).
[4] See Chapter 13 for Watts-Dunton's threat to denounce these two pamphlets.

and inquired about these two separate editions of the same poem printed by the well-known friends and collaborators, Wise evidently felt that some explanation was necessary. He told Barrie's bibliographer "... this pamphlet was originally printed with the intention merely of providing a text to accompany the MS which is also in my possession." The adroitness of the explanation and the way it is left in the air are characteristic. For the original purpose as alleged, it would be sufficient to print one copy of the poem not necessarily in pamphlet form. But Wise's edition bears a certificate of the number of copies printed—for what it is worth. In the not very likely event of his being challenged about the authority for the print when it was revealed in 1922, he would probably have said that it was printed by arrangement with Robertson Nicoll. Had this equally adroit explanation been offered, it would have been accepted by Barrie for the sake of the 71-year-old Robertson Nicoll, the author's friend and early patron.

IV

If Wise was unable to establish other than the most formal and infrequent relations with John Ruskin, far different was the association of that author and Dr. Furnivall. After Ruskin's unfortunate marriage in 1848 with Euphemia Chalmers Gray (Effie) had been annulled on the wife's unresisted petition (on the grounds of impotency), and she had married the artist, John Everett Millais, the devoted Furnivall received the poignant confidences of the divorced husband. Ruskin was, and continued to be for many years, much maligned; but he kept a chivalrous silence, allowing the scandalmongers to slander as they willed. The marriage was arranged by the parents. The young couple were incompatible. There is much in the theory that Ruskin married on the rebound, as his hero Sir Walter Scott had done; and that his life story would have been a happy one had he not been disappointed in 1847 in failing to secure Miss Lockhart, Scott's granddaughter. "As to the accusation of my having thrown my late wife in Mr. Millais' way," he wrote to friend Furnivall in a remarkable letter, "I should as soon think of simply denying an accusation of murder. Let those who say I have committed murder, prove it." He ended with the bitter philosophizing: "... for she hated me as only those hate who have injured."

When Furnivall, after Ruskin's death, showed that letter to Wise, the collector coveted it almost more than anything else he had ever sought. There was in it a dialogue which seemed to have a particular fascination for him. Furnivall, who lost his considerable fortune in a bank failure and was afterward a poor man, was persuaded to sell the original letter to Wise, who used to show it as one of the most dramatic documents in his store of manuscripts. For a reason not difficult to guess, he never made a private printing of this letter.[5] But he allowed Shorter to do so, freely quoting Clem's pamphlet in the *Ashley Catalogue* (from both of which my illustrative quotations are made). The passage that so irresistibly attracted Wise was written by Ruskin as an illustration of his wife's attitude and moods. It is:

> For instance, would the kind of temper indicated in the following dialogue—which I happened to put down one day as an example of our usual intercourse—be believed in a woman who to all strangers behaved with grace and pleasantness?
> Effie is looking abstractedly out of the window.
> John: "What are you looking at, Effie?"
> Effie: "Nothing."
> John: "What are you thinking of then?"
> Effie: "A great many things."
> John: "Tell me some of them."

[5] It was apparently printed under the "authority" described on page 95. Shorter's print is notable for his introduction, in which he makes a point that seems to have escaped biographers—namely, that the unresisted allegation of impotency was later disproved when Ruskin fell in love with young Rose La Touche and was prepared to furnish proofs that he had been cruelly slandered by his wife.

Effie: "I was thinking of operas, and—excitement—and (angrily) a great many things."
John: "And what conclusions did you come to?"
Effie: "None—because you interrupted me."

Dialogue closed.

Possibly the explanation of that letter's fascination for Wise [6] was the recollection of his own experiences. It was in 1895 that the difference in temperament and outlook of Thomas James (aged 35) and Selina Fanny (25) reached a crisis. Bibliography or what-not, the young wife had become increasingly restless of late; and, being spirited and energetic, and feeling neglected, she sought the distractions of a tennis club and other social amenities. But soon her young and impulsive being responded too ardently to the natural enthusiasm she inspired. And one day she blithely stepped out of Ashley Road ... out of Thomas's life ... into the blue.

"Into the blue" is not an extravagance. There was a considerable and costly quest for the five years' wife before the sequel—which was, of course, in the Divorce Court. This occurred on October 28th, 1897, when a decree nisi was made at the husband's petition for divorce on the ground of his wife's adultery with one Lionel Rogers. Selina's subsequent experience of life was far from being as happy as her prospects had appeared to promise. The fact is only mentioned to do justice to Thomas James Wise, whose compassion—and perhaps regret—were sufficiently touched, it is said, to make him responsive when the time came to be helpful to the first and disappointed sharer of his domesticity.

In the meantime, in 1896, Wise left forever the road whose name was given to his library of future fame. A bachelor

[6] There is a rare and mysterious pamphlet, *Ruskin's Romance* (1889), that purports to be a reprint "From a New England Newspaper," and contains at least two errors of fact that were for long in general currency. It has features characteristic of Wise's printings. He described it in the *Ruskin Bibliography* and sold a copy of it to his agent, Mr. Gorfin, for £1. 5. in 1910. Messrs. Clay & Sons, however, say that it was not printed by them. It is not included in the record of Wise's privately printed editions given in the Appendix.

again, he took up his abode at 15 St. George's Road, Kilburn (now called Priory Terrace); where he remained until he entered his second and more successful edition of matrimony.

V

Almost the last of his jobs before leaving Ashley Road was the printing of a 20-page booklet which has an importance greatly out of proportion to its small size. It bears the title:

THE/ASHLEY/LIBRARY/A List of/Books Printed for Private Circulation/by THOMAS JAMES WISE/52, Ashley Road, Crouch Hill, London. N./1895.

This title is ambiguous, whether intentional or not. The second title, "A List of," etc., may be taken as meaning either that the list was compiled by Wise, or that he had printed the books listed. Either way, the booklet has the apparent design of recording books in the Library. It details the titles, authors, dates, sizes, and limits of edition, of 47 items composed of 8 Ruskin titles, 6 Shelleys, 19 Shelleyana,[7] 11 miscellaneous, and 3 "in preparation." Among these titles are several piracies.

The items were those Wise had for sale; the booklet is nothing more or less than his bookseller's catalogue in a disguised form. As if the title were not sufficiently calculated to conceal the list's object, there is a statement on the reverse side of the title page which says:

The following list is printed as a Record, not by way of Advertisement. Books printed in short numbers for private circulation become so rapidly and entirely absorbed, that it is exceedingly difficult to obtain information regarding them when such is required for bibliographical or other purposes. Hence the necessity for the present Catalogue.

---

[7] These were off-prints of Shelley Society papers that he "took advantage" to make when in charge of the Society's printing as described (*vide* pp. 61-63 and Appendix), rigging them up with the usual preliminaries and labeling them "First Editions."

This is a statement in keeping with his angry protestation to me: "I am NOT a bookseller." But if it is only a bibliographical record, as suggested, and not an advertising medium, how strange that the bibliographer did not send a copy to the British Museum Library (which had later to buy one), and did not mention it in his exhaustive catalogues! This is the only printed bookseller's list issued by Wise that I know of, unless some of his larger publications—like the *Bibliography of Borrow*—were also intended to serve the same purpose. The necessity for such a list (which he reissued in 1897 to include publications he had produced in the meantime) indicates that his private publishing business was now in a considerable way.

VI

In the following year, 1896, as the result of the initiation of a Burns Centenary Club, appeared the pamphlet *Robert Burns. A Poem.* By Algernon Charles Swinburne (1896), which contains such fine stanzas as:

> *The daisy by his ploughshare cleft,*
> *The lips of women loved and left,*
> *The griefs and joys that weave the weft*
> *   Of human time*
> *With craftsman's cunning, keen and deft,*
> *   He carved in rhyme.*

Its title page said it was printed for the Club. Wise, describing his copy, says that 30 copies only were printed and the circulation limited to the 16 members, to which number the Club was "rigorously restricted." But the ultimate distribution of the precious first edition could hardly have been so rigorous or so equal; for I find that Wise kept three copies for the Ashley Library, two other copies found their way to his client, John H. Wrenn, and the collector-dealer had at

least one copy to sell to Mr. Gorfin fourteen years later!
Apparently the pamphlet was produced by Wise, who says
of the holograph MS of the poem in his possession that it is
of somewhat unusual importance, for it supplies a stanza
which was perhaps wisely deleted although restored in subsequent editions. The stanza, which—it may have been feared—
might have led to the drawing of claymores north of the
Tweed, runs:

> And Calvin, night's prophetic bird,
> Out of his home in hell was heard
> Shrieking! and all the fens were stirred
> Whence plague is bred:
> Can God endure the scoffer's word?
> But God was dead.

The pamphlet, however, follows the text of the poem as it
had been printed in the *Nineteenth Century* for February,
1896. If, as Wise affirms, Swinburne gave his "ready consent"
to the private printing, it is nevertheless exceedingly doubtful—all things considered—whether he agreed to the suppression of the stanza. Incidentally, the British Museum did receive a copy of this item, but it came from an anonymous
donor. Why it should not have come from Wise, why the
mysterious sending to the Museum—well, these are characteristic mysteries where Wise was at the printing press.

In January and February 1898 there was a curious correspondence in the *Athenaeum* about an 18-page pamphlet by
Robert Louis Stevenson entitled *Some College Memories*,
which purported to have been printed in Edinburgh for
members of the University Union Committee, 1886. It bore
neither printer's nor publisher's imprint. Messrs. T. & A.
Constable of Edinburgh wrote of this mysterious pamphlet,
"at present being offered at extraordinary prices," that *Some
College Memories* was first contributed by Stevenson to a
little volume called *The New Amphion*, which was printed

by them for the Edinburgh University Union in November
1886. They said that the pamphlet was unknown to them
or to Stevenson's friends, who would certainly be expected
to know of it; and the thing was pronounced to be "not a first
edition—merely a pirated reprint, of which the sale is illegal."

To this emphatic declaration the *Athenaeum* appended a
note saying that Messrs. Constable were in error, that Stevenson had some copies printed off in 1886 for his friends
connected with the University, and that they had been informed "by a bibliographer of note" that he had seen a copy
inscribed by R.L.S. Such a note not unnaturally angered the
Constables, who replied with truncheon strokes giving detailed reasons for their damning description of the pamphlet
as a pirated reprint.

Wise was almost certainly the "bibliographer of note" who
had inspired the *Athenaeum*'s editorial "reply," then entered the lists in defense of the pamphlet's genuineness; insisting, in a variety of vague and differing expressions, on
Stevenson's responsibility for the thing. It was a most unsatisfactory and side-tracking defense for any kind of bibliographer. But there are two strange features about his letter,
addressed from 15 St. George's Rd., N.W. *First,* that nothing
was said about the copy alleged to have been inscribed by
Stevenson, the production or corroboration of which might
have provided a clinching argument. If it ever existed, it has
never been heard of since. *Second,* that Wise, declaring the
pamphlet to be "no 'piracy,'" added, "neither is it in any
way a 'spurious print,' as it was printed in 1886, as duly set
forth upon its title page." No one had used the expression
"spurious print": the terms of the comment indicate the
trend of the writer's thoughts.

Then Mr. Frank T. Sabin, the bookseller, wrote a satiri-
cal skit which effectively showed up the hollowness of the
defense and the absurdity of linking the piracy with Stevenson. This pamphlet is now condemned in the terms of

Messrs. T. & A. Constable's censure. Even Colonel Prideaux, the innocent tool of Wise, could not swallow the "justification" of the "bibliographer of note"; as he showed when he came to compile his *Bibliography of Stevenson,* when he referred any "curious reader" to the pages of the *Athenaeum.*

While this affair was being thrashed out, Robert Proctor, the typographical expert and friend of William Morris, wrote to the *Athenaeum* (Jan. 22, '98) giving convincing reasons for describing as "an unauthorised and later reprint" a pamphlet entitled *Sir Galahad A Christmas Mystery.* 1858 (from Morris's *Defence of Guenevere.* 1858). This Christmas mystery is now completely cleared up by its inclusion by Carter and Pollard among Wise's forgeries, and condemning it on the evidence of its paper as well as on that provided by Proctor.

The "bibliographer of note" did not draw his pen in defense of *Sir Galahad.* He had the attack on *Some College Memories* to cope with—and that was more than enough. But these exposures in the *Athenaeum* (while not connecting the denounced things with Wise, of course) seem to have determined him for the future to keep out of controversy when he was on such dangerous grounds.

The closing years of the nineties found Wise at his temporary home in St. George's Road, producing bibliographies of Browning (1897) and Swinburne (1897) which were forerunners to the completer ones of the same subjects; and working on his Tennyson bibliography (1908). These advanced his reputation as a bibliographer and collector; they also publicized his forgeries and piracies, and assisted his bookselling to an extent that can be better guessed than definitely assessed. In the Swinburne work he announced as "in preparation" uniform bibliographies also of Robert Louis Stevenson and Dante Gabriel Rossetti. But these never materialized, probably because Colonel W. F. Prideaux was specializing in the former, and Rossetti's brother William in the latter. So that it may justly be said that there really were cases where Thomas James Wise did not ride rough-shod over all pioneers—as he did Harry Buxton Forman and Herne Shepherd, whose works he used without gratitude or even common acknowledgment.

CHAPTER 11

REMARRIAGE, AND THE WRITING
ON THE WALL

Belshazzar the King made a great feast. ...In the same hour came
forth fingers of a man's hand, and wrote over against the candle-
stick upon the plaster of the wall of the King's palace; and the
King saw the part of the hand that wrote....
Daniel v.

I

WITH THE NEW CENTURY came a new turn in the career of
Thomas James Wise. By this time he had probably finished
with the production of the forged pamphlets, although his
pirating continued as late as 1914. As a result of what could
only have been extraordinary labors and ingenuities in
bookselling and publishing since 1880, not forgetting his
City employment as cashier with Hermann Rubeck, he now
had capital at command and a considerable and growing
income. The time had arrived when he could build up the
Ashley Library on foundations already laid, out of small
savings and large discrimination. He had a reputation—even
then somewhat exaggerated—as a bibliographer; and as such
his plans were ambitious. Last but not least, at the age of
forty he was entering on a new matrimonial partnership, and
of course in a new home.

His second marriage, on June 27th, 1900, was to Miss
Frances Louise Greenhalgh, of Southend, who was his junior
by twelve years. Her father had been a bank manager. The
ceremony took place at the Register Office, Rochford, Essex.
The usual particulars, presumably supplied by the bride-
groom, are interesting. He described himself as a merchant;
his father's rank as that of "Gentleman"; and the bride's

deceased father as "Banker." For this marriage Wise had made a new home at 23 Downside Crescent, Hampstead, where he lived until finally removing to 25 Heath Drive, Hampstead, in 1910.

When in the course of time Wise's career blazed into such fame and his circle of friends and acquaintances extended, there were not more than half a dozen who were aware of his previous marriage. But those who met the second Mrs. Wise could hardly doubt that Thomas James had been as happy in his domestic partner as he had been successful in his worldly dealings. Added to the shrewd and practical virtues of a North Countrywoman, she brought a sympathetic interest in the higher and open activities of this, the second part of his career, and a particularly watchful loyalty in the final catastrophic years. Then, when he produced his last publication—the concluding volume of his formidable *Catalogue*—he paid a deserved tribute by gracing it with a pleasing portrait of her. She survived her husband by nearly two years; her death occurring on the 6th of May, 1939, at the age of 66.

II

It was during the first decade of the new century that Wise acquired most of his choicest books. These, together with his exceptionally extensive collection of nineteenth-century manuscripts, gave the Ashley Library its character and were to be the inducements that led to its acquisition by his country in 1937. Just as he had been fortunate in beginning to collect when first editions, in their original state, of such authors as Shelley, Keats, Wordsworth, and Byron, were to be got cheaply, so now again he was lucky in his opportunities—just when he had more money to command than in the earlier years.

For there now "dribbled on to the market" (to use Stock Exchange terms much affected by Wise, as also by others in the Rare Book Trade) a remarkable "run" of Elizabethan quarto plays in the fine original condition that means so much to students of old literature. Wise was one of the men foremost to appreciate the importance of copies as first issued, and in this regard his influence as a collector is a feature of his career. The precious printings from the Elizabethan presses that now came to light, fresh and eloquent witnesses to the English drama at its most virile epoch, were such as to excite the rivalry of long-pursed collectors. Rivalry there was, especially from such American millionaire bookmen as Robert Hoe (son of the famous inventor of the Rotary press), William A. White (a New York merchant), and later Henry E. Huntington (railway president and financier). The recurring fights over several years were not less keen because they were waged without fuss or publicity. But it behooved an Englishman to secure these treasures, or have them forever lost to his country. And Wise it was who, by his insistence and shrewd acceptance of expert advice, won the noiseless and unseen battle for books—outbidding his American rivals for the pick of the plays. In the final balance sheet of his career, it is this achievement that figures impressively on the credit side. His quiet collecting during this decade, often through agents, ultimately gave the nation possibly its last chance to secure in mint condition many of the important original editions in English poetry and drama from 1650 to 1900.

As that esteemed authority, Mr. Seymour de Ricci, has happily put it in a letter to me on the subject: "The British Museum numerically is rich beyond praises. But there are hardly a dozen of their English first editions which can compare in condition with the Wise copies. Many valuable 'firsts' in the Museum are in the sad condition of St. Peter's statue in the Vatican, slowly destroyed by the kisses of admiring worshippers. To add the whole of the Wise Library to the British Museum would be to give the Keepers of that Institution exactly what they need the most: books they might save from the hands of Twentieth Century readers for the benefit of the year 2,000."

Of this enthusiastic assessment of the entire Ashley Library, some qualification will be made. But it illustrates the arguments urged upon those responsible for buying the collection for the nation. A useful idea of his book buying during this important period can be provided by giving the following list of his acquisitions through one agency only, that of Messrs. Quaritch, between 1905 and 1908.[1] The prices are very interesting as indicating the small cost of his library compared with the sums at which, we shall see, it came to be valued and the amount for which it was bought for the British Museum. Within a few years he was to see the values of such books rise far beyond even his calculations.

III

In this list of Wise's acquisitions, all the books are first editions; and he had nearly all of them bound or rebound in whole morocco.

AUTHOR	TITLE	PRICE
		£. s.
Edmund Waller:	*Instructions to a Painter* (1666).......	6.
Sir W. Davenport:	*Poem upon his Sacred Majestie's Most Happy Return.* (1660).............	7.10.
George Wither:	*Vaticinium Causuale* (1655)	8. 8.
Ben Jonson:	*Ben:Jonson his Volpone* (1607).......	60.
John Day:	*Humour out of Breath* (1608).........	63.
Samuel Daniel:	*The First Fowre Bookes of the Civile Wars* (1595)	25.
Giles Fletcher:	*Christ's Victory over Death* (1640).....	20.
Sir W. Alexander:	*Doomesday* (1614)	24.10.
Drayton & others:	*Sir John Oldcastle* (1600) [2]...........	105.
William Cowper:	*Poems* (1782-5)	45.
Michael Drayton:	*Idea* (1593)	36.

[1] I am indebted for this list to the bibliophile, Mr. F. S. Ferguson, who is the present head of Quaritch's.

[2] Actually 1619. This is one of the Seven Spurious Plays attributed to Shakespeare, and reprinted in the Third Folio.

George Chapman: *The Conspiracie and Tragedie of Charles Duke of Byron* (1608).... 20.
Ben Jonson: *The Alchemist* (1612)................ 39.
John Still: *Gammer gurton's Nedle* (1575) [3]......180.
Thomas Preston: *A Lamentable Tragedie ... of Cambises King of Percia* (n.d.)................169.
Thomas Nash: *Have with you to Saffron-walden* (1596) 99.
"   " *Nashes Lenten Stuffe* (1599)..........111.
"   " *A Countercuffe given to Martin Junior* (1589) [4] .... 18.
[George Peele]: *The Battell of Alcazar* (1594)........ 60.
P. B. Shelley: *Queen Mab* (1812).................. 53.
Alexander Pope: *The Dunciad* (1728)................ 55.
Ben Jonson: *The Fountaine of Selfe-Love* (1601).... 60.
John Marston: *The Malcontent* (1604).............. 70.
Sir W. Davenport: [Various Plays in Three Vols] (1639-61) 50.
Shakespeare: *Romeo & Juliet* (1637) [5] .... 30.
George Peele: *The Love of King David and Fair Bethsabe* (1599)......................151.
Philip Massinger &
Thomas Decker: *The Virgin Martir* (1622)............ 30.
Edmund Waller: *Pompey the Great* (1664)............. 12.
John Bale: *Enterlude of Johan the Evangelyst* [?1560] .... 51.
John Cooke: *Greenes Tu Quoque* (1614)........... 49.
George à Green: *A Pleasant Conceyted Comedie of George à Greene* (1599) ....109.
Anonymous: *Everie Woman in her Humor* (1609)..103.
" *An Enterlude of Welth and Helth* (1558) ....105.

But, deeply satisfying though such buying must have been to Wise in the light of rare-book values after the World War, he did not always know what wonderful prizes were being thrust upon him by Fate. He was never really master of Elizabethan bibliography; and while he explored the physical make-up of his own rarities thoroughly enough as a rule, his knowledge and therefore his bibliographical works

[3] Attributed to Wm. Stevenson by Pollard and Redgrave (1926).
[4] Attributed to Pasquill of England by Pollard and Redgrave.
[5] Not kept for the Ashley Library.

often suffered for lack of studious comparison with other copies of the same rarities.

For example: it is a matter of history that when the trio of Elizabethans, Chapman, Jonson, and Marston, so brilliantly collaborated in the comedy *Eastward hoe,* played by the Children of her Majesty's Revels at Blackfriars, there was an unexpected and alarming sequel. Offense was taken by the Court at a gibe against the Scotch, and Chapman and Marston were thrown into prison. No doubt Marston was the offender. Ben Jonson, however, although he denied authorship, chivalrously joined his collaborators. Theirs was a pretty plight, for they were in danger of having their ears and noses slit—which is unpleasanter than having your purse slit in the law courts today in the rare cases in which authors have the courage to be bold. But Jonson and Chapman set influential friends to work; and the trio were released—the occasion being celebrated by Rare Ben feasting his partners in a proper Elizabethan merry-o. Perhaps they sang his song to Caelia that ends:

> *'Tis no sin, love's fruits to steal;*
> *But the sweet thefts to reveal:*
> *To be taken, to be seen,*
> *These have crimes accounted been.*

Anyhow, the gibe against the Scotch occurs in the scene where Seagull is telling vulgar fables about the wonders of Virginia and its fortunate inhabitants whose chamber pots and dripping pans were of pure gold, and who gathered rubies and diamonds by the handful on the seashore. "And then you shal liue freely there without Sergeants, or Courtiers, or Lawyers, or Intelligencers," says Seagull with a back-kick at the Court. Then followed the gibe:

Onely a few industrious Scots perhaps, who indeed are disperst ouer the face of the whole earth. But as for them, there are no greater friends to English-men and *England,* when they are out an't, in the world, then they are. And for my part, I would a hundred thousand of 'hem were there, for wee are all one Countreymen now, yee know; and wee shoulde finde ten times more comfort of them there, then wee doe heere.

This passage was deleted as soon as the play began printing in 1605. The only copy known to contain it is the very one that was acquired by Thomas James Wise; and to the Ashley Library the editor of Oxford University's magnificent *Jonson* edition had to go in 1932 for a complete version of the play. But, although in his *Catalogue* Wise briefly dismisses his copy as the first issue of the first edition (presumably because of the title leaf, about which he was mistaken), he was unaware of the treasure he possessed. With his fondness for ecstatically describing at length the reasons for the rarity of his acquisitions, it is inconceivable that he would not have brought out these facts had he known the full story about his unique possession. The truth is that he was all at sea about *Eastward hoe*. He indulged in what is known as "making-up" copies.[6] This is an example of a made-up copy in which the third title page issued has been put to the first issue of the text—and the only known copy of such first issue at that. His mortification when these things were revealed to him after the publication of the *Ashley Library Catalogue* must have been great.

An Elizabethan student, thinking to be helpful, once gently broke the "news" to him that one of his Massingers suffered from much the same defect. "Yes, I know, confound it! I made it up myself," was the candid avowal of the collector.

But Wise's library has many other good things, proving that he sometimes bought more by luck than by judgment, and that he was more fortunate than he knew. How cheap, for instance, his *Volpone or the Foxe* at £60! Here again he was unaware that, of all the copies known of this famous

---

[6] I.e., completing defective copies of rare books by transference to them of the required parts from other defective copies of the same books. Providing all such substituted parts are genuine and the result conforms to a known issue instead of fabricating something unauthenticated (which is the danger of the practice), this is considered allowable and often done, except by the purists of book collecting.

first edition, only his own and the British Museum's specimen (that is inscribed by Jonson to Florio) contains the shy and pleasing verses signed N. F.—the tribute of Nathan Field, an actor who had been given his chance to appear in one or two of the great dramatist's plays. Apart from this, Wise's copy of *Volpone* is distinguished for other features.[7]

His copy of Thomas Preston's *Lamentable Tragedie mixed full of plesant mirth . . . of Cambises King of Percia* (n.d.) is worthy of note for a reason other than its scarcity. It came out of a quarto volume containing seventeen plays of the late sixteenth century that for thirty years was bricked up in the chimney corner of an Irish farmhouse. The lucky find, when split into seventeen lots and sold by auction in 1906, realized £2602—Wise paying £169 for Mr. Preston's mixture of tragedie and pleasant mirth.

Wise's buying of rare books continued to about 1930, but decreasingly as he completed his individual collections of authors' original editions. Some of his later acquisitions before the rare-book boom included Charles Lamb's *Blank Verse* (1798), £45; George Chapman's *Bussy d'Ambois* (1607), £22, and his *Revenge of Bussy d'Ambois* (1613), £28.10.; Robert Greene's *The Spanish Masquerado* (1588), £43; and John Lyly's *The Woman in the Moone* (1597)—the last-named one of his costliest purchases and recaptured from America at $1320. A number of his Elizabethans came from the famous Rowfant Library that was founded on the collecting of that earlier delinquent Halliwell-Phillips; and others were from the library of Algernon Charles Swinburne, who loved Elizabethan first editions for their texts, not for their texture. Wherefore lamented Wise, who cared for condition above all things.

IV

It was in 1903 that Wise received the first shock of his career—a shock that must have been a premonition of the im-

[7] See Simpson in the Oxford *Ben Jonson*, Vol. v, *op. cit.*

pending Nemesis. In that year appeared the first volume of the standard edition of *The Works of John Ruskin* edited by Sir E. T. Cook and Alexander Wedderburn. It was a monumental work in 39 volumes exhaustively edited. Wise knew its able editors. As a Ruskin specialist himself, he had naturally been consulted by them; and, as naturally, he would be anxious to see what they had to say about certain rare pamphlets that he, and he alone, had been able to bring to light in his *Ruskin Bibliography*—although strangely enough they had not been known to his predecessor in that field, the pioneer Richard Herne Shepherd.

There was *Leoni: a Legend of Italy* (1868), a poem the 18-year-old Ruskin had written and got printed, by influence, in *Friendship's Offering* to recommend himself to Miss Adèle Clotilde Domecq, daughter of his father's partner in the wine merchants' business of Ruskin, Telford, and Domecq.[8] But Miss Adèle Clotilde Domecq was hardly one of the clotted-cream damsels who sighed and palpitated over the heartthrobs of *The Keepsake* and *Friendship's Offering:* she had laughed over it in "rippling ecstasies of derision, of which I bore the pain bravely for the sake of seeing her thoroughly amused."[9] There was not much likelihood of the pained young wooer having honored the derided poem by a separate printing. So also thought Cook and Wedderburn, who for various reasons doubted the authenticity of an alleged first-edition pamphlet, and its stilted preface in style so unlike Ruskin's.

Next, Cook and Wedderburn were obliged to "call in question" *The Scythian Guest* (1849), a poem which had also appeared in *Friendship's Offering*. As Ruskin's editors they were unable, they said, to guarantee the genuineness of this pamphlet purporting to be the first edition. Wise must have shivered. But worse was to follow.

---

[8] It was a useful combination which enabled John Ruskin to be a Samaritan and patron of the arts. Telford provided the capital; Domecq, the wine; and Ruskin senior, the brains.

[9] See his *Praeterita*.

In Vol. 12, issued the following year (1904), the editors dealt with another of these mysterious pamphlets, *The National Gallery* (1852), and showed by textual comparison that the producer of it had printed the material from *Arrows of the Chace* (1880), back-dating it 1852 in order to pass it off as a first edition. "It thus follows that the reprint '*of extreme scarcity*' is what is known in the trade as a 'fake.' "

But it was in their eighteenth volume that Cook and Wedderburn lashed out with the indignation of jealous editors. Of *The Queen's Garden* (1864), they said:

This pamphlet, which figures in dealers' language as "of the extremest scarcity," is—like the separate issues of *Leoni* and *The National Gallery* . . . a fake. It purports to have been "printed in aid of the St. Andrews School Fund"; in which case the issue would obviously not have been limited to a few copies. It bears the imprint of a firm which now at any rate is "not known" by the Post Office. The first copy of it to appear was elaborately described in the *Bookman* for February, 1893 [signed "W," is the later comment], with a reduced facsimile of the title page; [10] the facsimile was also given among the illustrations accompanying the bibliography, edited by T. J. Wise. Several copies of it subsequently appeared in the market, and changed hands at very high prices—copies in remarkably clean condition. . . . It is thus clear that the pamphlet is not what it purports to be, but is a clumsy "fake." The person who put it upon the market, not knowing that Ruskin had revised the lecture in 1871, had his "original edition of the utmost scarcity" set up from the later edition.

These four pamphlets were not friendship's offerings from Thomas James Wise. They were his productions done for commerce, and in his publicizing of them he stressed the fact that one had sold for £42—a figure that must have been considered very satisfactory for a thing whose cost price we can put at about half a crown. All four pamphlets are now condemned as forgeries on evidence independent of that of

[10] The impudence and cleverness of this "elaborate description," or puff, in friend Robertson Nicoll's *Bookman* is astonishing, but not untypical of Wise's advertising of his wares.

Ruskin's meticulous editors. The interesting point, however, is that the unmasking of Wise's spurious nineteenth-century pamphlets was really begun by Cook and Wedderburn in 1903; although some thirty years had to elapse before their damning verdict was upheld by typographical tests or paper analyses, and the forging was revealed to have been extended to other authors' works. Did Cook and Wedderburn suspect Wise of being the fabricator or concerned in the fabricating? And why did not their sarcastic rejection of these four pamphlets immediately lead to the exposure of the whole ramp, the evil traffic in which he continued until 1934?

These are questions that will naturally be asked. By the pointed way Cook and Wedderburn linked Wise with the pamphlets and quoted his publicizing statements as to their extreme scarcity, it does look as if Ruskin's editors had some sort of suspicion of Ruskin's bibliographer. But suspicion was one thing: tracing the origin of the fakes or making any charge, direct or indirect, against a man like Wise—a reputedly wealthy merchant and well-known collector—was another. They were doing their duty to Ruskin by branding the things. In the absence of more proofs (that thirty years later were to be obtained by methods they never dreamt of) they left the perpetrator to Time. As to the second question, the apparent failure of the book-collecting world to profit by the revelations of Cook and Wedderburn is a more complicated subject. Messrs. Carter and Pollard, who indicated their indebtedness to Ruskin's editors,[11] point out that the denunciations of the four pamphlets are "scattered in small-type notes" through Cook and Wedderburn's great work, and that collecting interest in Ruskin was beginning to diminish.[12] Cook and Wedderburn's startling discoveries were not mere

[11] A statement attributed to Mr. Graham Pollard by the *Daily Express* of August 17th, 1937, is: "I hit on the clue that there was something wrong with Wise's famous catalogue of books when I was doing some work on Ruskin.... Carter and I began an investigation...."
[12] The *Enquiry, op. cit.*

passing notes: to each of the four pamphlets a page or more
of some 800 words was devoted. In 39 bulky volumes, however, the revelations were somewhat buried, and doubtless
escaped general notice. Those who read them seem to have
kept their counsel, probably mystified and also impressed by
the absence of tangible proof against the perpetrator. Nevertheless, for a considerable time Wise must have been on
tenterhooks. But his luck held. The danger passed—though
the sight of that edition of Ruskin's works on his shelves must
have seemed like the writing on the wall to Belshazzar.

V

In 1905 and 1908 Wise produced the first of his two Catalogues of the Ashley Library. It was an imposing affair in
two large quarto volumes, with more margins than print,
and including 200 illustrations on vellum. The first volume
had for its frontispiece the well-known "true and livelie
portraiture" of Sir Walter Raleigh; the second, a lesser-
known but probably truer portrait of Thomas James Wise
(see plate opposite). The Catalogue describes some 700
items, compared with approximately 7,000 in the eleven-
volume *Ashley Library Catalogue,* which he produced between 1922 and 1936. Considering the comparative small-
ness of the Library at the beginning of the century, and the
fact that he was only then embarking on the ambitious plan
of rare-book buying for himself, it is not easy to account for
the sumptuous character of this earlier and obviously temporary catalogue. It may have been in the nature of a shop-
window affair in connection with his role of rare-book
dealer and collector. There may have been a secondary object:
to give some of the forged pamphlets an appearance of
authenticity by cataloguing them among the right things
forming the nucleus of the Library. Such condemned pamphlets as *Cleon* and *Gold Hair* (both works of Robert Browning) were not only described as first editions, but were given

Wise's portrait used as a frontispiece to Vol. II of his 1905-8
Ashley Library Catalogue. The frontispiece to Vol. I was of Sir
Walter Raleigh.

prominence by having their title pages reproduced from copies "in the Library of Mr. Buxton Forman."

Similarly, in publicizing his false Reading edition of Mrs. Browning's *Sonnets,* Wise reproduced the title from "a copy of the rare original in the Library of Clement K. Shorter." These were things that Wise alone had brought to light, the "discovery" of the purported Reading *Sonnets* being both highly important and romantic. Why not have reproduced the title pages of his own copies? The explanation is too obvious: the appearance of authenticity would be increased by showing them off in the libraries of other collectors. It was like slipping a naughty poem into a priest's pocket, and saying: "See! It is all right. Even the Church reads it."

VI

About 1906, Wise's long and successful association with the firm of Hermann Rubeck led to an important development. He entered into partnership with Hermann's son, Mr. Otto P. Rubeck, in another essential-oil business, with works at Rotherhithe and offices in Mark Lane. Of this business, W. A. Smith and Co., Wise was the chief of the two partners. It was a successful enterprise—especially in consequence of the World War, excess profits being paid. It contributed substantially to the fortune left by the collector-dealer.

Mr. Otto P. Rubeck is one of the very few people able to speak from close acquaintance with Wise in the fruitful period of his career. But an interview with Mr. Rubeck proved singularly unproductive. He thought there could be very little public interest in Wise's early life in the city. As to the activities which made Wise famous, Mr. Otto P. Rubeck was disappointingly unenlightening. Emphasizing that his own private enthusiasm was for farming, he conveyed the impression that book collecting and bibliography were things outside his knowledge. However, as he sold four of the condemned or suspected nineteenth-century pamphlets to the

British Museum in 1890,[13] appears as a member of the committee of Wise's Society of Archivists and Autograph Collectors, and was in the schedule of contributors to do a monograph on the autographs of Sir Walter Scott (a subject for an expert), it is presumed that before he passed to bulls he had an interest in books which has since faded. However productive the bulls may have been, the sterility of Mr. Rubeck's recollections did accentuate the remarkable way in which Wise's early career seemed to be veiled.

VII

Late in 1907, a mean-looking 4-page pamphlet measuring 6½ by 4¼ inches, gave to the collecting world *"A Song. By Elizabeth Barrett Browning. Privately Printed."* Here is the song, in which the poetess made amorous play rather more in the style of *The Keepsake* than in that of the better sonnets of her uneven poetry:

> *Is't loving to list to the night guitar,*
> *And praise the serenading;*
> *Yet think of nought when the minstrel's far,*
> *But of beauty and of braiding?*
> *Is't loving, to bask 'neath tender eyes—*
> *'Neath other, on their removing,*
> *And join new vows to old perjuries?*
> *Ah no! this is not loving!*

> *Unless you can think when the song is done,*
> *No other's worth the pondering—*
> *Unless you can feel when the minstrel's gone,*
> *Mine heart with him is wandering—*
> *Unless you can dream that his faith is fast,*
> *Thro' months and years of roving—*
> *Unless you can die when the dream is past—*
> *Ah no! this is not loving!*

[13] They were Swinburne's *Cleopatra* at £5.5.; Ruskin's *The National Gallery* and *The Nature and Authority of Miracle;* and Matthew Arnold's *Saint Brandon* at £2.2. each. See page 69.

This effort Mrs. Browning considerably altered and expanded into the poem "A Woman's Shortcomings." The tiny 4-page pamphlet of the original *Song* was issued without any statement as to printer or publisher; it was still in copyright in 1907. Wise describes his copy without indication of his having any connection with it. But he is able to say that it is in the original state as issued, and (although there is no certificate) that it was limited to twenty copies. He gave copies to Gosse, Wrenn, and the British Museum. Gosse, sending his thanks (Aug. 3, '08) for the E. B. B. stanzas, says: "I have determined ... to begin buying books again, so as to fill up some of the gaps in my little collection. I know you have your special friends to think of, but if you would occasionally think of me, I should be grateful. I feel that I have been falling rather out of the game. But these things, nowadays, never seem to offer themselves." Wise, in sending Wrenn his copy four days later, threw in this letter from Gosse as one would throw a scrap to a good dog, suggesting that the two might be bound up together, as the letter would add a bit to the importance of the poem. Nothing wasted. Every lump of sugar goes to make a pound. Apparently he got hold of the original manuscript of the *Song*[14] and could not resist the temptation to put it into print and make a first-edition trifle. But from the facts of the covert publishing and the existence of the copyright, it is presumably a piracy. It is not unfair to class this "shortcoming" with printings by others that Wise loftily sneers at as "miserable things."

As for Gosse's request to be remembered, that came timely. For within a few months Wise was almost neck-deep in a treasure trove such as book dealers dream of after halcyon nights with the clique.[15] And then it was that Gosse was so useful.

[14] In the letter to Wrenn, he says he is binding it up with his own copy. But this MS is missing from the Ashley Library.
[15] "Clique" is the term for the fraternity of antiquarian booksellers in England.

CHAPTER 12

THE TRIO AT THE PINES AND THE
SECRETS OF THE VATICAN VENUS

Up jumped, with his neck stretching out like a gander,
Master Swinburne, and squeal'd, glaring out through his hair,
"All Virtue is bosh! Hallelujah for Landor!
I disbelieve wholly in everything!—there!"

With language so awful he dared then to treat 'em,–
Miss Ingelow fainted in Tennyson's arms,
Poor Arnold rush'd out, crying "sæcl inficetum!"
And great bards and small bards were full of alarms;
Till Tennyson, flaming and red as a gipsy,
Struck his fist on the table and uttered a shout:
"To the door with the boy! Call a cab! He is tipsy!"
And they carried the naughty young gentleman out.

Robert Buchanan: *The Session of the Poets* (1860).

I

ALGERNON CHARLES SWINBURNE was a physical wreck when in September, 1879, with the consent of his mother, Lady Jane Swinburne, he went to live with the literary critic Theodore Watts (who later changed his name to Watts-Dunton) at The Pines, Putney. For some twenty years Swinburne had been living a Bohemian life, chiefly in London. It had been a life of intense creative effort as a poet and student, mixed with periods of the wildest excesses—also of illnesses. In the early days, his original and vitriolic personality, his brilliant and amusing conversation, his gifts as a poet, had caused him to be hailed and petted by men of reputation long before he was discovered by the public. The little man with the enormous mass of flaming hair, green eyes, large head, and slight body and limbs—the poet who could caper so funnily and

142

write such deadly invective—the frail elf who could outshriek Hitler, swear like any East Side youngster, and pen exquisite verse to childhood,

A baby's feet, like sea-shells pink,

was described as a "tropical bird," a "crimson macaw among owls": terms which have become permanent labels for that eccentric and lovable character.

But his trouble was, he would but he couldn't emulate the free robust lives of his heroes among the Elizabethan poets and dramatists. He was akin to his admired Villon, Baudelaire, Rimbaud, and Mallarmé, and would be as Bohemian. He wanted to drink and love with the zest with which he talked and hurled off his poetry. He had the spirit; but, for one thing, he could not cope with the spirits. There was his boon companion, Sir Richard Burton, one of the few men who could fire the old type of elephant gun from the shoulder; who could get up from a long spell of translating the *Arabian Nights,* and drink a bottle of brandy at a sitting: whereas Algernon was under the table after a few glasses.

He was, as he said, "a bit of a bibliomaniac"; not much of one, but enough to have responded to Wise's curiosity about his Elizabethan quartos, and to have taken a temporary interest in the collector. I used to frequent a rare-book shop, now no more, where Swinburne was remembered as a regular customer, always arriving in a cab for his usual afternoon with the proprietor. He would descend, uttering torrential maledictions on the fog or something, trip into the shop, and through to the private room at the back. There, books would be produced, together with—in view of the young gentleman's known habits—bottles. The spirits flowed with the talk, which was glorious when it turned as usual to the Elizabethans. Nothing could restrain Swinburne on his pet theme—at least, not until the spirits and his legs began to disagree: also as usual. Then, making a faltering exit, he would be assisted by the bookseller and his staff into his waiting chariot; the while he cursed cab, cabby, cabhorse, and cabstand, in one magnificent flow that would have left "foul-mouth'd" John Marston, Ben Jonson, and Chapman envious and speechless with laughter.

Probably Swinburne then went to his lodgings in Great James Street for one of those apologies for a meal of which Justin Huntly MacCarthy had an unforgettable experience. "Come to lunch," the poet asked him with more cordiality than calculation. On the appointed day MacCarthy arrived, to find that lunch consisted of a tin of biscuits, a pot of jam, and a bottle of Hock. The poet's landlady was wont to lament: "Mister Swinburne, Sir! he haven't eat anything for days. A nice beefsteak 'ud do 'im a power o' good."

This way of living could not go on: he hadn't the physique to keep pace with Burton and his sturdier cronies. The brilliant tropical bird was a jaded macaw—a bedraggled, dying creature—when rescued by Watts-Dunton: to be wheedled from brandy to two bottles of light beer daily because ale had been Shakespeare's drink; and to enter on a new life of serenity and health that lasted for thirty years in the peaceful haven of The Pines. There, says Sir Edmund Gosse, he was "The book-monk of a suburban Thebais. All the charming part of his character blossomed forth anew.... He became less amusing and stimulating, although perhaps more lovable than he had been in his tumultous youth." [1] Of that tumultuous youth that gave us the noble lines of *Atalanta in Calydon* and the lyric passion of *Poems and Ballads,* Swinburne once wrote from The Pines to his cousin, Mrs. Disney Leith: "What stuff people talk about youth being the happiest time of life! Thank God ... I am very much more than twice as happy now as I was when half my present age."

The loss of Swinburne from his circle of Bohemians, however, led to stories comparing him to a songster that had been captured and was pining silent and sad in its cage at The Pines. After the deaths of the poet and his "devoted

[1] *Life of Algernon Charles Swinburne* (1917).

companion" (Gosse in the *Dictionary of National Biography*), these stories were resurrected and pointed with sneering criticism of Watts-Dunton—culminating in the conversational scandal in George Moore's *Avowals*. These glimpses of Swinburne are by way of introduction to the full account of Wise's remarkable coup at The Pines. This is not the place to settle that other mysterious controversy.[2] But one of these days the full history will be written of The Pines and the enigmatic character of the unpicturesque Watts-Dunton, to whose helpful friendships with Swinburne, Rossetti, and Tennyson there are plenty of tributes by the sharers of them.

II

Swinburne, who died at the age of 72 on April 10th, 1909, left to his friend and housemate, Watts-Dunton (aged 77), all his property: a large portion of it consisted of his library and his papers and copyrights. There at once followed a great clearing-up at The Pines, of which business Wise in the second volume of his *Swinburne Bibliography* gives but an incomplete account. "Immediately after the funeral Watts-Dunton invited me to join with him in the examination of the books and papers...." The fact is that it was an old-standing arrangement for him to have first hand in the deal for the realization of the estate. On his few visits to Swinburne he had formed a shrewd estimate of the contents of the poet's library, and had staked first claim with Watts-Dunton, to whom he gave the usual privately printed pamphlets, and generally made himself agreeable. The elderly critic shared the common idea of Wise as being a wealthy merchant and keen collector.

That clearing-up in Swinburne's library was a revelation—

---

[2] John Lawrence Lambe wrote a long letter to the *Morning Post* of Jan. 9th, 1920, headed "Swinburne and Watts-Dunton. 'A Campaign of Slander.'" The differences between the references to Watts-Dunton in Gosse's D. N. B. article on Swinburne, his *Life* (*op. cit.*) of the poet, and in his correspondence are striking.

even, apparently, to Watts-Dunton after thirty years of life with the poet under the same roof.[3] It was a most exciting experience for Wise; he never forgot his astonishment and delighted to give descriptions of it to his friends. The poet had been a prolific worker, and from the time when he left Oxford—on Jowett's advice, and without a degree—he had preserved the bulk of his original scripts, so many of them on the favorite blue foolscap. They included much that most men would not have cared to preserve. The library's lower bookshelves and the corners were heaped with parcels containing letters, MSS, circulars, bills, and printers' proofs bundled away from time to time as Swinburne cleared his study table. Among the manuscripts was much unpublished— and in some cases unpublishable—poetry and prose from the poet's best period. The selecting and editing of these for publication meant a long-drawn-out task: Watts-Dunton was an old man.

So in the room where the poet had spent the long and peaceful autumn of his life, still pouring out his lyrics and his learning, the old critic and the middle-aged bookseller and collector sat them down and did their deals. Wise's account—as usual when it comes to personal matters—is not very clear. But in the result, over a long period of visits, he got all he wanted: the bulk of the papers, including everything unpublished, and some copyrights, for a sum of "about £3,000," which figure may safely be taken as the maximum. The treasure was removed in cabs to the Ashley Library at Heath Drive; but, for much of it, only temporarily.

There was also Swinburne's collection of books that included Elizabethan quartos and other fine things. Wise had his pick of these at prices satisfactory to him; then, for the second helping, he introduced his client, John H. Wrenn of Chicago, spending his annual holiday in England.

---

[3] Watts-Dunton seems to have lived a busy life as critic, student, etc. In a letter to Wise he speaks of three persons working in a secretarial capacity for him at one period.

First of all Wrenn was shown over The Pines. To the Chicago business man it must have been impressive: heavy with comfort, bestrewn with Victorianism—knick-knacks, antimacassars, and all—the walls and passages were crowded with Pre-Raphaelite art, that of Dante Gabriel Rossetti predominating. The summer scene from Swinburne's window, the garden away from the madding crowd of Putney Hill, was something to make the heart leap. The narrow lawn backed by trees formed a natural setting for a life-size statue— a replica, formerly in Rossetti's garden, of the Vatican Venus, whose chaste whiteness shimmered against the brilliant verdure.

Wrenn now attuned, as awed as a girl at her confirmation, the three settled down to business in the library, unconscious of the mocking spirit of Swinburne, who couldn't be bothered to cash his publishers' checks.[4] "After some pleasant conversation," records Wrenn in a solemn declaration, "he allowed me to purchase ... the poet's own copy of the original Quarto Edition, printed at Pisa in 1812, of Shelley's *Adonais*. ... I also obtained from Mr. Watts-Dunton the holograph manuscript, fully signed, of Swinburne's Sonnet on Shelley, which has now been added to the Elegy. The whole forms one of the choicest and most attractive souvenirs imaginable of the two great Poets."

It is the simple phrase "he allowed me to purchase" that makes the American's record so likable. After Wrenn had finished writing this statement on the binder's blank flyleaf of the *Adonais*, Wise indited, signed, and dated a corroborative note that he had been present on the above occasion, etc., etc. With two such testimonials Wrenn replaced the immortal elegy in its fireproof case, morocco-bound, and re-

---

[4] When Mrs. Watts-Dunton was left a widow, she scrapped the remainder of Algernon's books, and converted his library into her bedroom. Some of the visitors to The Pines were shocked, and showed it. But, as she observed when displaying to me the charms of the boudoir: "After all, Swinburne's gone. It is I who am living here."

turned to America—a happy man, whatever the relics cost him.

Indeed, all three were happy, Wise most of all. Throughout the restricted account of his £3,000 deal for the Swinburne manuscripts there is an undertone of vaunting it as a matter of only literary importance to him. To be fair, doubtless many an author would be glad to know his literary remains were to be so carefully preserved, even though he might pray for sterner discretion. But it is fair to do justice also to Wise's commercial ability.

The £3,000 outlay to Watts-Dunton was soon recovered. Within a short time Wise had resold some fifty of the manuscripts, mostly published, to Frank T. Sabin, a leading London bookseller, for £3,213.7.! He had a side interest in Watts-Dunton's sale of 102 manuscripts for about £2,000 to "a London dealer" that eventually found their way to a bookseller of Chicago (whence came Wrenn), to be priced to the public at nearly £6,000. From William Heinemann, who paid Watts-Dunton £5,000 for the Swinburne copyrights, Wise received £900 in respect of the publishing rights in the new MS material he had acquired, in addition to other sums. There were considerable sales of single MS pieces by Wise among his private clients, including Wrenn. Last, but not least, came the proceeds of printing the unpublished material in 76 of the privately printed Ashley Library pamphlets— the figure of 76 does not include his Swinburne forgeries and suspects. And after his Pines account had shown a handsome profit in cash transactions, the "residuary legatee of the so-called Pre-Raphaelite School" (as Gosse flamboyantly described him) was left with his own superb collection of original Swinburne manuscripts—and first editions into the bargain. It was a profitable clearing-up.

As an example of Wise's commercialism in dealing with Swinburne's MSS, that of the poet's important *Essay on Blake* (1868) was broken up, and leaves inserted in some 25 Swinburne first editions (genuine and spurious) sold to Wrenn "to add a bit to their value"—as the dealer explained in another similar instance. The fact that the Blake manuscript showed considerable differences from the printed text did not save it. Nor was even this piece of vandalism skillfully done. Four pages of the Blake material were inserted in *A Midsummer Holiday and Other Poems* (1884), whereas a MS sonnet from this book of Swinburne's verse was placed in his *Bride's Tragedy* (1889).

III

While this chapter is being written, there is another clearing-up taking place at The Pines, consequent upon the death of Mrs. Clara Watts-Dunton. Her mother, Mrs. Reich, was an old friend of the bachelor Watts-Dunton. Clara Reich was a small pretty golden-haired girl, all dimples and curves, when she was taken by her mother to the "great critic," to whom she went, some years later, as his secretary. Then in 1905, when she was about 27, she married the 72-year-old Watts-Dunton of the solemn air, the kind, soft manners, and the walrus mustaches. Thus "I—little more than a girl in years—became chatelaine at The Pines"; [5] though it may be doubted whether she kept many of the keys. For four years the young chatelaine and the two old men lived their lives regulated by The Hours—a timetable sacred at The Pines; then Algernon departed. Five years more of The Hours, then Watts-Dunton followed.

Now, only the draped Venus remains: so chaste, so unlike Rossetti's "stunners" [6] of whom she had seen more than enough for her Vatican purity. But she will never tell about his ménage in Cheyne Walk, or about the strange trio at The Pines and Wise's visits. No! Not this Venus!

---

[5] *Home Life of Swinburne,* by Clara Watts-Dunton (1922).
[6] As he used to name his beautiful models. The Pre-Raphaelites, according to Violet Hunt, went out into the streets in groups of twos and threes, searching for suitable subjects for their brushes and for their amateur "rescue" experiments.

IV

Wise says "fortune smiled upon my adventure" because Gosse became interested in the haul of the poet's literary remains, and offered editorial help. Fortune not only smiled but had a hearty Olympian laugh over what was a sensation in its day.

In 1897 Wise had included a tentative bibliography of Algernon Charles Swinburne in his *Literary Anecdotes*, giving the titles of four poems which "A. C. S." had contributed to *Fraser's Magazine* between 1849 and 1851. The bibliographer seems not to have fully appreciated the significance of the dates. In 1912, however, something made him search still further in the files of the magazine, there to find more poems by A. C. S. The earliest had been done in 1849, when Swinburne had just completed his eleventh year. At last Wise realized the full interest of his discovery, and its possibilities for him. It was not quite a record in precocity, he calculated. Chatterton had begun poet at the age of ten years and six weeks; and Ruskin when ten years and eleven months. Nevertheless, it was pretty close.

The discoverer exulted, "hurried the good news" to Gosse, and rushed transcripts to the printers—to make two of his privately printed "first editions" entitled *Juvenilia*, by Algernon Charles Swinburne; and *The Arab Chief A Ballad*, by Algernon Charles Swinburne. "These Swinburne juvenilia are imitative in the extreme," pontificated Wise in his preface (using Gosse's information without acknowledgments), "and exhibit small promise of the wonders to come. But they are biographically interesting, and, after all, are immeasurably superior to the incoherent vaporings of Shelley's early muse."

Gosse was also excited over Wise's discovery. "I have little doubt of their being by our A. C. S.," he wrote to Wise (Aug. 2, '12) "... half of them are quite new to me, and I am unable to guess what induces you to attribute them to Swinburne ... I demand from you as full information as it is in your power to supply. ...." But the little doubt was pooh-poohed away. Certainly the poems came in the nick of time. Gosse was just sending his memoir of the poet to the *"Dictionary of National Biography,* and was able to include the discovery thus: "He [Swinburne] was ... now writing verses, some of which his mother sent to *Fraser's Magazine* ... but of this 'false start' he was afterwards not pleased to be reminded."

What a day was that, my countrymen! when Wise through his private printings, and Gosse through the D. N. B., could display dear little Algernon as a poet-just-turned-eleven! And what a nuisance it was that he never wrote those poems! Oh, Algernon! After all Uncle Tom's trouble!!

No sooner were the Ashley booklets and the D. N. B. article off the press than Gosse realized there had been a ghastly error—as did others, including Watts-Dunton, who was a very wideawake veteran.[7] Then began a dithering exchange of daily letters between the biographer and the bibliographer; interspersed with charmingly polite missives from Watts-Dunton about that "monstrous attribution." "I am altogether in your hands," wrote Gosse to Wise (Mar. 29, '13). "Your judgment is paramount. Only I should hate that anyone but ourselves should reveal the mistake. Fancy how it would look to wake up and read, 'Messrs. Wise and Gosse know so little of their business that ... [etc.].' Keep the Old Man of Putney Hill quiet."

Wise would have liked to keep the whole "damned thing" quiet. But Gosse insisted on writing a formal letter to *The Times,* in which he announced the new discovery that the "discovery" was not really a discovery. But the Press and

7 He was at first led into the error of supposing that the wrongful attribution was originally due to Herne Shepherd in his pioneering *Bibliography of Swinburne.* But he went into the matter more closely, exploded the charge against Shepherd, and blew up Thomas James Wise instead. He wrote (Apr. 10, '13): "By the by, the familiar adage, 'Give a dog a bad name,' &c, can certainly be applied to Shepherd. ... I have pretty well ascertained that the first ascription of the *Fraser* poems to Swinburne does not lie at the door of this man. I cannot trace it earlier than 1896, in the second volume of *Literary Anecdotes.*"

critics were not to be put off: the D. N. B. had been made the vehicle for false history. Those were days when a literary problem or discovery had not such formidable rivals of topical interest as, say, the particular complexion favored by some third-rate film actress. The controversy over the injured "A. C. S.," and the other mysterious "A. C. S." grew hot.

The now defunct *Globe,* printed on pink paper, became almost crimson in its furious efforts to solve the identity of the other "A. C. S.," whose verses had been fathered on Swinburne. After much Sherlock-Holmesing, the *Globe* did it (Apr. 8, '13), perhaps inspired by Watts-Dunton, who had solved the riddle a few days earlier. The "A. C. S." who had actually written the *Juvenilia* and *The Arab Chief* was triumphantly proved to be Sir Anthony Coningham Sterling, K.C.B.—a minor poet, but a major soldier: he had been Brigade-Major and Assistant Adjutant-General of the Highland Division in the Crimea, and had also served under Lord Clyde in India.

The curious feature of the whole affair, and the one most relevant to this study, is that Thomas James Wise, the cause of all the trouble, never himself emerged to take his major share of responsibility. Gosse was hard pressed by severe critics, including the poet's sister, Miss Isabel Swinburne, who was furious with him, and James Douglas. What was Gosse's authority for the attribution and for the tale of the poet's cultured mother sending such rubbish to *Fraser's?* What did he mean by it, eh? Edmund remained silent and suffering under the storm. As he said (and unfortunately believed), Wise was paramount. But bibliography is the handmaid of biography; and Gosse was entitled to state his authority—as he briefly did in the letter to *The Times* announcing the discovery that the "discovery" was not really a discovery. Except for this one reference, Wise escaped; thus proving once again his peculiar elusiveness in avoiding the consequences of his errors.

V

All the same, it was very mortifying. When he came to correct the attribution in his later works, Wise made the peevish comment: "It is difficult to understand why Swinburne, when the poems were brought directly under his notice in my *Bibliographical List* of 1897, and there distinctly cited as his, did not himself deny their authorship." Perhaps not so difficult. If he ever saw Wise's *List,* he would have noticed that two of the poems fathered on him at the tender age of twelve, just when he was a queer little elf going to Eton, were titled:

> *Where shall I follow thee, wild floating Symphony?*

and

> *Oh! Sing no Song of a joyous mood.*

Another specimen of the minor A. C. S.'s muse:

> *Then don't despise the working man, he's strong and honest too,*
> *And he would rather governed be than seek to govern you;*
> *But lack of proper guidance at last may make him mad,*
> *And when the best don't govern him, he'll call upon the bad.*

Algernon, even when settled down to the light beer and the heavy sobriety of the peaceful Pines, retained enough of the elfin spirit to enjoy such delicious jokes— Yes! and to leave them for posterity to enjoy.

*   *   *   *

And when in the Shades they heard the rumpus on Earth, Swinburne screamed again with laughter; and Sir Richard Burton, felling the Sultan Shahryár with an empty brandy bottle, took the jolly Shahrázád into a Grove, to tell her this Thousand and Second Tale.

CHAPTER 13

THREATS, COUNTER-THREATS, AND MORE MYSTERIES ILLUMINED

He's tough, ma'am, tough, is J. B. Tough, and de-vilish sly.
Charles Dickens: *Dombey and Son.*

O, what a tangled web we weave
When first we practise to deceive. `
Sir Walter Scott: *Marmion.*

I

"You ARE a consummate diplomatist, and in your skilful hands everything in our tangled skein is coming straight," Sir Edmund Gosse once wrote to Wise (June 6, '15) with reference to some trouble with Miss Isabel Swinburne concerning the critic's *Life* of the poet. How consummate, how astute even, Gosse amply experienced in his collaboration with Wise when the collector-dealer came to turn his rich haul of manuscripts from The Pines into hard cash. A lively correspondence ensued between the two men. It shows how Gosse reveled in editing Swinburne's unpublished work, writing prefaces, and detecting his collaborator's howlers; while Wise got on with the sorting of his haul, the printing, and the dealings—about which the literary partner was not told what has been revealed here. Wise had his own tangled web from which to extricate himself.

There was a fearful instance in the early days of his negotiations for the Swinburne treasures. It is reported to Gosse in the following letter:

23 Downside Crescent,
Hampstead. N.W.
July 10. 1909.

My dear Gosse,

Many thanks for proof of 'Twilight.' I spent all last evening over the MS of this, & it now reads quite differently. Will send you revise next week.

Bought some more MSS from your "Reptile" friend [1] on Thursday, & am going on Monday for more. He rather pressed me to take the autographed "Tombeau" at 12/12/—. But I stuck to 'No,' and told him "all or none." It ended looking very much like *"all."*

Now for some fun. He had got a copy of my S[winburne]. Bibliography,[2] & pointed out to me

"Sonnets on Browning"
"Grace Darling"
&
"Bulgarie"

"These are *damned* things [said Watts-Dunton]: they are all 3 forgeries & piracies. I shall write to the Athenaeum & denounce them!"

I told him that to do so would do him much harm, as his note would be replied to, & it would end by being shewn that he knew nothing about S's books at all.

That I could produce S's *written permission* for the Br[own]-ing Soc[ty] to print the Death Sonnets, and also a copy with presentation inscription to Christina Rossetti, bought by me from Wm. R. after Christina's death.

That I could also produce *S's letter to myself* giving me leave to print "Grace Darling," & a second letter thanking me for copies of it.

"Oh, yes," he said, "I remember, they are all right."

As to "Bulgarie," I said, the MS. was sent for publication to the P[all]. M[all]. G[azette]., but held back from publication. Possibly the P.M.G. people may have struck off a few copies

---

[1] I.e., Watts-Dunton.

[2] Wise's original and tentative *Swinburne Bibliography* (1897). Was he surprised to find Watts-Dunton had it? This letter is reproduced literally from Wise's script. Italicized words represent words underlined by him. My interpolations made for clarity appear within brackets.

before returning the MS. to S. *That* would not be either 'forgery'
or 'piracy'!—"Yes, I do remember something of the sort: I think
I wont trouble about them"!

Ever yours

Tho°. J. Wise

However much Wise might pretend that this episode was
funny, it can hardly be doubted that it came as another horrid shock to hear Watts-Dunton threatening to denounce
these "*damned* things" in the Press. It was another warning
of the coming Nemesis. But Wise soon recovered his aplomb.
The way this unexpected indictment was met provides a
remarkable and all-sufficing revelation of his diplomatic
technique, and is worthy of a Ribbentrop. Let us first ex-
amine the things with which he counter-threatened Watts-
Dunton.

If, as he alleged, he could show Swinburne's authority in
writing for the Browning Society to print the *Sequence of
Sonnets On the death of Robert Browning,* that document
could only have referred to the quoting of the Sonnets in the
Society's annual *Papers* (see No. XII, 1890) among a collection
of obituary notices and poetical tributes. It is doubtful
whether he possessed even that authority, for he was not the
editor of the *Papers* (his interest in the Society had waned
by 1890); and the document was not among his Swinburne
correspondence in 1937. Moreover, although two annual
volumes of *Papers* were issued after Browning's death in
1889, they contain no reference to any such pamphlet having
been produced for the Society or for anyone else. That it
was *not* done for the Society Wise himself revealed ten years
later in his 1919 *Swinburne Bibliography* (Vol. I, p. 427)
when he said the pamphlet was seen through the press "upon
the poet's behalf" by Harry Buxton Forman.[3] Therefore, if
the thing was printed for the poet and not for the Society,

---

[3] Forman had died some two years previously. When Wise described the
pamphlet in 1896 in his List of Swinburne's Scarcer Works (*Literary Anecdotes*), he said nothing about Forman having seen it through the press for
the poet.

the tale to Watts-Dunton about the letter was misleading. Wise backed up the threat about the letter by suggesting he had the copy of the pamphlet presented by Swinburne to Christina Rossetti, which copy he described in his catalogues as "highly treasurable." It is indeed very interesting. But the nation, which bought it with the Ashley Library, will hardly treasure it so highly, because it is another fake— and a clumsy fake too.

In the first place, it is not, as implied, an inscribed presentation copy at all. There is no inscription on any page of the pamphlet itself. What is there, is a shingle sheet of Pines notepaper pasted on the first leaf; and the sheet bears the following note in what appears to be Swinburne's handwriting:

> The Pines
> Putney Hill. S.W.
> Oct. 3—90

Dear Miss Rossetti
I send you a little poem of which the subject may perhaps interest you, and am always
> very sincerely yours
> A. C. Swinburne.

Now, if Swinburne wrote that note, it is almost a certainty that it does not refer to the pamphlet in which it is pasted. He would not refer to an important sequence of seven sonnets, written on so memorable an occasion, as "a little poem"; and it is hardly likely that he would make the casual and not very complimentary suggestion that the subject "may perhaps interest" the poetess. Moreover, if the pamphlet really was privately printed for him, and if this letter dated October 3rd, 1890, really does refer to it, there was a curiously long delay in sending the gift. Robert Browning died on December 12th, 1889: the sonnets appeared in the *Fortnightly Review* issue for January, 1890, from which the pamphlet was probably printed. Wise says that Harry Buxton Forman was concerned in its production; and it is on record that his agent, Mr.

Gorfin, bought twelve copies from Forman's widow—though this circumstance does not necessarily make Forman the pirate; because there is Wise's statement (page 75) of the stock of one of his forged pamphlets being shared with Forman, and because in this case Mr. Gorfin's purchase from the widow was effected through Wise. Strangely enough, if the pamphlet was regular and was seen through the press for Swinburne by Harry Buxton Forman, the British Museum did not receive a copy from either the author or the producer. Its copy was the gift of Mr. G. A. Phillips, of Ilford, Essex, together with three other items, on May 9th, 1891.

Whoever was responsible for the printing, it is clear Wise knew that what he put forward as an author's inscribed presentation copy of *A Sequence of Sonnets* was a fake. When he came to boost it in his *Swinburne Bibliography,* quoting the poet's purported inscription, he was shrewd enough to see that the reference to "a little poem" would not pass muster. So he altered the telltale word—the all-important one in a note of one sentence—and printed "Dear Miss Rossetti, I send you a little book . . ." etc. He says he bought this copy now shown to be a fake from William Rossetti. Be that as it may, whoever was the fabricator, (1) Wise misled Watts-Dunton about it; (2) he gave two conflicting accounts of the pamphlet's origin; (3) the fake presentation copy does not prove that Swinburne knew of or consented to the private printing. These circumstances, together with the probable reproduction from the *Fortnightly Review,* strongly suggest that the thing is a piracy.[4]

It seems as if Wise was determined to catch at every thread, no matter how weak, to link the private-pamphlet issue of the *Sequence of Sonnets* with Swinburne. He records in the *Ashley Library Catalogue* (VI, p. 177) the possession of an-

[4] When Harry Buxton Forman's "magnificent copy" of this "excessively rare" item was sold for $45 by the Anderson Galleries, New York, in 1920, nothing was said in the catalogue description about Forman's having seen it through the press for Swinburne.

other copy, and says: "Inserted at the commencement of the pamphlet is an A.L.S. of three pages from Browning's son to Watts-Dunton, conveying his thanks for the gift of a copy of the Sonnets." But examination of the letter shows that Browning's son neither conveyed thanks nor mentioned any copy of the sonnets. All he did was to add to the main and quite different subject of his letter this sentence: "I have been deeply moved by Mr. Swinburne's beautiful sonnets." As he was writing from a London address on January 2nd, 1890, and as the sonnets had appeared in the *Fortnightly Review* of the previous day's date, there can be little doubt that he was referring to the publication in that periodical. Had he been acknowledging the gift of a presentation copy of a private pamphlet, he would have been assuredly more explicit.

Next we come to the *Grace Darling* pamphlet. Reasons have already been given in Chapter 10 for inferring that this is also a piracy. But Wise held over Watts-Dunton the threat that he could produce Swinburne's letter giving permission to print it. In none of the poet's few letters to Wise, printed or unprinted, in the Ashley and Wrenn Libraries, is there any such permission. Wise must surely have known that he could not produce such authority, because, for the purpose of printing, he handled his brief correspondence from Swinburne in the same year (1909) in which this episode with Watts-Dunton occurred.

As to the *Ballad of Bulgarie* pamphlet, Wise's plausible surmising that possibly the *Pall Mall Gazette* people may have struck off a few copies is proved by himself to be false because in his *Swinburne Bibliography* (Vol. I, p. 450) he jocularly admits that he printed it without the poet's consent. The absurd suggestions that the *Pall Mall Gazette* might have printed the thing after rejecting it, and that that would not have been piracy, should be noted, in view of what follows later.

In short, then, Watts-Dunton was right to describe all three pamphlets as "damned things." They were not both "forgeries *and* piracies," as he loosely said; they will henceforth be classed as piracies. But the point as illustrating Wise's consummate diplomacy is that in each case he warned off Watts-Dunton's threatened denunciation in the Press by counter-threats based on falsehoods and misrepresentations. It may be wondered why the indignant housemate of Swinburne retracted his charges (if he did) and allowed himself to be coerced into silence. He was an old man of 77, described at this very time as shockingly feeble and helpless, though amazingly wideawake. But he was faced by a younger man—one clever and formidable, who was, moreover, buying the bulk of the inherited treasures. So, what with Wise's counterthreats and his gold, the aged Watts-Dunton wilted and surrendered.

In view of what has been said in Chapter 7 about Swinburne's brief correspondence with Wise, and in view also of how he held it over Watts-Dunton, it is interesting to see Gosse's reaction to the collector's proposal to rush the letters into print and to show them off in one of the earliest of his 75 privately printed Swinburne pamphlets. It is not unreasonable to say that the letters were drawn from the poet by the gifts of reprints and the suspect *Cleopatra* pamphlet. Wise much desired a preface to them written by Gosse. But the critic was not obliging to that extent. He perhaps guessed what Wise would expect him to say. Anyway, the request was emphatically refused in this significant reply (Jan. 2, '10):

...Don't you think before working off these seven letters of Swinburne, it would be worth while to look still more carefully for the 6 or 7 other letters which you have mislaid? You cannot have lost them, and the collection would be so much more valuable if it contained 14 than 7 letters. There cannot be any cause for hurry, and I would suggest that it would be far better to wait while you hunt your papers thoroughly.

These letters, of course, are of great biographical and bibliographical value; you have however used much (or nearly all) of this already in your "Bibliography." . . . I do not see my way to writing any prefatory words.

But Wise did not wait to hunt further for the missing letters, probably for good reason. With the exception of a short note of thanks (for a "beautiful and curious" Shelley reprint) left unprinted, none was found among his papers on their removal to the British Museum; although he had years earlier sold to Wrenn one of the so-treasured letters which was also an acknowledgment for another Shelley reprint.

II

The accounts Wise gave to Gosse of his dealings at The Pines after the deaths of Swinburne in 1909 and Watts-Dunton in 1914 make a rather sordid tale, and the vituperative epithets he applied to "W.-D." come ill from the writer who says of him (Preface to the *Swinburne Bibliography:* Vol. I): "I am glad to take this opportunity of expressing the gratitude I feel to my dead friend for the kindliness and goodwill he at all times exhibited in his transactions with me," etc., etc. If Watts-Dunton, critic and ex-attorney, was old and feeble, he was fairly shrewd, and obviously anxious to get as much money as he could for the literary property Swinburne left him. Wise came to the conclusion that he was being squeezed; and he admitted that he determined no longer to consider his old friend's interests, but to make as good deals as he could. They were exciting months in 1909, during which the bargaining ensued in Swinburne's once peaceful library. Wise was jubilant and uncontainable about the glorious things he was bringing away in cabs. Gosse thought the prices paid for them were generous. But he was assured that they were ridiculously low. How well founded was the dealer's confidence is proved by the financial success achieved.

When Watts-Dunton died, Wise again busied himself in

affairs at The Pines, chiefly for the purpose of securing what treasures remained after the former clearing-up. As a rule his letters compare unfavorably with those of Gosse; but the scenes of jealousy and hysteria at Putney prompted descriptions from which Hogarthian pictures may be conjured up. The Pines was likened to Hell, with the three females then resident (the widow and two sisters of Watts-Dunton) continually on the verge of coming to blows, labeling this and that as theirs, pulling Tom here and there to secure his championship.

"Your reports of the Watts-Dunton ménage are marvelous," once commented Gosse. "Now people seem to be getting a little over the sort of terror which W.-D. managed to spread around him, I receive from strangers as well as friends dreadful stories of the way in which—of late years particularly— he bullied A. C. S., whose patience and modesty were heavenly. Still it is possible to write as that man ******* ******** does somewhere this month, as if W.-D. was a great gentleman, putting up with an eccentric pauper!"

As The Pines ménage has already been a subject of controversy, and as Wise was concerned to show that Watts-Dunton had hardly any financial resources of his own and practically lived on Swinburne, the unpleasant affair shall be dismissed here by giving the gross results of the scramble for the poet's fortune.

Swinburne's effects were sworn for probate at £24,282.10.8., Watts-Dunton being the sole legatee. But Wise estimated that with the subsequent sale of the MSS and books, the estate realized about £35,000—a likely enough figure.

Watts-Dunton's estate in turn was returned at £22,934.6.10., which in Wise's opinion was a considerable undervaluation.

Wise's profit from the resale of the MSS, books, and copyrights, plus the proceeds of his publishing, was probably little short of £10,000. This is a reasonable estimate based on known transactions, the chief of which have been mentioned.

III

It is in connection with the private printing of the un-published Swinburne manuscripts that the Gosse-Wise corre-spondence is such a revelation—not merely of the enterprise itself, but of the characters and relationships of the two friends. Sir Edmund Gosse was as intimately acquainted with the literary development of the poet as with the man himself. He was most eager to assist with the maze of material unexpectedly brought to light. His warning to Wise (Apr. 18, '13) is significant and important: "Remember! that I know more about Swinburne than any other man living—more than his sister, more than Watts-Dunton, more than even you. I know much that will die with me. I have an almost religious wish to leave for posterity the materials for a genuine picture of him at his best."

How much more Gosse knew of the poet's work and life than did Wise, the latter came to appreciate. He was fre-quently rescued from errors by his collaborator from 1909 onward, during the years in which the Swinburne pamphlets were privately printed by Wise from his acquired MSS. The results of his adventuring alone and unaided were the pro-duction of at least two pieces—including the *Blest* (1912) pamphlet—as first editions, only to be told that they had already been published. Gosse's friendship was one of the luckiest of the many boons that befell Wise. There were times when he was positively humble to the "literary gent" as he described the critic. An instance is contained in a very illus-trative letter from Wise (Oct. 18, '12) that gives this faithful self-portrait:

No: I am by no means "gracious." On the contrary, I fear that I am frequently pugnacious to a militant degree! But my mind is not altogether in a state of atrophy,—and I am sufficiently acute to be able to perceive when, and to what degree, I fall short of par. When any matter of mere business regulation is before me, I cannot help but lean upon my own opinion; &, when op-posed, I quickly develop into a pig-headed and obstinate beast. But, on the other hand, I do not fail to appreciate how terribly short I fall of the standard necessary to the holding of any opinion on matters or questions of literary expediency, or of critical judgment. Thus, when you (who are overlord in all that pertains to literature or criticism) are generous enough to express an opinion, I appreciate that the opinion you express is a correct one, even though it does not coincide with any determination at which I may previously have arrived. Hence I naturally follow without question whatever path your finger points to!

Nothing could be truer: except that, unfortunately, he did not always follow the path. Here, for once, Wise draws aside the veil and reveals himself. After examination of many of his own papers, the foregoing is the only example of introspection and humble confession I have found. The correspondence of the two men devoting their energies to Swinburne for such opposite purposes resembles a game of battledore and shuttlecock in its exchange of thanks and compliments—from the one side, for the prefaces, notes, and information which Gosse bestowed with enthusiastic generosity, interspersed with sundry rarities for the Ashley Library; from the other side, for pamphlet first editions (genuine and spurious), "lovely" grapes, and an occasional manuscript. "You really are a very terrible man," Gosse wrote innocently (Apr. 9, '01), acknowledging some gifts which included the pamphlets *Laus Veneris* and *Samuel Prout* now classed as suspected forgeries. Again (Aug. 19, '09). "But I know your masterly way, and that it is useless to resist you."

But for all the other's masterly way, it was Gosse who held the whip hand in their literary partnership; and he sometimes flicked the whip smartly about the "obstinate beast." For example, in an undated letter: (July 19, '19?):

What an extraordinary man you are! You will leave nothing untouched, and you not merely rub the dust off the butterfly's wings, but you scrub them to a skeleton. What is this that you suddenly start on me about a *translation* of Swinburne's pleasant

jest? And why in the name of ******, do you apply to *****
***** in the matter? If there is a question of this kind, am not
I, as your colleague, worthy to be consulted? A man like *****
*****, a quite inferior person, should not be consulted on a deli-
cate point of this kind. I cannot understand you having any dealings with him at all. Why do you do so?

"La Fille du Policeman" was a joke, a piece of playful extravagance. Such a merry trifle cannot be "translated"! The whole
fun of the thing was the bad French, the absurdity of the supposed Parisian view of English social life. What on earth has
driven you to the amazing proposition of having it "translated"?
You seem to me sometimes, in regard to Swinburne, to have
immersed yourself so long in the merely bibliographical labour
of dealing with his MSS, as to have lost all sense of humanity, of
reality, in connection with him. You will leave nothing alone.
It is incomprehensible to me that your sense of humour does
not prevent you from crushing the very life out of the poor old
poet by these pedantries.

It is high time that you put Swinburne altogether out of your
view for a while, for you are losing all sense of proportion and
all range of values in connection with him.

There were some values whose range Wise was never in
danger of losing—whoever the authors concerned might be.
In this case his project to make a pamphlet of *La Fille du
Policeman* was abandoned in the face of Gosse's caustic
criticism.

Here is part of a letter (June 22, '24) which can hardly
have pleased the man who years earlier edited the *Faerie
Queene:*

My dear Wise, Let me at once express my horror at finding
the author of the *Faerie Queen* called
                    Spencer
in your proofs, as if he were a cunning bookseller or an effete
philosopher. My first idea was that the c was a printer's error,
but no! it is repeated. What possible authority can you have
for spelling Edmund Spenser with a c ? It looks horrible. I entreat
you to correct it in every case. . . .

Now do, I entreat, restore Spenser to his proper spelling. You
might as well write

                                Biron
                                Coalridge
                                Driden
                                Po
                                Chawcer
as (oh ye Gods)
                                SpenCer.

There was a startling revelation of Wise's ideas of annotation in a proof which drew this objection from Gosse (Apr. 6, '19):

...But why...do you consider this anecdote "a myth"? I can conceive no possible reason for doing so. But as you do hold this, you ought not to say "is almost certainly true."

And a few days later (Apr. 16, '19):

...What on earth do you mean by: "It is Leslia not Lesbia, Brandon"? You are surely not ignorant of the reason why Swinburne chose the name Lesbia?

Whether at their next meeting the critic enlightened Wise about Sappho and the Isle of Lesbos is not revealed. But the correction saved him from appalling error in one of the most notable of his bibliographical records; and a year later, in Vol. II of his *Swinburne Bibliography*, he was able to pull Shorter's leg for suppressing the passage about "The small dark body's Lesbian loveliness" that has already been commented on.

Gosse supplied prefaces for the writings of other authors that Wise printed, in addition to numerous notes. What literary man will not recognize the peculiar attitude of mind and approach that drew this mild protest (Nov. 30, '30)?:

My dear Wise, I was amused at your suggestion that it would only take me "ten minutes" to write this introduction!! It has taken me many days and numerous visits of reference to public libraries. There is no single work in any language where all the information I have brought together here is to be found. "Ten minutes," indeed!

Swinburne and Watts-Dunton in the garden at The Pines.

This preface will be of use to whoever ultimately collects Borrow's *Kjæmpeviser* into one volume. If that is Clement Shorter, I daresay he will steal the greater part of it, and forget to acknowledge the source,—in the true Borrovian manner.

Again and again Gosse vehemently protested against Wise's habit of rushing pieces of poetry and prose to the printer to turn into privately printed first editions, without saying anything about their origin, or where they had appeared serially, or giving them proper editorial treatment. For example, thanking Wise for the pamphlet *Pericles and Other Studies* (Febr. 27, '14):

... This is a delightful addition to Swinburne literature. But I must gently,—yet earnestly,—reproach you for putting it out without any explanation whatever. ... The value of the volume is, therefore, very much diminished. To myself, for instance, in writing Swinburne's life, it has hardly any value. You must be punished for bringing out a book in such an imperfect form, and the punishment is this: you must write out on a sheet of paper exactly where and when each of these papers appeared first, and send it to me that I may bind it into the "Pericles" volume, which will then become useful as well as curious.

IV

The fact is that Wise did not always know what treasures his great coup at The Pines brought him, or (more frequently) how to deal with them when he had got them. A bundle of MS poetry proved that he had been "entertaining a bevy of angels unawares" when it was examined by Gosse. No wonder that the critic was hailed as a wonderful chap. Strictures on and punishments for Wise's failings notwithstanding, the correspondence became affectionate, expressing the most tender solicitude for each other's health and well-being. Wise would lament the plaguiness of his "local trouble," as he called it; and Gosse, with more humor, would report: "What is the matter with me is gravel in the kidneys. I must exercise patience. I shall meditate on the verses you have sent me, and sketch an introduction in my head. As the hymn says, 'Out of my stony griefs Bethel I'll raise.' " The collaboration between the two friends seemed to be of the happiest and most genuine character.

And yet, the "extraordinary man," who would leave nothing untouched, must needs rub the bloom off his most valuable friendship. Gosse lent his unpublished MS of Swinburne's *The Cannibal Catechism* to Wise, who said he would get Clays to produce for them ten copies—unseemly and unreprintable as it might be. But he printed at least double the number.

Of the proofs of another proposed private printing, Gosse wrote (Dec. 13, '09):

> I wish I could persuade you to destroy this utterly valueless fragment, which ceases before it begins, and is neither intelligible nor characteristic.
>
> I will have nothing to do with it, and I think [the] presence of it among the valuable and interesting posthumous pamphlets which you have brought out would be a calamity.

The fragment referred to was Swinburne's *A Criminal Case*. In reply to the critic's emphatic condemnation, Wise promised to have "the types dispersed," implying that he would give way to his friend and adviser's urgent entreaty, and not produce the thing. Yes! the types were dispersed—but only after Wise had printed off his usual edition.

He occasionally sold to Gosse a rare book. Probably the "duplicate" explanation came in here: Gosse would have been shocked had he known that his friend and collaborator was a secret book-dealer. Very friendly it was of him to spare his duplicates from the wonderful Ashley Library. On one occasion Gosse wrote (July 25, '14):

> ... But a bookseller called Gorfin has offered me a collection of eleven early Landors, quite an interesting lot (he says you know them) for which he wants £85. I have told him that I must wait a little before deciding. Do you think they are worth that, and

that I ought to give it? I have got the money, but I am not in the habit of going busters. I shall be most grateful for a word of advice.

Wise agreed that he knew the Landors, and advised his dear friend to buy them. So the unsuspecting Gosse went "busters." It is now revealed that the books belonged to Wise all the time, that as his agent Mr. Gorfin offered them to Gosse for sale on commission, and never actually handled them himself!

V

The original arrangement with Watts-Dunton (who also inherited the Swinburne copyrights) was that Wise should, in addition to the purchase price for the manuscripts, pay a fee for the right to produce them as his private pamphlets (see the Preface to Vol. II of his *Swinburne Bibliography:* 1920). After this plan had been working for some time, Wise proceeded to make printings without Watts-Dunton's knowledge and without payment of the agreed fee. One reason he gave to Gosse (Nov. 13, '13) for this procedure was that the illicit printings included material which would lead Watts-Dunton (now 81 years old; his health fast breaking up) to express undesirable views! Wise claimed, moreover, (Nov. 15, '09) that although Watts-Dunton could prevent publication he had no legal rights over private printing. His attitude rather than his actual knowledge of Copyright Law is shown in this extraordinary letter to Gosse:

23, Downside Crescent,
Hampstead. N.W.
27-10-09

My dear Gosse,
    You ask why I pay W.-D. for printing these tracts. I do so because I feel morally bound to do so. He has no legal right or power to stop me printing them privately. As I bought "unpublished poems" without executing any legal instrument reserving to him the copyright, I have full legal right to PUBLISH them,

& to register the copyright against him. He would have no claim upon me at law.

But I happen to conduct my actions upon the lines proscribed [sic] by my own ideas of right & wrong. I'm not going to be a cad because he has been a cad. When I bought those MS. [sic] it was under the distinct verbal understanding that I was not to publish one. Of course a "verbal understanding" could not be maintained in a court of law. But the old man accepted my word as being as good as my bond, & my word is sacred. I have never broken yet a promise I have once given.

I asked him "May I privately print [?"] He replied "not without my consent." Naturally I imagined that such 'consent' would be freely given. When I had made arrangements I asked for consent. He replied "Pay: those proposed pamphlets will be very valuable: what do you offer to give me?" Hence my flow of £20 cheques to Putney.

The foregoing refers to the series of *Border Ballads* & the two *prose stories*. The Mazzini and the prose essays were sold to me without one word of comment or restriction. Thus with them my hands are free, & I'll see him ———— before I pay him a Cent for their a/c. But as a fact I don't propose that he shall see them at all.

Ever your
Sincere Friend
Tho⁸. J. Wise

I will now put the *Mazzini Ode* to press, & send you proofs in due course. I mean to print a pamphlet or two of *Letters* also. No use to ask his consent for this, so shall do *without it*.

————

On Saturday I mean to talk as a *business man* in regard to the remaining MSS and the Books. It's got to be "All *or none*"!

There is no doubt that Thomas James Wise did, as he says, conduct his actions by his own ideas of right and wrong. Here we have his own expression of those ideas. But he knew the law, especially regarding copyright, better than this. He knew that he was privately printing the pamphlets for sale, although Gosse did not understand the trading aspect of the affair. It may be wondered why Wise went to all the trouble of this specious arguing. Was he again exercising his "consummate diplomacy" to hoodwink Gosse, or doping his conscience? The things he produced without Watts-Dunton's knowledge or consent would be piracies. How many there were it is difficult, perhaps impossible, now to say. They were, according to him, a minority of the 75 privately printed Swinburne pamphlets. Gosse's faith in Wise's integrity was above suspicion. Nevertheless, he was obviously perplexed at times, as when he wrote (Oct. 10, '09):

...As long as there is a mystery about these books, I should be sorry to cause you any possible inconvenience by distributing or even showing them. I keep my own copies locked up. ...

VI

The correspondence on which this chapter has been based is in the Collection bequeathed by the late Lord Brotherton to the Library of Leeds University, and was made available to me after my book was written. It was particularly interesting to find that many of my impressions and conclusions already recorded were confirmed by the documents from Leeds University. But it is unfortunate that the correspondence is incomplete, especially as to Wise's side of it. Did he diplomatically hint at some suppression? There is a suggestive postscript in one of Gosse's undated letters (? 1914): "You are *so* right about destroying papers. I have a daily holocaust." If this explains the gaps in the Wise correspondence, it is not the only instance known to me, and now regretted by the destroyers.

CHAPTER 14

PAYING OFF OLD SCORES AND FINDING
A SCAPEGOAT

Had I the gifts of wealth and luxury shared,
Not poor and mean, Walpole, thou hadst not dared
Thus to insult me. But I shall live and stand
By Rowley's side, when thou art dead and damned.

Thomas Chatterton.

I

IN TELLING of the sequels to The Pines coup, the year 1910 has been skipped. It marked the final stage in Thomas James Wise's residential progress from Holloway to Hampstead— the once favorite dwelling place of London's merchants and authors that has almost been converted into an alien quarter. Wise bought a house in Heath Drive—No. 25—"a devilish difficult place to find on a foggy night," E. V. Lucas described it truly enough; as was found also by others who approached it the wrong way, whether or not in the state of happy fogginess in which E. V. L. at times was found. Heath Drive is a quiet dignified road that, like Keats Grove on its southeastern side, slopes to the top of the hill whence Joanna Baillie's Georgian house views with sleepy contempt the sprawling monstrosity of London. The casual stranger passing No. 25 Heath Drive, standing dull and respectable behind its stout, well-groomed hedge and square of sacred turf, would have been astonished to learn that people journeyed across the seas to visit it: that its first-floor back room housed one of the world's finest private libraries. What masks are the house fronts of mankind!

Here celebrity came to Thomas James Wise and his Ashley books and manuscripts—that family of his dreams, of his toils, and of his pleasures.

These were still laborious days for him. He plunged into his varied pursuits with the zest of a healthy man who has disciplined himself to waste nothing of energy or time, each day adding to his fortune, to his library, and to the fast-accumulating piles of booknotes and descriptions. We get a glimpse of the chubby human dynamo in one of Gosse's notes (Apr. 26, '13): "Please read this letter carefully. You must forgive me for saying that I think, in your excessive haste about everything, you do not take the trouble to read my letters." The admonition was a little exaggerated in its severity. Gosse's letters were not neglected. They brought too much valuable information to the often perplexed bibliographer.

It was perhaps in one of these "excessive hastes" that Wise refused a bundle of Robert Louis Stevenson manuscripts offered for the comparatively trifling sum of £125 ... only to see R. L. S. a few years later become a rabidly collected author, and these same MSS to realize thousands of pounds. Such tales of lost opportunities can be told by all collectors and dealers.

II

The year 1912 [1] inaugurated an important phase in the career of Thomas James Wise; for it was now that he began to occupy himself almost exclusively with enterprises that were to bring him fame beyond his pleasantest dreams, although they were followed by shocks unequaled in his worst nightmares. For the present, he was in comfortable circumstances financially; thanks to the success of his book-dealing and publishing, and also to his own City business of W. A. Smith & Co. In the previous year he had confided to Gosse that he was going to withdraw from commerce, and devote himself to his cataloguing. "I shall be glad when you can

[1] While distinguishing this as the year in which Wise began his ambitious series of bibliographies and catalogues, it will have been noted that he had already compiled bibliographies of Ruskin (1893), Browning (1897), Swinburne (1897), and Tennyson (1908). Those of Browning and Swinburne, however, were preliminary studies—now to be greatly expanded.

throw off the burden of business and live entirely with the muses," replied the critic, who on August 12th, 1912, was hailing the news "that you had freed yourself from the chain of business. You are so wise to do this betimes."

His enterprises now were the production of the bibliographies and catalogues which form such an imposing monument to his industry and skill—to his astuteness and unscrupulousness. These works, with all their faults, are unmatchable as the performance of one man. There is nothing like them for range of interest in the whole of the vast literature of literature. "See Wise" will be one of the commonest references made by researchers and students.

All his life he had been learning about rare books and their authors. Every volume bought, whether for himself or for one of his private clients, had taught him something. As Sir Bernard Spilsbury examines a human body on the mortuary table, so Wise would lay each book before him, probing, exploring, collating—until all the secrets of its mechanism, as created by the printer and author long ago, were revealed to him, and described in his scrawling script. Thus were his data accumulated as the result of long nights of concentration.

Now that he had a library full of scarce editions in the finest state and manuscripts of great curiosity and literary value, there remained the last part of his life's work: to compile records that would accomplish the twofold object of making his collection more widely known, and of making available the information it yielded. That was to be his crowning achievement. His catalogues and bibliographies would be the coping-stones, stuccoed with romantic decorations, to the library he had built up with such patience and shrewdness.

Incidentally, they would afford him the opportunity to pay off old scores against men with whom he had worked, and to whom he was indebted for services and inspirations which he did not deem it convenient to honor lest, perhaps, his own achievement was diminished. And, remembering those forged pamphlets and piracies, he determined to have a scapegoat at hand to plant them on when need should arise.

III

Wise once said in an interview: [2] "I am a bibliographer by choice and intention. I simply drifted into book-collecting because books and manuscripts formed the tools necessary for my job—and so tools had to be acquired."

The latter part of this statement is an example of his aptitude for giving a twist to facts according to circumstances. At other times he would declare that he was first a collector—as early as in his teens. This was the fact: his ideas about bibliography were then negligible. What happened is that he first began collecting and dealing in books. Then he developed the ambitious plan of forming a collection that centered more and more round first and early editions of English poetry and the poetic drama. But he was soon faced with a most perplexing and formidable difficulty—the lack of information; although in the cases of a few authors he had the original efforts of pioneer bibliographers (Forman's Shelley work has been cited) to build upon.

Having decided upon the authors he would collect, how was he to know all the works they had written, and their earliest appearances? An author might have written a score of known books; but he also might have written a dozen unknown works—juvenilia and anonymous pieces. How could he say he had a complete collection of this or that author's works if he lacked the fugitive writings?

It was then that Wise came to appreciate the need of authoritative and exhaustive bibliographies that would tell him these things, and provide him with exact descriptions of rare books and pieces. With the knowledge came also the realization that he would have to compile his own. Now to compile

[2] In *The Strand Magazine* for September, 1930.

a really serviceable bibliography you must have before you not only all the author's first editions in their original variations and in the finest state, but also as much of his manuscript material as possible—since clues to fugitive pieces are often only discovered in letters and obscure references. Thus Wise found himself compiling bibliographical data to further his book-collecting and dealing, and collecting books and MSS to help his bibliographies. It was a bibliophilic merry-go-round, on which he was always going to the end to reach the beginning. It was a highly exciting game. To discover a work that an author has slipped surreptitiously into the world of letters has an inexpressible thrill.

What allurement would there be in the drudgery of literary research if authorship were without its freakish moods and hidden impulses?—if Shakespeare had not written the *Sonnets* to the still mysterious "Mr. W. H."; if the marvelous boy Chatterton had not written the poems fathered on the antique and imaginary "Thomas Rowley"; if Shelley had not made into paper boats a proscribed and anonymous pamphlet to float on the hazardous sea to Ireland; if Sir Walter Scott had not baffled a delighted world as "The Author of Waverley"; if ... but the adventurous tale is unending.

"When I was a young man," Wise said, "bibliography was something new. Scholars spent their days in linguistic research—tracing the history and origin of words. The Oxford English Dictionary of 1888 is an outcome of this activity.... The study of the texts of the Classics was what everybody went for: look at the enormous number of reprints that came out then. But the editors were compelled to ask themselves what text was the most reliable one to reprint. Who could tell them? The bibliographer! Nowadays, the good editor has to be a good bibliographer. And that—that is my answer to the man who cries 'First editions! What a lot of nonsense it all is!' Sweep away into the dust heap the early editions of our English classical writers, and in many cases you destroy the records of the intimate history of their mental and spiritual development."

That was a characteristically energetic defense of book collecting in which is much truth. If bibliography was hardly new in Wise's day, it was certainly circumscribed—both in its information and in its use. And its development into the science it has now become, with such magnificent results— by scholars like A. W. Pollard, W. W. Greg, and J. Dover Wilson—dates from the eighties. In that development Wise was to play his part—a rather more popular part, perhaps, as appealing to the wider interest of book collecting.

He had been fortunate. In the seventies and eighties his contemporaries—all older men—like Dr. Furnivall, Dr. Richard Garnett, Richard Herne Shepherd, Harry Buxton Forman, F. S. Ellis, Colonel Prideaux, Walter Slater, Stopford Brooke, R. A. Potts, Wm. Rossetti, H. B. Wheatley, John Morgan, Professor Dowden, and Thomas Hutchinson, were all concerned in the awakened interest in bibliography. Some of these made an informal committee to advance the subject, one of the chief objects being to arrive at a common system of recording bibliographical descriptions.[3]

These enthusiasts, with others, used to meet at the house in South Audley Street, London, of R. A. Potts—a connoisseur who paid all the costs of printing specimens, etc. It is not difficult to conjure the picture of Wise in this conclave of ardent bookmen gravely discussing whether line endings should be distinguished by vertical or sloping strokes, whether advertisement pages should be counted as part of a book, and such minutiae of the subject. Wise, the junior member, was all ears and eyes—tremendously keen, but modest and deferential in the presence of his elders and betters, some of whom were famous men of letters. He bided his time.

The day of his dominance was to come.

    [3] Wise told me that the "final" plan then drawn up was the one he had always adhered to in his own works. There are many more arguments for than against the general adoption of a standardized form of bibliographical description—as I have urged elsewhere.

There are some people who are successful only in turning knowledge into more knowledge; there are others who have the knack of turning it into hard cash. Wise, collecting books and compiling his bibliographical data on wide and original lines, determined that the knowledge he set himself to gain should enhance the value of the rarities he acquired to get that knowledge—with a substantial side credit on account of his private book deals. The data had assisted him in his collecting and dealing; now, set out in imposing volumes, that data would make impressive advertisements of his library and publications.[4]

These pursuits, subtly interdependent, thus served a double purpose.

IV

One of the first scores he was to settle, after he began in 1912 to devote himself to his compilations, was with Dr. Furnivall, from whom he received his first instruction in bibliography—the very man who had greatly favored him by the introduction to Browning. Wise, in his tentative work on Browning (1897), had been obliged to catalogue Furnivall's earlier *Bibliography of Robert Browning* (1883); and he did so *without comment*. But now that his master had passed away (Dr. Furnivall died in 1910), he vented his feelings in the added note:

Although the name of Dr. Furnivall alone appeared upon the title page as the compiler of the Bibliography, the spade-work was done almost entirely by me under his direction. It was my first lesson in bibliography. But it was always Dr. Furnivall's habit to take full credit for any undertaking in which he was the smallest degree concerned. In the present instance Dr. Furnivall's share of the labour mainly consisted in "compiling" and annotating the work done by Mr. J. T. Nettleship and myself.

---

4 An example occurs in Wise's preface to his *Borrow Bibliography*, in which he draws attention to the "attractive series of Pamphlets" comprising his own privately published issues.

The custom whereby the pupil makes some return to his tutor by doing anonymous spadework has the sanction of antiquity. The system does not work out so unfairly in the long run. The master uses his pupil, who derives practical experience thereby; the pupil, in the fullness of time and with the privilege of age and reputation, uses his own students likewise. And so on—like Swift's fleas.

But examination of Dr. Furnivall's original work of 1883 reveals that he was most punctilious, not merely in making acknowledgments of assistance, but in specifying the individual contributions of his helpers. In his forewords he thanks eleven of these helpers, including Richard Garnett, Austin Dobson, J. T. Nettleship (whose name appears as the author of one section), and especially "Mr. Richard Herne Shepherd, the well-known bibliographer"; the extent of whose honorary efforts is indicated by nearly forty notes. Wise's name is not mentioned; nor is there a single note initialed as contributed by him—though he may have been included among the "and other friends" thanked.[5] If it is really true that Wise played the part he suggests in this pioneering bibliography of Browning, Furnivall possibly considered that, since he was giving him his first lesson in bibliography, the pupil was sufficiently rewarded for his spadework. The keen young merchant would have his own chances, and would seize them. But Wise was very careful not to write that splenetic note until Furnivall was out of the way.

The doctor was a big man in more than one sense. He could get very angry indeed, and hit hard.

V

Another score to be settled was with Fred Hutt, the youngest of three brothers—all booksellers. The story is a revelation of Wise's psychology; it also illustrates how cheaply he acquired some of his greatest rarities.

[5] That Furnivall was not ill-disposed to Wise, however cautious, see the episodes related in Chapters 3 and 10.

One day in 1888 he had called at Fred Hutt's shop, which was situated in Clement's Inn Passage. The bookseller knew where was a copy of that excessively scarce book, the original edition of *Pauline* (1833), Browning's first work.[6] Would Wise give £15 for it? "Yes! gladly," replied that excited customer, who departed rejoicing (like the fellow in Job) and thinking Fred a fine fellow. When Wise went the next afternoon for the book, Hutt was very sorry, but the owner had held out for £20, which he (Hutt) had paid, knowing how much Wise wanted the item. He trusted there would be no objection to a charge of 10 per cent for his trouble. "Certainly not," said Wise, who was just going to write a check when, he says, it evidently dawned upon Hutt that he had "let me off too lightly." He applied another "squeeze," mentioning 10/- paid in cab fares to secure the prize, and hoping that there would be no objection to refunding this. "Of course I will," replied Wise; who adds that he "gaily" handed over his check for £22.10.

Very gaily, we may be sure; for the astute collector-dealer was confident enough of the bargain he had got. Six years later, as he himself records exultantly in the next breath, he was to see £325 given for a copy of that same first *Pauline,* whose market price eventually reached the fantastic height of over £3,000 in 1929.

But a week or two after he had gaily paid £22.10. for a potential £3,000 book, Wise alleges that he learned from another bookseller that Hutt only paid £2.10. for the rarity and that it was in his possession all the time the business was under discussion. "I was perfectly satisfied with the price I paid," comments Wise, "but was naturally annoyed at having been the victim of lies and trickery. I made it my business to call upon Hutt and tell him what I had heard. Instead of flushing with shame and embarrassment, his face assumed a radiant look. . . . He was proud of his 'smartness.'"

There is something comic about the virtuous indignation

6 See *A Browning Library* (1929).

of the last sentences. But there is something more in the incident. A bookseller has to make his profit. It is precisely on the occasional purchase of rarities that he expects to recoup himself for months of labor, continuous buying, and perhaps poor enough daily sales of small items. Moreover, if it is correct (and we have only Wise's ex parte version) that Hutt paid £2.10. for the book, he could hardly tell that to Wise, who, being a keen buyer himself, might well have jibbed at paying £19.10. profit, plus the cab fare. Wise, with all his experience of Mammon and the market place, of its lies that are never believed, and of its "oiling" commissions rarely revealed—Wise, after declaring that he was perfectly satisfied (as well he might be), must thus vent his spleen on the poor dead bookseller, who had but followed the normal ways of business and had contented himself with a modest profit compared with the gigantic coup of his client—for it must be remembered that he wrote this account years after his purchase, when he knew how well he had done.

Nor does the story of petty revenge end here. Three years later Wise found occasion for another kick at the bookseller. In his *Byron Bibliography* (1932) he says: "Charles Hutt commenced business as an employee of Hodgson, of Chancery Lane. Unlike his brother Fred, he was a 'straight' man in every way," etc.

And that was Fred Hutt's account settled.

VI

It was Richard Herne Shepherd who seems to have been selected by Wise to be the scapegoat at hand in case of emergency. Shepherd has a place in the *Dictionary of National Biography* as a bibliographer and man of letters. It was largely he who, in the seventies and eighties, turned the interest of bibliography to modern authors; whereas formerly collectors and builders of libraries had confined themselves to the old and classical authors. With his *Bibli-*

ographies of Ruskin (1879), Dickens (1880), Thackeray (1881 and '87), Carlyle (1881), Swinburne (1883), and Tennyson (1886) he explored uncharted fields. Nor was it in bibliography only that Shepherd was a pioneer. By editing the then comparatively unknown Elizabethan dramatists Chapman, Dekker, and Heyward, he brought these authors to wider recognition. Strangely enough, all his bibliographies appeared without his name on their title pages; and his valuable work for Elizabethan literature was similarly veiled. Whether this was due to his own modesty or to the begrudging spirit of his publishers it is difficult now to say. He was a publishers' hack and a handyman to antiquarian booksellers. Few publishers' hacks get their reward, either for merit or otherwise.

An eccentric character was Shepherd,[7] a tall, angular man, with shoulders rounded from long nights of poring over books. He dressed little better than a beggar; and he was remarkable for the possession of a most beautiful voice and gentle manners. One of his idiosyncrasies was his persistence in walking always in the middle of the streets—in defiance of the shouting and gesticulating jehus of London's cabs and other horse vehicles. His familiar figure, as he made his perilous perambulations from his home (at one time in Chelsea, and for years at the Bald-Faced Stag in Finchley Road) to the British Museum, would be pointed out with the mixture of respect due to scholarship and with contempt for misfortune and eccentricity that was the snobbishness of Victorian London.

But snobbishness and meanness are not confined to any age. When Wise came to publish the correspondence of Swinburne in a series of little books, he entitled them respectively *Letters from Algernon Charles Swinburne* to Thomas J. Wise —to Edmund Gosse—to William Morris—to Sir Richard Bur-

---

[7] Little of a personal nature has been recorded of him. The picture here is derived from details supplied by probably the only man now living who knew him well.

ton, etc., etc.; while the poet's correspondence with Richard Herne Shepherd is merely *Letters on the Works of George Chapman, With an Introduction by Edmund Gosse*. However, Gosse did the gentlemanly thing, acknowledging the recipient as a pioneer, and our indebtedness to "this unfortunate man" for a "most valuable contribution to literature."

Shepherd's was a pathetic case of a kind only too common in literary history. Grandson of a clergyman, he was a man whose learning and devotion to literature were more profitable to others than to himself. Many another man has boomed himself into repute and affluence for achieving far less in literature than did Richard Herne Shepherd—the anonymous toiler. His whole career was one long desperate struggle for a precarious livelihood. It was a struggle not made easier by resort to alcohol—that mocking comfort which stimulates for an hour the will to endure the misery of the next two. He died in 1895, poverty-stricken, in an asylum.

When Wise, always loath to admit he owed anything to this unfortunate man of letters, came to compile his *Swinburne Bibliography*, he made the following carping reference to the dead pioneer:

> Against the errors in Herne Shepherd's elementary Bibliography Swinburne himself afterwards warned me.[8] But I had already gleaned sufficient knowledge ... to make me aware that the gleam of light thrown from the lamp of Shepherd was far too dim to enable me to espy the smaller trifles which ... had been dropped by Swinburne, and were rapidly sinking beneath the accumulating dust. Of these—then unheeded, and unless promptly rescued, soon to be forgotten, waifs, but now highly valued treasures—Herne Shepherd knew nothing.

For very good reasons! Shepherd's *Bibliography* knew nothing of those forged or doubtfully authentic "trifles"—Swin-

---

[8] Swinburne seems to have been unfortunately prejudiced against Shepherd's *Bibliography*, compiled without any assistance from him. He was annoyed to find himself wrongly described therein as editor of *Undergraduate Papers*, and possibly also at the details given of Robert Buchanan's successful libel action arising out of the *Devil's Due* row. Swinburne's prejudice was made the most of by Wise.

burne's *Dead Love*, the *Laus Veneris*, the *Cleopatra*, the *Siena*, and the *Dolores*. How could Shepherd, who died in 1895, guess what "highly valued treasures" they were to become, even had he got to know of them? As for their "sinking beneath accumulating dust"—surely this was the wrong figure of speech. Wise meant "salt," not "dust"—that useful commodity to which Mr. Maurice Buxton Forman referred in *The Times* Literary Supplement (July 12, '34), when he made the revelation of how "remainders" of pamphlets were salted down pending appreciation of their values.

It was Wise who knew all about those "waifs"—whose values were to be artificially created by his authoritative descriptions in the Ashley Library Catalogues.

VII

One of Shepherd's predilections was for hunting after Press contributions by authors, like Tennyson and the Brownings, in whom he was interested. This recording of juvenile and anonymous trifles hidden in magazine files is valuable enough. But Shepherd's obsession for printing some of his finds and perhaps making a few hard-earned and badly needed shillings eventually secured for him the sobriquet of "literary chiffonier" by his biographer in the D. N. B.—a description which, when applied in his lifetime by the outspoken *Athenaeum* (together with more offensive epithets), was punished by a British judge and jury's awarding him £150 damages for libel against that paper.

It is a fact, however, that Shepherd did make a few unauthorized printings of this sort of trifles; to which proceeding the authors objected.[9] It was on these cases that Wise

---

[9] The few things Richard Herne Shepherd printed were mostly often out of copyright. The position was clearly stated by the judge in his summing-up in the case against the *Athenaeum*, when he said "The legal right of the plaintiff [Shepherd] to publish Mrs. Browning's earlier poems was undeniable; but there were some rights which it was very bad taste to assert." This case was decided in 1879; yet two years later Dr. Furnivall was under the necessity of acknowledging Shepherd's generous and voluntary contributions to the first *Bibliography of Browning* (see above, p. 179).

fastened greedily—gloating over the few indiscretions of the penniless scholar as a spider gloats over the enmeshed fly before demolishing it.

Outside, as well as in the Ashley Catalogues, their compiler built up a tale of rascality and untrustworthiness against Shepherd, suppressing all credit due to him as a pioneer. The charges were supported by little or no evidence. An example is provided by the 4-page Swinburne item entitled *Unpublished Verses,* of which Wise contemptuously says that, though "constantly offered as a 'First Edition,'" it is the "merest rubbish" and an "impudent piracy." Shepherd is saddled with responsibility for the thing; and Wise asks:

"Did Shepherd find some scraps of Swinburne's rough draft carrying the lines, and, ignorant of them, imagined them to be unpublished? I think not; but if so—how did he in 1888 know that they were written in 1866? My own opinion is that he traded upon the frequent ignorance of collectors concerning the contents of the books they buy, and carefully selected an extract from one of the Poems which should read pleasantly, and at the same time not readily be identified."

The sneer at ignorant book collectors being imposed upon comes oddly from Wise. But why did he put forward the theory of *Unpublished Verses* originating from a rough draft, only to reject it? His alternative theory may be dismissed. The stolen poetry was not a "carefully selected" extract: it consists of a jumble of lines in an order different from, and some of them in versions far inferior to, those in Swinburne's published poem *Hesperia;* they might well have been the rough draft of part of that poem. From Wise's suggestion it looks as if he knew more about the matter than he said. Of this there is a curious piece of circumstantial evidence. In the catalogue of books and MSS sold at Sotheby's on March 15th, 1911, was described a copy of *Unpublished Verses,* with the statement that the following notes appeared on a fly leaf:

These verses were originally intended for *Poems and Ballads,*
Second Series [this was a slip], but the MS. sheet was mislaid.
The MS. afterwards came into the possession of Mr. Wise, who
had 50 copies printed for presentation. Mr. Wise tells a very different story to the above.

Where that important copy is now, who was the writer
of those explicit notes, and what was his authority, it would
be highly interesting to know. Since Wise asked questions
incriminating Shepherd, here are three more: (1) What evidence had he that Shepherd printed the leaflet (several reasons can be advanced against the supposition)? (2) How
comes it that he who described it as the "merest rubbish"
and an "impudent piracy" was formerly trading in the fake?
and (3) Is the truth of the matter this: that, eventually discovering that the jumbled lines had formed part of the composition of *Hesperia,* and were therefore liable to be recognized as neither unpublished nor a first edition, Wise denounced the fake, using it as another means to belittle and
besmirch Shepherd? There is no evidence to convict him.
But there is the circumstantial evidence of that copy catalogued by Sotheby's; and there is also the evidence that Wise
sold copies of the piracy to his agent, Mr. Gorfin—once in a
lot of fifteen.

Thus in his books and in conversation Wise lost no opportunity of making out Shepherd to be worse than he was—
pursuing with relentless design a pioneer bibliographer to
whom he was greatly indebted, but whose lamp, as he
cynically complained, was "too dim" to expose some of the
very "trifles" Wise himself had imposed upon the book
world.

An even more remarkable case is that connected with
Tennyson's poem *The Lover's Tale,* of which Herne Shepherd reprinted unauthorized editions in 1870 and 1875. The
earlier was voluntarily withdrawn; and against the later an
injunction was obtained by the poet. Shepherd was perfectly
frank in his *Bibliography of Tennyson* about these printings

of his, and gave the details of their suppression. But he defended himself strongly against the charge that he printed these things to cater for collectors of rare and curious books. "What he was interested in was poems which were unobtainable among their authors' current volumes, and his whole series of reprints reflects this harmless passion for 'literary rag-picking'" [Carter and Pollard's *Enquiry*]. But about 1890 his 1870 edition was copied with a predated title page by the manufacturer of the nineteenth-century forged pamphlets; and Wise in his Catalogues was at great pains to plant this forgery of his also on Shepherd. It is a case of a forger cutting the throat of a not very wicked pirate.

When the bubble was pricked in 1934, Wise brought out the scapegoat ready at hand—as we shall see when that year is reached in this history. The scapegoat was also produced then by Mr. Maurice Buxton Forman, who theorized:

I wonder whether Herne Shepherd, and possibly others, knowing how keen he [the writer's father] was, manufactured small pamphlets with the sole object of planting them on him? It is not a nice thought, but it seems to me by no means impossible.

Mr. Buxton Forman is right. It is not a nice thought. All things considered, it is indeed a very ugly thought—to suggest the poor unfortunate scholar as the villain of the piece, or pieces. And if Richard Herne Shepherd did put out a few unauthorized printings, who was Wise to stone him? —Thomas James Wise, the plump and prosperous dealer, with his twenty-nine forgeries, twenty suspected pamphlets, and his career of piratical publishing extending from the eighties to 1914.

CHAPTER 15

REVELATIONS GRAVE AND GAY

*The truth seems to be that it is impossible to lay the ghost of a fact.
You can face it or shirk it—and I have come across a man or two
who could wink at their familiar shades.*

Joseph Conrad: *Lord Jim.*

I

IN ADDITION to the general cataloguing of his books and MSS,
Wise was now compiling exhaustive bibliographies of Coleridge (for the Bibliographical Society) and of George Borrow.
His interest in the Romany lad was largely the result of
another Shorter-Wise haul of an author's manuscripts through
tracing the writer's descendants. In this instance the unpublished MSS were bought *en bloc* from the executor of
Borrow's step-daughter, Mrs. MacOubrey, and were now being
sent hot to the press for publication by Wise in 1913 as first
editions in 44 of his privately printed pamphlets. His *Bibliography of Borrow* (1914) followed close on their heels, and
may be described not unfairly as a sale catalogue of the
pamphlets. It doubtless helped him to get the profitable price
of £80 for ten of the titles, as already related. "I confess that
the *Borrow Bibliography,* where half the "first editions" are
Wise pamphlets, makes me furious," Mr. William McCarthy,
one of the librarians of the University of Texas, writes to
me.

One of Wise's Borrow items has a threefold interest. It
illustrates firstly, John Gibson Lockhart's little way with
his contributors when editor of the *Quarterly Review;* sec-
ondly, Borrow's sturdy independence; and thirdly, Wise's
little way with his possessions. Lockhart in 1845 sent a copy
of Richard Ford's *Handbook for Travellers in Spain* for

Borrow to review. It was just the thing for the happy man who had sold the Bible in Spain and bought adventures cheaply at the same time. Besides, Ford was his friend. To his dismay, Lockhart found that while Borrow had sent him a delightful paper, really another "capital chapter" of his *Bible in Spain,* there was "hardly a word of 'review,' and no extract giving the least notion of the peculiar merits and style of the *Handbook";* so he confided to Ford wistfully. Editors, of course, are the accursed darlings of misfortune. The well-minded Lockhart braced his shoulders, and decided that "I could easily (as is my constant custom) supply the humbler part myself, and so present at once a fair review of the work, and a lively specimen of our friend's vein of elo-quence *in exordio.* But, behold! he will not allow any tam-pering." Ford grinned. Borrow blasted Albemarle Street to Gibraltar, and wrote the following skit:

> *Would it not be more dignified*
> *To run up debts on every side*
> *And then to pay your debts refuse,*
> *Than write for rascally Reviews*
> *And lectures give to great and small*
> *In pot-house, theatre, and town hall—*
> *Wearing your brains by night and day*
> *To win the means to pay your way?*
> *I vow by him who reigns in ——*
> *It would be more respectable!*

The manuscript of this skit and Borrow's "review" as set up in type in 1845, but not published, were among Wise's acquisitions from Mrs. MacOubrey. He says that this 1845 review, of which only "two copies would appear to have been struck off," is the rarest of all Borrow's first editions. So! if it is a first edition, then he is wrong to describe (as he does in the *Ashley Library Catalogue:* Vol. I) his 1913 privately printed publication of the review as the first edition: that publication, titled *A Supplementary Chapter to the Bible in Spain,* would be merely a reprint. The 1845 review, however,

appears to be one of the specially pulled proofs returned by
Lockhart after he had supplied his "humbler part" by in-
serting some quotations from Ford's *Handbook:* in which case
Wise's 1913 publication happens to be the first edition
proper. In book collecting there can only be one *first* edition.
There cannot be a dead heat—not even between something
proofed in 1845 and the same thing printed by a stout little
runner panting behind Borrow, and catching him up in 1913.
Wise could not have it both ways.[1]

In this same year—1913—as the Borrow publication, Wise
was apparently concerned about the vacant Laureateship. Surprising as it may be, he seems to have written to Gosse on
behalf of someone (a pity this is one of the missing letters!),
to receive this bland but definite reply:

> ...Asquith has sent for me to talk to him about the L'ship,
> to-day. I suspect he is a good deal pressed. The person you so
> kindly name is not a candidate, and could not be thought of.
> Nor is Y., so far as I know, in "the running" at all....

II

But perhaps the most important event of the prewar years
was connected with little "Herby," whom we left in Chapter 9
helping Mister Wise, the cashier at Hermann Rubeck's, to
dispatch books to his American and other customers. In the
years that followed, the small office boy advanced in station
as well as in stature. "Herby," sharp and intelligent, picked
up a knowledge of book collecting and selling, largely from
Mister Wise, who, needing an agent, encouraged the youth.
He would be useful.

From 1898, therefore, young Gorfin was permitted to sell
on commission books and pamphlets for his master. Gorfin
found that certain pamphlets by the Brownings, Swinburne,

---

[1] It is evident that he had his doubts about the propriety of his classifica-
tions; because he does not describe the 1913 publication as a first edition
in his *Bibliography of Borrow,* but only in the *Ashley Library Catalogue.*

Ruskin, and others, sold very well to collectors and dealers if only a copy or two were available at a time. They were somewhat vaguely referred to as "remainders" of small editions, often printed apparently for their authors' use. He knew also that Mister Wise, who was so clever, had quite a stock of these easily handled booklets. The junior having decided to launch out for himself as a bookseller (but with a shop, for the world to see): "Look here, Herbert," said Wise to him one day, "as you know, I've been dealing in these pamphlets now for quite a long time, have made plenty out of them, and am getting a bit tired of them. What about taking the remainder over from me at a nominal price, and dealing with them in future on your own?" So the industrious apprentice, eager to become a rare-book seller, laid out his savings and capital—over £400—in Mister Wise's nice "clean" little pamphlets, the majority of which were either forgeries or piracies.

Then came Herby's third great adventure in life—having first been born, of course; and then having come under the Star of the Wise Man of E.C. 3. In 1912, backed by a small stock of books (including those "gilt-edged" securities, the forged pamphlets) and a large stock of confidence, Herbert Gorfin opened a secondhand bookshop in Charing Cross Road, London.

Confidence? Why not? His destiny seemed set as fair as any barometer could promise sunshine. Had he not a powerful friend and backer—Mister Wise, so prosperous, so well in with all the best collecting people? There followed two years of successful building-up of the Charing Cross Road business, during which Mister Wise kept close touch, visiting the young bookseller several times a week to sell items and to arrange deals on commission. All was going fairly for young Herbert, although there were times when his confidence was shaken.

He gives this example. Wise had an option on a rare first edition which he suggested that Gorfin should offer to a

West End firm for £180. Gorfin protested that the price was not nearly enough for a book of which less than half a dozen copies were known. He spent several strenuous hours negotiating with the rival bookseller, who eventually agreed to buy at £460. Young Gorfin joyously proceeded to find Wise, who became "purple and speechless with surprise and annoyance that he had made such an undervaluation." He said he would consider the matter, and finally decided not to sell. His agent, who presumes that the rare book was afterward sold to America direct, described this episode with bitterness—not only because he had come to terms with the other bookseller, but because he received no consideration in respect of his dealing.

Suddenly the barometer of friendship and fortune fell to zero. In 1914 Gorfin's association with Wise became less cordial and useful owing to the former's dissatisfaction over the Landor deal with Gosse already mentioned; Gorfin objecting that he was asked to sell Wise's books without handling them. Then came the World War—to swamp the young bookseller's business, as it did so many businesses.

Asked about their personal relations, Mr. Gorfin said that when they were alone Wise was most charming in his attitude to him. His disposition was so friendly, indeed so affectionate, as to be almost paternal; and with it all a jocular intimacy that was born of their long office familiarity at Hermann Rubeck's. "But the moment we ceased to be alone, when it came to showing and proving friendly relations before others, then Wise's attitude changed. His manner became cold and aloof. He was the client and master; I was the servant. Before long I realized that I was merely regarded as a tool."

Thus the experienced bookman of many parts and the young bookseller of the dashed hopes went their ways—the former heading for celebrity; the latter for the trenches. But destiny had not done with their association.

Sign printed at the
e n d of many of
Wise's publications

MR. HERBERT E. GORFIN

Photographic study by himself.

Wise about the age of 40. Photograph by Mr. Gorfin

Wise's Bookplate

III

On the 29th of July, 1913, *The Times* achieved one of its historic coups by publishing under the heading "Charlotte Brontë's Tragedy" a series of long-hidden love letters from the authoress to Professor Constantin Héger, the originals of which the professor's son had just lodged with the British Museum as a gift to the nation. So the secret was out at last. Something of it had been guessed for a long time. Mrs. Gaskell, Charlotte's biographer, had allowed too much to be read between the lines of her last-minute account of Miss Brontë's two years as a teacher at the Brussels *pensionnat*, which ended with Madame Héger's estrangement and the suffering girl's departure. Now here was the story: revealed by the heroine, not by the novelist, in all the intensity of her passion and anguish—when she could find "neither rest nor peace day and night" for the longing to hear from her professor; when, if she sleeps, *"Je fais des rêves tourmentants."* The "Reason" she also puts into verse that is little known, and not yet included in her works:

> *Unloved I love, unwept I weep.*
> *Grief I restrain, hope I repress;*
> *Vain is the anguish fixed and deep,*
> *Vainer desires or means of bliss.*[2]
>
> *Have I not fled that I may conquer?*
> *Crost the dark sea in firmest faith,*
> *That I at last might plant my anchor*
> *Where love cannot prevail to death?*

This first publication of the love letters was the literary event of the decade. As they were read, men in their club chairs uncrossed and crossed their stiff legs, women schoolteachers thrilled, and Brontë enthusiasts hurried to *Villette* to fit the poignant letters into the blank spaces of that autobiography.

---

[2] This, of course, did not appear among the newly revealed love letters. It comes from the Ashley Library MSS.

There were two persons who, when they saw those generous columns in *The Times,* were also thrilled, but by far different emotions from those that stirred the sensibilities of learned clubmen, and also the repressions of spinsters who understood *ever so well.* Those two persons were Clement King Shorter and Thomas James Wise, who—as we have seen in Chapter 9—had made something like a "corner" in Brontë manuscripts. *The Times* appended to Charlotte's letters (they were in French) English translations and notes by that authority Mr. M. H. Spielmann—prefacing the whole with the word "Copyright." Shorter was very angry, puffed down to Printing House Square, and raised loud protests. These were promptly silenced by the "Thunderer," which next morning came out with this withering announcement:

Mr. Shorter, while raising no objection to the acquisition of the letters by the British Museum or their publication by "The Times," was a little disconcerted by the fact that the warning word "Copyright" was added to our headline yesterday. Some while ago he purchased from Charlotte Brontë's literary executor [referring presumably to his deal with Bell Nicholls, see p. 100] all legal rights in her unpublished correspondence, and he suggests that this would vest the copyright in the newly discovered letters in him. Whether this is legally correct in the case of letters now 70 years old, Mr. Shorter must settle, if he cares to, with the British Museum authorities. So far as "The Times" is concerned, it was not intended to claim permanent copyright in the letters themselves, but only in the matter which accompanied them.

Whereupon King Shorter abdicated, retiring within himself; for which there was ample room. Wise, of course, did not go down to Printing House Square: he was not so concerned; and, as we have seen, he preferred to lie low when any bother was about. But a few months later he sent *The Times* transcripts and Mr. Spielmann's translations and notes to his printers, to make another of his privately printed first editions, *The Love Letters of Charlotte Brontë to Constantin Héger* (1914), maintaining in his prefatory note that the copyright was the property of his friend Shorter, whose generosity, etc., etc., etc. But it was not until 1938 that Mr. Spielmann knew of the Wise publication and its wholly unauthorized use of his translations—"the cool bagging of my Brontë work," he wrote to me.

It is unexpectedly late in Wise's career, now verging upon rectitude, to find him producing a piracy. But there it is: the philosophy of "What's yours is mine, and what's mine is my own." So once again he could wink at his familiar shade.

IV

There came the World War. Its horrors did not touch him very closely. He had no sacrifices to make: no children to risk in its raging hell. As relentlessly as death swept over the stricken fields, he pursued his own aims. After the works on Coleridge and Borrow, he was able to publish in 1916 his *Bibliography of Wordsworth;* in 1917, that of *The Brontë Family;* and in 1918, that of *Elizabeth Barrett Browning;* in addition to a regular flow of his privately printed first-edition pamphlets. Also during these years good bargains were to be had in books and manuscripts, for the luxury trade was badly hit; and so the Ashley Library increased its treasures. Amid these activities he was very active again in the City; for the War prospered his business in spite of the difficulties of the times. Even these were smoothed out by that valuable friend of whom he could secretly take advantage. The essential-oil dealer told his troubles about shipment. Whereupon Gosse wrote:

I am deeply concerned by what you tell me about the export of spice ... Can I be of the slightest use to you in bringing your case before the authorities?

He could be, and was: not only in that case, but over a cargo of olives—not olive branches, however.

All was fair in bibliography and war.

As he worked in his comfortable library, sorting and cataloguing his treasures of 35 years of collecting, he might well pride himself on his skill and acquisitiveness. Closer study of the contents of his shelves surprised even him. The Ashley Library has two independent appeals: its magnificent first editions of early English poets and dramatists; and its wealth of manuscript material of the nineteenth century. Comparing one with the other, and considering all circumstances, my own opinion is that the collection of MSS represents the greater triumph.

Wise had a partiality for what are termed "human documents" telling of the scandals, the private confessions, the secrets of authors. Now he had only to stretch out a hand and open his bookcases to expose the quivering souls, the comic figures, the ghastly skeletons that always have made and always will make up the literary world. From these he covered the dry bones of his book descriptions with the living flesh of biography, giving life to his catalogues that will long outlast their purely bibliographical interest. What materials his eager hands had gathered! Documents in which men and women are stripped naked, souls searched and revealed—a welter of idylls and passions, jokes and despairs. I have handled many of these fragile letters and discolored papers. And although some of them are now mockingly shrouded in the finest silk and morocco blazing with gold, it has seemed as if they were still wet with tears and kisses, or else shaking with the laughter or anger of their writers. Let us take a few glimpses at some of the lighter revelations. At—

SHELLEY'S noble generosity when expecting Keats in Italy: "I intend to be the physician both of his body and soul. . . . I am aware indeed that I am nourishing a rival who will far surpass me; and this is an additional motive and will be an added pleasure."

CHARLOTTE BRONTË, about her dead brother Branwell: "All his vices were and are nothing now—we remember only his woes."

KEAT'S suppressed poem entitled "Sharing Eve's Apple," beginning:

> *"O blush not so! O blush not so!*
> *Or I shall think you knowing;*
> *And if you smile the blushing while,*
> *Then maidenheads are going."*

MARY SHELLEY telling Mrs. Leigh Hunt as one woman to another: "If it were of any use I would say a word or two against your continuing to wear stays. Such confinement cannot be either good for you or the child; and as to shape, I am sure they are very far from becoming."

TRELAWNY philosophizing to Jane Clairmont: " 'The dream we call life' is a farce. . . . The only solace is that we are all in the donkey race."

JANE CLAIRMONT, the discarded mistress of Byron, in her diary: "I have nothing left to do but fry in the sun for your amusement."

THOMAS HARDY recalling the traffic perils in the London of 1867: "It carried me back to the time of 30 years ago when I used to read your [Swinburne's] early works walking along the crowded London streets to my imminent risk of being knocked down."

BYRON, as Mrs. Leigh Hunt saw him: "Like a schoolboy who has been given a plain, instead of a currant, bun."

ROBERT LOUIS STEVENSON'S delightful letter in verse to his friend Charles Baxter, beginning:

> *"Blame me not that this epistle*
> *Is the first you have from me,*
> *Idleness has held me fettered;*
> *But at last the times are bettered,*
> *And once more I wet my whistle—*
> *Here in France beside the sea."*

CHARLES DICKENS back at slavery, after a jolly tramp and dinner with Leigh Hunt: "Oh Hunt, I'm so lazy, and all along o'you. The sun is in my eyes, the hum of the fields in my ears—

and a boy, redolent of the okam engine and sweltering in warm ink, is slumbering in the passage, waiting for 'copy'."

GEORGE BORROW, who liked to air himself as a philologist: "It must not be supposed that 'Will' is the abbreviation of William; it is pure Danish, and signifies 'wild'."

GEORGE MEREDITH anticipating Swinburne's poems coming out: "I have heard 'low mutterings' already from the Lion of British prudery."

SWINBURNE, with a typical characterization: "Swift, I take to have been Dante's bastard by a daughter of Rabelais."

HARDY, again, on the riddle of Browning: "The longer I live the more does Browning's character seem the leading puzzle of the Nineteenth Century. How could smug Christian optimism worthy of a dissenting grocer find a place inside a man who was so vast a seer and feeler when on neutral ground?"

ROBERT BROWNING, reporting that Landor is established close at hand (in Italy): "I believe I am to have the poor dear old man permanently 'added to my portion,' as the Methodists phrase it."

WILLIAM ROSSETTI, hugging himself upon the reflection that he had got portraits of his sister and his "dear loving old mother" into the National Portrait Gallery: "Christina had to be there one day, as a matter of course; but I greatly applaud myself on having thus wafted in my mother by a side-wind."

Limerick writing was one of the milder amusements of Victorian authors and artists. D. G. Rossetti was always doing it. Here is one against him by his friend, John Payne—him of the emasculated *Arabian Nights:*

> *There's a joker called Dante Rossetti,*
> *Who thinks he paints better than Etty.*
> *His ladies in paint*
> *Look all ready to faint*
> *But* au fond *they're plain Molly and Betty.*

which was true enough, as Gabriel would agree; for did he not know his "stunners" *au fond?*

The Ashley Library material is remarkable for its light on the curious recreations of the Pre-Raphaelites. Wise says in his prefatory note to the privately printed *Letters addressed to Algernon Charles Swinburne* (1919): "All are interesting, but some of the expressions and allusions contained in three from Sir Edward Burne-Jones and D. G. Rossetti render the publication as a whole of these particular letters impossible. But the letters are by no means unimportant, and cannot be entirely disregarded. I therefore see no sufficient reason why they should not be preserved in the pages of a private pamphlet [for which, of course, Wise found a ready sale]. The only alternative is to destroy them." The arguments contain the usual proportions of Wisedom and hypocrisy. He did not print the Swinburne effusions that prompted these letters. Nor did he destroy the equally scabrous replies they drew—all of which remain in the Ashley Collection at the British Museum. When, as is probable in the course of time, the Wise collection is split up, these things will go to their final resting place on the shelves *Librorum Prohibitorum* in the Bloomsbury mausoleum.

There was an occasion when William Morris, on approaching the age of 30, suddenly grew so very stout that he burst a pair of trousers. This was an undying source of merriment for years among the grown-up children of the Pre-Raphaelite Brotherhood. Burne-Jones and Rossetti drew realistic pictures of the "Affair of the Bags" after Swinburne had exploited it in a squib "which," says Wise after printing it as one of his publications, "can never be included in any edition of his published verse."

In a letter from one of the Brotherhood (circa 1886) to "My Dear but Infamous Pote," he acknowledges the "dreadful" gift of Swinburne's last letter, and his own fearful anxiety lest it should get out of his pocket and be seen. For "its genius, my dear Sir, is such that I wouldn't destroy it for the world, and to keep it is destruction. It lies before me now with its respectable edge of black, and its wicked contents, like—if the simile may be accorded me—a sinful clergyman." Apparently the enjoyment of the artist friends (including the "Jewjube"—i.e., Simeon Solomon) at the effusion was so intense that they spent the morning in drawing pictures "such as Tiberius would have given provinces for." The classical allusion explains why sending them through the post "seemed dangerous," and so "we burnt them." To show how much Tiberius, and Swinburne, and Thomas James Wise would have liked his Pre-Raphaelite illustrations, the correspondent describes one:

It was my own poor idea, not altogether valueless, I trust. A clergyman of the established church is seen lying in an extatic dream in the foreground. Above him a lady is seen plunging from a trap door in the ceiling, about to impale herself upon him. How poorly does this describe one of my most successful designs. But you shall yet see it.

Nice goings on among the Pre-Raphaelites. But the point is that nothing of this stuff is fit to be published among the works of the respective authors, says Wise unctuously. It could be privately published for his gain, however; and the copies of his pamphlets are now scattered far and wide, for any unscrupulous person to reprint and disseminate the rubbish for their gain also.

V

While Wise was busy during the War, there appears to have been some disposition to be faithless to his old printers, Clay & Sons. Between 1916 and 1918 nine of his publications were produced by another firm. These may have been experiments with a view to a change. However, he returned to Clays until 1922; when came the break with the good printers who had innocently served him so long and so well in producing his "private" pamphlets—both illegitimate and legitimate. On this subject the comment to me of Mr. Cecil Clay is interesting. "There was no official break with Clays as far as I know, and you see after 1921 we had no printing works in London. The manager whom Wise always saw died in '28 or thereabouts; but this should not have stood in Wise's way if he was prepared to go out of London. . . . Whatever the cause of Wise's change of printers you can rest assured it was not due to any suspicion on the part of the firm that its previous transactions with him were of an unsatisfactory nature." (Mar. 10, '38.)

But we have only arrived at 1918 in the chronology of Thomas James Wise, for whom the postwar years were to hold such remarkable developments.

CHAPTER 16

WAR AND EXPLOITATION

The story [of the faked first edition of Chance] once more proves what I have before asserted, that easy as it appears to be to fabricate reprints of rare books, it is in actual practice absolutely impossible to do so in such a manner that detection cannot follow the event. Even when the volume is of so recent a date that the necessary types and paper are both procurable, the human element fails, and, as in the present instance, a blunder is committed in spite of the exercise of the most meticulous care.

Wise: *Bibliography of Joseph Conrad.*

I

AFTER THE world conflagration came the boom that follows war as vultures follow the dying beast to gorge on its still warm carcase. Europe passed from a nightmare of bloodshed to an orgy of gambling, dissoluteness, and extravagance. There were plenty of people who had amassed money out of the horrors of Armageddon, out of the slaughter and maiming of over 27 millions of young manhood. Now, when wealth was distributed as never before in history, was the fever of spending and the delirium of making. Get rich quick while the boom lasted and prices soared—that was the spirit of the Great Peace—except for a few emotional hours on every eleventh of November. Win fair, win foul, and the devil take the hindmost when the slump comes.

After the Napoleonic Wars the nation that came out most advantageously began coveting and buying the treasures, artistic and literary, of impoverished countries. Now history was repeated—with this difference: after dictator Napoleon had run his short and fearful course, it was the English who could buy the Continent's illuminated manuscripts, Velasquez

Venuses, and Elgin Marbles. Now it was America who could swoop down on Britain to gratify the desires of her culture for treasures in which she had a family interest. Vastly poorer in those treasures than was the Britain of a century earlier, she was much wealthier financially. So books, MSS, pictures, sculptures, even some of England's lovely old buildings, were captured by the irresistible dollar: many of them to be formed into magnificent collections, and finally swept with princely gestures by their millionaire-owners into the State's keeping for the benefit of the people.[1]

It was wonderful history-making in those ten years that followed the World War; future generations will be grateful to the United States of 1918 to 1929 for her enterprise. Although the ignorant lamented and protested against the transfer of cultural possessions from the old country to the new, it can be proved that Britain could well spare the greater part—even 95 per cent—of what America gained; for which, let it be emphasized, she paid well. That the exchange was a fortunate one, those familiar with American scholarship are well convinced by what has already been done with the English books, MSS, etc., acquired in the historic ten years.[2]

In the boom the rare-book field became affected with much of the gambling fever of the Stock Exchange. Collecting, for a time, ceased to be the exclusive pursuit of booklovers and students, rich or poor. Into the arcadian field came bustling speculators ludicrously disguised as bookmen, who grasped the possibilities of the American demand and the popularized interest in old books and MSS due to the rising

[1] During this period I broadcast a series of talks on book collecting. One was on the subject of America's rivalry in scholarship, as a result of acquiring our book and MSS treasures (vide *The Listener*, August 14th, 1929). When, in accordance with custom, the script was submitted, the B. B. C. censor deleted my comment: "What a happy part for these old books to play in the relations of two great English-speaking nations!" The reason given for this curious suppression was that the sentence touched on international politics!!

[2] American acquisitiveness in respect of English literary treasures continued to a decreasing extent after 1929, and of course it had been successfully active long before 1919; but there never was before, and probably never will be again, such a period as the ten years of the boom.

prices. They bought and bought with abysmal ignorance of what they were buying, in order to unload at the right time.

Many books that formerly were priced in shillings were now cheap at as many pounds. Others, the first editions of immortal authors, that used to sell—and slowly enough—for a few pounds, now sold for hundreds. The exciting competition was increased, and values were forced up, by the elaboration of minute points of difference between copies of the same first edition due to accidents of printing, by the discovery of freak copies, and (more justifiably) by the appreciation of volumes bearing some association with their writers or their celebrated friends by reason of inscriptions, corrections, etc. As for original letters and MSS, fantastic prices were commonly reached—the amazing record being that of £15,400 paid by A. S. W. Rosenbach for the script of *Alice in Wonderland*. How that must have startled the author looking for Alices in the Wonderland of the Shades! How it amazed his jolly nieces, my neighbors of boyhood days.

In the wider distribution of wealth that followed the World War, many of the old rich became the new poor. In old English homes a long reign of cloistered calm and careless affluence ended with the new economic conditions and the alarmingly increasing demands of taxation. Some of their little-known libraries, long matured like wine in sacred cellars, were broken up and cast into the welter of the London sales rooms. Others—more than we yet realize—were ravished secretly, the old volumes, in their mellowed calf or original boards, packed into metal cases and rushed across the Atlantic. No one was wiser, except the dealer with his cigar and the straitened landowner left with a fat check and an uneasy mind. Ruffled and bewigged ancestors looked down fearfully from their frames: for the next visitors were to be the picture dealers.

Oh, yes! they sold well. The Americans loved anything from a turreted and famous old Hall. Why not? Here were good things: to covet them was a grace, not an offense. "What remarkable prices to pay for those old books, Agatha, my dear," an owner would say, patting the antique silver teapot. Poor things! They needed it. By the time the prosperous family lawyers had paid off mortgages and arrears or war-income tax,[3] and allowed for the death duties staring in the face of the living, there was not much left. The libraries crossed the Atlantic; to be, on the other side, marveled over and superbly indexed by experts whose care and efficiency would have left gasping the learned but easy-going librarians of the Stately Homes of old England.

But it was not only the veteran first editions of mellowed libraries that went soaring in value. There were not enough of them to meet the hungry demand. So the first editions of contemporary authors were seized upon as the next best things—a few justly enough; more with little reason. It was in this traffic that the silly limit was reached. Some of these books had been published only a short time before in first printings known to have run to hundreds and thousands of copies. The supply at all times exceeded the demand, temporarily inflated though it was, and "forced" by those who hoarded copies. Sums ranging from £50 to £200 were frequently paid for first editions of popular novelists and dramatists that before many years were to be hardly salable at prices about 75 per cent less.

With all the publicity these ephemeral wonders obtained, there were even some writers with aspirations to be best sellers who thought that the collecting field was a short cut to their goal. I could name more than one pushful author who endeavored to stimulate artificially the collecting demand for his very mediocre writings. It was a crazy time, the most cynical comment on which was that made by George Bernard Shaw, who advised Mrs. Patrick Campbell to sell the personal letters he had written to her and make money while the going was good!

[3] The British war bill was the heaviest of all combatants—13,578 million pounds, against Germany's 10,341 and America's 8,000 millions.

II

All this is very interesting history, the reader may say; but where does Thomas James Wise come in? The answer is that he had come in before the history-making began. With his shelves well-filled with rare first editions and MSS, he could watch the soaring prices of the boom, knowing that the value of his library was being doubled, quadrupled, and more. Except for an item now and then to fill a gap, some desirable thing here and there that would round off a collection of some author's works, he could keep out of the mad competition and its fancy prices. Furthermore, he could sit back and see the labors of his earlier years bearing remarkable fruit. The concentration on books having special points of interest, on freak copies, on original issues in fine state, etc., was partly the result of his influence.

Those who were selling and buying in the feverish rare-book market eagerly consulted the bibliographies he had so far produced. In these, the points were elaborated with all Wise's enthusiasm and that lavishness of evidence (drawn from MS sources) which gave his reference books much of the interest of biographies. His authority was increasingly cited; and he himself was frequently referred to personally by strangers—rarely in vain. Thus, whereas formerly Wise and his collection had been known to only a small circle of connoisseurs, now his name as a collector and bibliographer became familiar to many people in Britain, the Empire, the United States, and other countries. To this larger public he loomed out of an obscure past—affluent, successful, a genius at the collecting game, a wizard at bibliography. And so, his fame spread on the wings of a boom.

He held aloof from the new craze for collecting almost every contemporary author who got into the newspapers. His shrewd judgment as a rare-book dealer warned him that many of these boosted first editions had only a passing interest and value. Nevertheless, although he had chosen to specialize in the old poets and dramatists, the great fame of men like Hardy, Conrad, and Kipling, and the amazing prices paid for copies of their rarities, caused him to tack to the fashionable wind—led to the opening of his library to a few selected rare first editions of modern novels. Here he was following the crowd. His literary perception and his scholarship have been much vaunted. But no instance can be found—not even that of Swinburne—in which Wise saw the promise of an author's early work and backed his judgment by collecting him when he was obscure and unheralded. *A Pair of Blue Eyes* did not lure him at first; the original *Almayer's Folly* was like any other man's; and certain lilting songs and amusing barrack-room tales (that came in paper-covered booklets and quickly disappeared) found no welcome in the Ashley Library—not until they had become desirable things to be dearly bought.

III

In one of his compilations Wise makes reference to the merciless exploitation of Joseph Conrad after his death. Just that: no other information is vouchsafed. I have a memorandum of Wise telling Edmund Gosse: "I'm *sick* of the way these brutes are trading on Conrad—particularly the ******* crowd, who are selling to the Yankees everything they got out of him, or can scrape together: books, letters, and ought else." But he said nothing of what happened *before* the author's death.

Wise's interest in collecting Conrad first editions was excited by Mr. Richard Curle, who was well known to both parties. Mr. Curle had himself been assiduously engaged in making a complete collection of original Conrad editions, etc., the author generously assisting and inscribing many of the volumes. Immediately the boom began, the values of Conrad first editions soared. Wise, realizing the possibilities, determined to include him among his collected authors (see his note on "ever-increasing prices" in the preface to his *Bibliography of Conrad,* which duly resulted in 1920). In this case, however, he did not want mere first editions: he wished to emulate the example of Mr. Curle and to have a collection of inscribed copies—which are much more valuable. This was arranged in a way that was made worth while to Conrad, who also sold to Wise all his manuscripts done from 1918 onward—at least eight of which, in addition to a case of original letters from the author, were disposed of privately by the collector-dealer.[4] The former merchant-captain had had a lean time after he left the sea to become an author. Now, with an increasingly expensive family, it was not surprising that he should avail himself of some of the side profit of the enthusiasm for his writings. But Conrad fondly believed the MSS he sold to Wise were remaining in the Ashley Library.

The inscriptions written by the author for Wise in his Conrad first editions were often of a bibliographical character. Actually the old sea rover so brilliantly metamorphosed into the novelist was about as qualified to make such bibliographical statements as was the essential-oil merchant to handle a windjammer in a typhoon. Conrad's occasional irritation with the business can be surmised from the style of some of the signatures to the inscriptions, such as:

Signed for T. J. Wise
Joseph Conrad.

The baldness of that statement in what was desired to appear like an inscribed presentation copy may be best interpreted in seaman's language. Of course, the mood varied in other cases, and the author would perform his well-paid task with more "friendly regards." As an example of the inscriptions, take this one in Wise's copy of *The Inheritors:*

---

[4] One other, that of *Laughing Anne,* was retained in the Ashley Collection. I find Conrad writing to "Dear Mr. Wise," sending the 53-quarto-page MS and also the corrected typescript, of the play, and asking £100 for them, the letter being signed "Yours faithfully." Wise's check was sent by return mail.

This is a copy of the first American edition, which was before the English edition, the imprint of Heinemann being merely stamped for publication purposes.

So this is Joseph Conrad, the sensitive temperamental writer, who, ever since he left the sea, lived for his art, developing a secret self in which he lived to weave his pictures and fantasies. So this is Joseph Conrad solemnly writing his own bibliographical data. My own laughter at the thought, echoing round my library in the stillness of the night, startles me. I try to imagine Conrad as I have seen him in his study, bending over his table, the powerful shoulders hunched, the hand with its long fingers and whipcord veins seizing that fat fountain pen—for what? To compose bibliographical certificates to the rarity of copies of his own books! The mockery of it all. For the true picture is that of a calculating expert behind the half-bewildered author, dictating the careful inscriptions which in Joe's generous script make the volume so valuable.

Thanks to the continuance of his commercial good fortune, Wise never knew what these inscriptions he got Conrad to write meant to him in cash. But he had a shrewd idea when, within three years from Conrad's death, at the height of the first-edition boom, Mr. Richard Curle sold by auction in New York his collection of Conrad's books, etc., which the author had inscribed for him. The sum realized for the Curle collection was nearly £8,000.[5]

When the news of this sale was announced, Joseph Conrad's widow wrote to me: "Perhaps you would like to see the Curle catalogue. It is disconcertingly complete. So much so that I feel almost guilty of bad taste to be still in the land of the living."

IV

The popularity of authors is not always due to readers' recognition of their best work. The sickening and grossly

[5] This sale took place at the American Art Association Galleries on April 28, 1927.

overrated *John Inglesant* was made a best seller by a photograph showing Mr. Gladstone holding a copy in his hands. It was *Chance* that raised Conrad into the ranks of best sellers; and it is *Chance* that provides a remarkable illustration of how chancey a bibliographer Wise could sometimes be.

The novel was first printed with a title page dated 1913; but, publication being postponed until the following year, that title page was removed and replaced by one dated 1914. A number of copies, however—some 50, says Wise—got into circulation with the 1913 title; and these constitute the first issue of the first edition.

Then comes a mystery about which there have been many rumors and head-shakings. A forger got to work, printed off leaves reproducing the 1913 title page, and inserted them in copies of *Chance* in place of the 1914 title. By chance, it was none other than Thomas James Wise who first revealed the hidden hand of the forger; and it was the forger's failure to reproduce exactly the genuine article that led Wise to write the weighty pronouncement which I have selected to head this chapter. It is possibly the sardonic echo of his regret, remembering his efforts with sundry nineteenth-century pamphlets, and the exposure of some of them by Cook and Wedderburn.

Once informed of the foregoing facts, no one need be gulled. In copies of the genuine and valuable uncanceled 1913 issue of *Chance*, the title page bearing that date is part of the sheet on which that section of the book is printed. On the other hand, the forged 1913 title page and also the publisher's substituted 1914 title page are both inserted leaves pasted on to stubs in the joints, or back of the books. Wise made the matter crystal clear in his *Bibliography of Conrad* (1921) when he said:

The separately inserted title-pages with the note dated 1913 ... are forgeries. Regarding this there can be no question, and copies of the book in which they occur are worthless from the point of view of the collector.

Nothing could be more explicit, or Wisely dogmatic.

But by still stranger chance, it was Thomas James Wise who later, in his *Ashley Library Catalogue* (1926), described a remarkable copy of *Chance* in his possession. It had the "right" 1913 title page, but *pasted in;* and this he accepted as a genuine first issue.

A copy such as the present [he adds in the catalogue], the genuineness of which is supported by the author's signed certificate, is good enough. But in view of the doubt and uncertainty which must necessarily cling to any copy not certified in this manner, the only safe plan to follow is to accept no specimen of the book [he means as a genuine first issue] in which the title-page does not form an unsevered portion of the first half-sheet.

In brief, let Wise's copy be the unique exception to his own despotic rule: all because the obliging Conrad had been procured to write in the volume:

The title-page of this book is a genuine copy of the original title dated 1913, at first removed, and subsequently restored to the volume.

If there is one thing certain in this uncertain affair, it is that this is not Joseph Conrad speaking and certifying, although the statement is in his script. The voice is that of another dictating to the novelist; and the point of psychological interest is: why this forcing of things to the extent of getting Conrad to write a certificate of genuineness for which he was hopelessly unqualified as compared with Wise? For that certificate to have any bibliographical value it needed to be signed by the expert, by Wise himself, who was able to expose the *Chance* forgeries. Did it never occur to the shrewd collector that the ruse was transparent: that as a guarantee, it was sheer humbugging? Or did his desire for inscribed rarities become such an obsession as to overwhelm his judgment and make him oblivious of the farce?

The final light exposing the hollowness of the business is

this: that when the Ashley Library came to be moved to the British Museum, this strangely exceptional copy was missing. The inference is that, notwithstanding what he had set out in his Catalogue, Wise was taking no chance with his very extraordinary *Chance*.

Another first edition of a Conrad novel came under suspicion as having been the subject of a book faker's attentions. This was *A Set of Six*, a doubtful copy of which had been exposed through my Journal [6] as differing from Wise's volume. "I do think that these frauds should be prevented—if it be possible to stop them," he observed to me when expressing a wish to see the copy. This was duly borrowed from the obliging owner, Mr. J. C. Thomson; and "a sort of inquest" was held on it by Wise, Clement Shorter, and Mr. Webster of Methuen's. It is not for the verdict that the case is mentioned here, but for the sequel in the light of subsequent events. Mr. Thomson, a typographical and paper expert of 35 years' experience, wrote to me: "I neither agree nor disagree with Mr. Wise's conclusions, but his reasons are ludicrously inadequate. It is but too apparent that he has no practical knowledge of printing and no technical knowledge of paper."

Wise's connection with Conrad did not end with the collecting of the highly manufactured association items as described. There was the usual burst of privately printed first editions. Clement Shorter was, for once, first in the field in 1918 with five of the booklets. But Wise came along with a rush in 1919, producing ten over his imprint—none of which he sent to the British Museum. Then, ten more of these privately printed Conrad first edition pamphlets were produced (1919-1920)—strangely enough, although from the same printing press, over the imprint of Conrad this time. I sought an explanation from Mr. Richard Curle, who was for years on the friendliest terms with Wise. His reply, while missing the chief point of inquiry, supports some of my contentions:

[6] See *The Bookman's Journal*, Nos. 59 and 62 (1920) and 63 and 65 (1921).

I presume that the reason why no copies were deposited at the British Museum was that there was quite a run on the pamphlets and that a number were given to Conrad. I was out of the country when the first series was done, but I remember that Mr. Wise paid Mr. Conrad a handsome fee for permission to do the second series. In fact the whole relationship was friendly from beginning to end. I can only suppose that no more pamphlets were printed partly because twenty seemed quite enough, and partly because there was practically no more available material.

The law's obligations apart, the fact that there was "quite a run" on the pamphlets seems a curious excuse for failing to send copies to the British Museum, considering that these things were usually purported to be done from idealistic motives of preservation. The printings were mostly of contributions written by Conrad for periodicals. It is an extraordinary thing that they omit to state where the pieces first appeared—as one would expect a bibliographer to be most careful to state.

V

In 1920, Mrs. Flora Virginia Livingston, of the Harry Elkins Widener Memorial Library, Harvard University, wrote and printed a 32-page pamphlet entitled *Bibliographical Data Relating to a Few of the Publications of Algernon Charles Swinburne*. Mrs. Livingston's notes were the "outcome of a painstaking examination" of Wise's *Bibliography of Swinburne*. As a result of checking the bibliography by various Swinburne collections in the United States, "information has been gathered which was not known to Mr. Wise." In spite of her painstaking examination, however, the true character of certain Swinburne publications now condemned as forgeries or suspects was not revealed.

But the significance of the pamphlet is that it was respectfully but determinedly critical of one who was widely accepted as an infallible authority above suspicion. To Wise it may well have seemed the horrid writing on the wall again—not so clear and denunciatory as when Cook and Wedderburn's work was done; but still a hint of the kind of investigation that might follow any day. In print he dismissed his critic with "A thoughtless suggestion was made by Mrs. Livingston in her hopelessly ill-informed and misleading pamphlet."

Subsequently Mrs. Livingston compiled an admirable *Bibliography of Rudyard Kipling* (1927), in which she boldly stated that two Kipling pamphlets, *White Horses* (1897) and *The White Man's Burden* (1899), now classed among Wise's productions, were piracies. It was more writing on the wall; and Wise's reaction is not surprising. In 1937, Mrs. Livingston wrote to me:

I was unfortunately one of the first persons who criticized his work in print, and he never forgave me. I proved all my statements by the books themselves in our library, and he afterwards incorporated all of them in his own bibliography.... But he never forgave me, and considered me an "ignorant, ill-informed person...." My experience with him is very interesting, but what I could say, and think, would hardly be fit to appear in print. He was a great man, and a curious one—a *mystery*. But why get angry when errors are pointed out? We all make them, and most of us are only too glad to have them pointed out.

CHAPTER 17

PORTRAIT OF A DICTATOR

They dwell in the odour of camphor,
They stand in a Sheraton shrine,
They are "warranted early editions"
Those worshipful tomes of mine;—

In their creamiest "Oxford vellum"
In their redolent "crushed Levant"
With their delicate watered linings
They are jewels of price, I grant.

 ** * * **

For the row that I prize is yonder,
Away on the unglazed shelves.
The bulged and the bruised octavos
The dear and the dumpy twelves

 ** * * **

And the Burton I bought for a florin,
And the Rabelais foxed and flea'd
For the others I never have opened,
But those are the books I read.

From *My Books,* by Austin Dobson.

I

MENTION of Wise once provoked Joseph Conrad to an unexpected outburst on an occasion when I was visiting him at Bishopsbourne. At the time there was a proposal under discussion that I should produce something of Conrad's in a little series of unpublished works I was then editing. When we came to the subject in the course of conversation, the *Secret Agent* was mentioned. This led Conrad to suggest that I should include his unpublished play *Laughing Anne.* Suddenly there came to me the recollection that Wise possessed the original script of the piece. I was a young man with a considerable appreciation of the respective achievements of these two who were so much my senior; and, lest anything should be done which might lead to misunderstanding, I recalled that Wise was the owner of the original manuscript.

In an instant the calm of Conrad's study was broken as by a tropical storm. "Wise! Wise!! What has it to do with Wise?" exclaimed Conrad with a passion that startled me. "Wise! Wise!! he only owns the paper. The work is mine"— and Conrad's powerful shoulders went up: his face was tense with emotion. I began to say something tactful. It was no great matter anyhow.... Moreover, I was a guest. But before I could say much, Conrad's momentary irritation vanished; and, flinging himself on to the settee beside me, he put his arm round my shoulders: "Of course I must have *Laughing Anne* now ... poor dear Anne ... he would let Thomas Wise know his intentions.... There would be no need to trouble him for the manuscript ... another copy was available." Then came the summons to lunch; and we joined a merry family group.

It seemed as if in this matter I was fated as Laughing Anne herself. No sooner was I back in London than the storm blew up from another quarter. Wise wrote (Mar. 14, '23) furiously upbraiding me because, instead of consulting him, I had discussed the printing of Conrad's play with the author; adding that I had given him a lesson, and henceforward he would take care to keep unpublished things out of his catalogue. Being able to reply that I knew of the unpublished work long before his catalogue appeared, that the choice of *Laughing Anne* was Conrad's, and that it was no concern of mine what was omitted from the Ashley Catalogues, I could write with calm confidence. By return mail came an apology and an assurance that *it was not on my account that he had resolved not to catalogue anything unprinted by either Rudyard Kipling or Robert Louis Stevenson*. It was a complete

JOSEPH CONRAD: the last photograph of him to be taken, and hitherto unpublished. "I'm sick of the way these brutes are trading on Conrad." —Wise.

about-face. These uncatalogued MSS he presumably sold. Anyhow they were not retained in Wise's collection.

But there was always something curious about his attitude towards unprinted material; especially in the cases where he had acquired the paper on which it was written.

II

One certainly needed to have Laughing Anne's sense of humor when dealing with Wise. His talks and correspondence with me suggested the acrobatics of a thermometer plunged alternately into boiling and iced water. One day I might be a "wonderful chap." Another day: "If you had only referred to my bibliography, you would have saved ****** making yourself and the magazine ridiculous." Another day: "You are doing a useful work...." And another time: "Why do you do this?" So the weathercock of praise and criticism revolved. The great thing in life was to keep your eyes glued on the score or so works by Thomas James Wise. Then you and everybody who wrote for you would be infallible. One of his habits when dealing with correspondence is illustrative of his character. In his impetuosity he would sometimes reply to a correspondent by writing—in his slapdash script—terse and not always polite remarks in red ink on the margins of their letters. The addition of a line or so at the end, and his signature, completed the reply. The lurid result may be easily imagined. He liked to look on the ink when it is red: he often saw red.

But if his correspondence was stimulating, there were some who must have found his hasty letters a serious matter—judging by the stories he told me. If a book whose bibliographical points had been elucidated by Wise was contrarily described in a bookseller's list, the perpetrator was always likely to receive a stinging letter. And the merest suspicion of a "wrong 'un" (i.e., a spurious MS or a faked book) raised the devil. At least two prominent members of the admirable trade were politely summoned to the Presence, and, concerned for their reputations, attended: to spend an embarrassing half-hour in the Ashley Library—that is, according to its owner.

Such episodes as these were described to me by Wise with a show of righteous indignation, mixed with quizzical enjoyment of the discomfiture caused. They left the impression that, had he been the Mikado or the King in *Wonderland,* instead of the dictator of bibliography and a London produce merchant, all the suspects, guilty or innocent, would have had their heads chopped off within 24 hours of the receipt of their catalogues.

But there was something in his exultant accounts of such inquisitions, usually with some inexplicable hiatuses, that made me resolve never wholly to believe, still less to repeat, them. Nor was I the only visitor to the Ashley Library to make such a resolution. In print, the case was different. There, when it came to personalities, Wise either damned with safety or was caution personified. For he early in his career informed himself with great nicety respecting the laws of libel, slander, and copyright.

One of these stories concerned a London bookseller who was invited to the Ashley Library to produce some original Shelley letters he allegedly had for sale, the genuineness of which Wise suspected. The manuscripts were accordingly produced. "I immediately saw that they were forgeries," Wise told me. "So I tore them up, handed the fragments back to ******, and said: "Now then! You are at liberty to sue me for destroying your property.' " [1]

This dramatic affair is in the most sensational Lyceum traditions, and could only have been improved by the inclusion of a "curse you, villain" and heavy breathings. I have made an exception to my rule by repeating the story because Wise himself told it to so many of his friends that it has become a legend in the rare-book world—a legend calculated to be

[1] It would be interesting to have the pretty legal point involved decided at one of those Moots they hold in the Inns of Court.

highly creditable to Saint Thomas James. Side by side with it ought to be set these facts: that this bookseller, whose name has always been freely mentioned in the telling of the story, was one of Wise's best customers for the Ashley Library private printings; that he enjoyed Wise's hospitality; and that he was the recipient from the compiler of a copy of the *Ashley Library Catalogue*. The regard was evidently mutual, for he once, in a book, gave a testimonial to the destroyer of other people's forgeries, describing him as "that most dignified and honoured of book-collectors, Mr. Thomas James Wise."

III

As he was in his correspondence, so he appeared in personal intercourse. His talk was voluble, and often amazingly free in criticism of other people and things that roused his quick temper. At this time (from 1919 onwards) when he was widely regarded as a sort of bibliographical Sherlock Holmes or a Napoleon of book collecting, I was seeing him with fair regularity either at his house or in town—almost invariably to discuss some matter of bibliography. He was, both in manner and actuality, a dictator; and—like all dictators—during his little reign he wore the mantle of autocracy and omniscience with superb confidence, assisted (though not always) by diplomacy and also by a joviality that came of natural pleasure in his success. Neither in appearance nor in personality was he the mellowed, dreamy, philosophizing bibliophile of fiction and occasional fact. No Sylvestre Bonnard was he. He looked, in truth, what he was: the astute business man, but a business man with an instinctive and remarkable flair for book collecting.

He was short and plump. His chubby face was pink and shaven. The small shrewd eyes could laugh humorously behind their spectacles, but they could also glitter mercilessly. The mouth and chin were of determined set. But it was the eyes that mirrored the man himself. An interviewer, Augustus

Muir, said that Wise "Looks at you as though reading a date on a title page." True, but a date can be read at a glance. Those suspicious eyes probed, fathomed, weighed up with the same intensity that revealed to him a book's bibliographical secrets from its make-up. Behind them was the opportunist experienced in pitting brain against brains.

His memory was prodigious. To date a book or event was as easy as striking a match. His brisk movements about his library, the way he would take a book from here and there, reeling off a fund of anecdotes, were things that rarely failed to impress a visitor, and sometimes left him bewildered.

There was one theme on which loquaciousness dried up: that was the subject of Thomas James Wise himself. In my anxiety to do justice to the subject of this biography and to test my personal judgment of the man by that of others, I have sought the opinions of several who could justly describe themselves as close friends of the collector-dealer. All have remarked his reticence about himself—especially about his early days—and their inability to draw him out on any matter relating to himself on which he did not choose to be expansive.

One of the friends and admirers of Wise in his later years was Mr. de Vincheles Payen-Payne, who supplied valuable information for the *Swinburne Bibliography* and voluntarily gave much experienced help with the proofs of the *Ashley Library Catalogue*. Mr. Payen-Payne's impressions were so typical and admirably crystallized, that I give them in his own words:

The revelations about Wise came as a painful shock to me, and the whole thing is such a mystery that I do not dwell on it. I visited him frequently—usually on Sundays. I always found him most charming. He was very entertaining and full of talk. But somehow, when you had left him, and came to think over the talk, you realised that he hadn't told you nearly as much as you thought he had; that the things you expected and wanted to hear, especially about himself, never followed. He was *un faux bon-homme.*[2]

IV

My impression on first seeing the Ashley Library was one of surprise. It was at Heath Drive, Hampstead, that it was seen as the fulfillment of a long-worked for ideal: it was there that visitors from many lands saw it in its penultimate glory. It seemed to me, at first, incredible that his thousands of treasures were contained in that one comfortable room of some 25 by 20 feet—that the closely packed bookshelves in the ornately glazed cases embraced all the brilliant eloquence of the verse and prose, all the burning passion of those human documents, described in the owner's catalogues.

Truly here was "infinite riches in a little room." But the Ashley books are rarely of the bulky kind, the most corpulent and imposing of them being perhaps Wise's own catalogues. The poetry and drama of his collecting often made their shy appearances in the world thin and poorly clad. Garbed anew in rich Levant moroccos of many colors, with gold decoration and lettering, they became outwardly as well as inwardly "slim gilt souls" of literature. And packed in scores to the yard of shelf room, they presented an unnatural air of newness and serried splendor—a marshaled and imposing array, but lacking the warm and careless intimacy, the literary atmosphere, of other private libraries I have known.

Binding and rebinding became something of an obsession with Wise. Far too few items were kept in their original condition; for the exceptions the best slip cases or book boxes were made. His bookbinders' bills in themselves must have represented a small fortune. Few collectors achieve success without making blunders that later are smiled at and blushed for. Wise tells this story against himself. In his early days he bound his original collections of Shelley and Byron first

2 "One who affects to be a good easy man: a hypocritical old fellow"—Clifton and Grimaux's *Dictionary* (1923).

editions in red and blue moroccos respectively; and, as he said—"mighty proud I was of them. But not many years had passed before I appreciated my folly; and the lesson once learned, I lost no time in discarding the lot. . . ."—which appeared to him years afterward on the shelves of booksellers and collectors, like ghosts to remind him of his error. Morocco is excellent in its place and in due proportion. But his passion for it never moderated. The lesson of the socialistic red Shelleys and the aristocratic blue Byrons was never wholly learned; for Elizabethan plays issued without covers and merely stabbed, were later bound for him instead of being preserved in slip cases in their original and interesting condition.

Mr. A. E. Calkin, of Rivières, who did much of the Ashley binding, recalls that Wise never kept receipts for the large and frequent payments he made always immediately on receiving his accounts; but that he relied on his remarkable memory and his check counterfoils. Of the former he once gave effective proof. At the bindery one day, after the object of his call had been achieved, he asked if his account was ready. As it happened, it was just then waiting to be mailed. It included among numerous items the charge for a binding at which Wise instantly demurred, saying that it had been paid on such and such a date. Inquiry at once showed that the charge had been included by accident, and that the client's recollection was correct. In view of the mass of diverse detail he had to keep in mind: Hermann Rubeck's business, his own City company, his private bookselling, and the tremendous ramifications of his bibliographical pursuits, the little incident is illuminating.

The Wrenn collection, so largely formed by Wise, also gave scope for his binding and rebinding obsession. The considerable work involved was nearly all done by Wise's binders, and paid for by him. The settlement with friend and client Wrenn was a private matter.

V

During the years covered by this chapter—namely, 1918 to 1921 inclusive—the production of the privately printed Ashley Library pamphlets practically came to an end. In 1918 there were nine; in 1919 thirty; in 1920 fifteen; and in 1921 two. In addition, with Gosse he edited Swinburne's *Contemporaries of Shakespeare* (1919) and *Selections from Shakespeare* (1919), and in 1920 he completed his edition of the 5-volume Wrenn Library Catalogue. Also in this period were published his *Bibliography of Landor* (1919), the *Swinburne* (1919-20), the *Conrad* (1920-21), and the *Keats* (1921), which works put him on a still higher pinnacle of fame and authority. Materials for the last-named works had been accumulating for years.

Like most of his compilations, these four met nothing but praise in the limited specialist Press in which they were reviewed. It is a characteristic of bibliographies that their merits are readily perceivable, whereas it takes time and usage to reveal their defects. I once asked Wise of which of his compilations he was proudest. He shied at the question, and countered by asking which of them appealed most to me. At that time his *Bibliography of Byron* had not appeared, and I plumped for the *Swinburne* because of its added biographical interest. The choice seemed to please him. The *Byron* (1932-3) is a rival for the same reason; although both works have faults that a more judicious and less dogmatic bibliographer would have avoided.

After 1921 less than half a dozen of the privately printed pamphlets were issued. For this there were several reasons. For one, his easily handleable material was giving out. Then his financial position was flourishing, thanks to the war. With his growing reputation in the rare-book and literary worlds foreshadowing honors and still dizzier heights of attainment, he doubtless felt that his smaller trading ought to be dropped

—as the production of the nineteenth-century forgeries had been at an earlier stage in his career.

There was one other reason. He was about to begin the production of his magnum opus, to crown a life's successful effort achieved by sheer industry, not a little genius, and ruthless determination.

CHAPTER 18

FIRSTS, AND SUPER-FIRSTS

For, whosoever hath, to him shall be given, and he shall have more
abundance: but whosoever hath not, from him shall be taken away
even that which he hath.

Matthew 13:12.

I

WISE'S MAGNUM OPUS was, of course, his *Ashley Library Cata-*
logue in eleven bulky quarto volumes, the first two of which
came off the press in 1922, and the remainder at fairly regular intervals between then and 1936. It was meant to be an
imposing affair that would enhance the value of his collection; and it received a most flattering welcome. He afterward
said that he had no idea the *Catalogue* would meet with such
success; and, as it was to cost £500 a volume to produce, most
of which he expected having to pay, he originally intended
to confine the work to five volumes. Finding that all the
copies for sale were promptly subscribed, he allowed himself
to "spread a bit"; and in the end the eleven volumes only
"landed me," he added, "in a loss of £100 each." Even if
that was the balance-sheet result, it was a profitable invest-
ment.

It is Wise's own testimony that every word of the *Cata-*
logue, as well as of his other formidable bibliographical
works, was written by him. The wonder is that they were
not more inaccurately done.

He secured such well-known bookmen as Augustine Bir-
rell, Edmund Gosse, John Drinkwater, E. V. Lucas, R. W.
Chapman, A. W. Pollard, Sir J. C. Squire, and Arundell
Esdaile, to write introductions. Gosse's advice and help was,

of course, in request; and his letter on the subject has several points of interest:

> ... Now, as to the preface to the new volume of your catalogue, I feel very much puzzled what to say. It is a great compliment for any one to be asked to write an introduction to one of your volumes, and would be a still greater compliment if you had not made (in your too-easy good-nature) such a mistake with the first introduction of all.... You are, of course, quite at liberty to tell them that you write at my suggestion. But, I assure you, there must be no suggestion of payment. The whole point of these little introductions is that they are voluntary....

Wise, thus directed by his faithful guide, found that the bookmen generously responded to his invitations, inspired no doubt by the wealth of treasures being revealed in the *Catalogue.* With the exception of a few good-humored reservations, these learned introducers presented handsome tributes. In fact, the eleven volumes provide one of the prettiest assortments of such bouquets ever brought together. Such was the chorus of appreciation, often elegantly and wittily turned, that when poor Drinkwater's turn came he was handicapped because the "thunder of praise" ... had been stolen by his predecessors. Everyone was pleased—most of all Thomas James Wise.

But it takes time to digest a feast such as he had put before his kings. For the present, the horrid skeleton was locked in the cupboard.

II

Wise's bibliographies of a few authors had given a good idea of the quality of his collection. Now that all his treasures were described under authors' names arranged alphabetically, a highly colored picture of the Ashley Library was presented. Very few great collectors—and Wise was one of the greatest—have been their own cataloguers. He did not make a very successful job of it. Apart from his judgments on major problems, his efforts to cope with Elizabethan typography reveal his limitations; some of the reproductions of title pages even show errors of transcription in the text; the indexing is most faulty and inadequate. The collection deserved to have been catalogued by an expert, but in that case we should have missed many naïve revelations of the owner's character.

In pursuance of the Bible's unidealistic principle quoted at the head of this chapter, Wise was the recipient of many gifts of rarities. In some cases the donors were named; in others Wise is silent. Whatever the reason for acknowledging some gifts and not others, the discrimination is unfortunate, to say the least.

"A book which has been admitted, in equal terms, to this Valhalla," wrote Drinkwater, "takes on something of the divinity of its surroundings. . . . It is in a fair way to being a collectors' book." Perhaps it was in this large hope that certain authors were so lavish in sending him presentation copies of their writings. Even George Bernard Shaw, Wise's playboy acquaintance of former Shelley Society days, joined in adding "more abundance." He wrote in a gift copy of *Saint Joan* (referring to a recent Academic honor bestowed on Wise): "Worcester ought to make ME an honorary fellow for supplying you with so many crude attempts at my masterpieces." But if every author who presented his "crude first attempts" had been so honored, Worcester College would have had a surfeit of Hon. Fellows.

Another G. B. S. "masterpiece" was inscribed "Hot from the press"; and another "To T. J. Wise—absolutely the first copy"—conjuring up a picture of the impatient author waiting at the printer's for the first turn of the press, then hurrying with the ink-wet sheets to the folders and stitchers, to ensure that the Ashley Library got the *absolutely first* copies of the editions printed.[1] Nothing less than this could have assured the strict accuracy of Shaw's laughing claim.

[1] They were mostly the author's private editions, as he himself has described (see Chapter 2).

Here it must be recorded that the highly gratified and lauded collector-dealer was himself generous in presenting his own bibliographies and catalogues to those who had been, or might be, useful. If not all the recipients could be expected to use them as he hoped they would be used, he liked to have their recognition in full measure. One well-known author whom he named to me "did not seem to care, so I ceased sending him my books." For ever after, the bibliographer spoke of that author in the most disparaging way.

Wise was not very tolerant—least of all outside his enthusiasms. For instance, he did not care for Anthony Trollope, and, unlike other collectors, refused to find a place in his library for a single book or MS of that author. His typical comment to me was that "all the fuss about him is simply due to one man"—a singularly ungenerous reference to Mr. Michael Sadleir, Trollope's biographer and bibliographer, and also a shocking exhibition of ignorance.

III

A feature of Thomas James Wise's library was his method of rounding off a collection of an author's first editions by gathering all important books directly relating to them. These he called "-ana." An example is that of the Shelley section, in which his Shelleyana, excluding documents, number approximately 150 items. If there is anything in Drinkwater's pleasant theory that the mere inclusion of a book in the Ashley Library made it partake of something of the greatness of Wise's illustrious editions, then the presentation copies of contemporary authors and the items constituting the considerable "-ana" were indeed richly endowed.

These "-ana" became the fellows of Wise's superb Elizabethan first editions, of his Popes, Drydens, Priors, and other authors already dealt with here. They shared the glory of the only perfect copy of the second earliest English comedy, *Gammer gurton's Nedle* (1575), of the best copy extant of

Milton's *Comus* (1637), of one of the two known copies of Dekker's *A Rod for Run-awayes* (1625), of the only known copy of Pope's indecent parody, *A Roman Catholick Version of the First Psalm. For the Use of a Young Lady* (1716), of one of the two known copies of Congreve's *An Impossible Thing* (1720)—the authorship of which he claimed as his discovery—and of the only known copy of Edward Fitzgerald's first and suppressed book, *Casimir Delavigne*.

But it is invidious to single out a few titles, or even authors. An idea of what are the riches made known by the *Ashley Catalogue* can be conveyed more quickly by the following figures. Of 88 first editions described, 37 are claimed by Wise to be the only known copies; of 18, he claimed that only one other copy of each was known; of 10, that only two other copies of each were known; and of 23, that less than half a dozen copies of each were known. More important still, of these rarities, 58 were said to be not in the British Museum Library. As to manuscripts, he had amassed over 300; while the autograph letters in the Library ran into thousands.

Considering the importance of many of the Ashley books, and also the doubts about others, it is regrettable that Wise did not make a general practice of giving the provenance of his rarities. And had he emulated the example of Narcissus Luttrell, the seventeenth-century collector, in stating the prices he paid for his books, what an astonishing difference would be revealed between the cost of the Library and the unofficial £250,000 valuation subsequently put on it. But to have given provenances and prices would have been awkward in some cases, and especially undesirable in the event of having to change his secret plan for the ultimate destination of the collection.

Some comparisons of the prices and ultimate values of individual items have already been given here. Walter T. Spencer, the bookseller, recorded that the earliest book he remembered selling to Wise was a perfect copy of Keats's

Poems (1817) for ten pounds—a work for another copy of which, years later, £380 was paid by the bookseller, who added: "Mr. Wise once chaffed me about his 'bargain' over tea when I visited him and Mrs. Wise at his charming house in Hampstead. . . . To me he has always been a true friend."

It has been shown, in the case of the Ben Jonson (page 132), how Wise erred through not sufficiently comparing his rarities with others. His reputation as a bibliographer, and therefore the authority of his catalogues and bibliographies, suffers because of his judgments and his prejudices in favor of his own copies. Of the two issues of Thomas Middleton's *A Trick to catch the Old-one* (1608) Wise claims his example to be the first issue of the first edition; and he alleges that the copies in the British Museum, the Bodleian, etc., are of the second issue. But Mr. A. W. Pollard, one of the most able Keepers of Printed Books the British Museum has had, objected (in the Introduction to Vol. IX) to this classification, considering it probable that the two variant issues were produced simultaneously. This was not the only instance in which Mr. Pollard showed the weakness of Wise's theorizings in favor of his own specimens. It takes a clever trick to catch the old-ones.

Wise could be amazingly inconsistent—the greatest sin in a bibliographer. There was the question of proof sheets. In 1907, when Robert Louis Stevenson's works were being edited, it was left to Edmund Gosse to decide whether or not a drama, *The Hanging Judge* (which had been set up in type), should be included. The decision was against it. "A few copies of the proofs, printed upon one side of the paper only, were preserved," says Wise, adding: "In recent years these proofs of 1907 have come into the market and have realised prices far above their worth." These proofs were thus frowned upon because seven years later Wise himself produced a private pamphlet of *The Hanging Judge* (1914), describing it as the first edition.

But see how he veers round when he comes to collate a

4-page item—Swinburne's *Russia: An Ode* (1890). "Three or four proof copies only were struck off," he says in his note, "and of these but a single example is at present known to have survived." It is clear from Wise's further annotation that these were only proofs, yet in this case his "unique" copy is labeled a first edition.

The naïvest revelation Wise ever made in his *Ashley Catalogue* was: "To suggest that the correction of every trifling error made whilst a book is at press constitutes a fresh 'issue' is childish: such emendations furnish 'minor varieties' of a volume: they do not result in fresh issues." Yet it was precisely by such "childish" arguments that he represented some of his copies as being rare first issues of first editions.

His notes reveal some curious lapses, although Edmund Gosse repeatedly saved him from committing howlers. Of Dante Gabriel Rossetti and Swinburne meeting at Oxford in 1857 he says: "Their intercourse soon developed into a more than fraternal comradeship." Elsewhere he speaks of something written "on each side of the page." As an example of inaccuracy, an undated note from Swinburne to Payne is quoted. But, although it contains only fifty words, including a postscript, the transcription shows two omitted words and four variations of punctuation. He was not shy about himself. The result of obtaining an introduction to Ernest Hartley Coleridge is this comment: "It is pleasant to reflect that until death brought it to an end the friendship thus formed remained mutually stimulating and agreeable." And he was not always careful in his attributions. Under Matthew Prior he catalogues his copy of a rare little book, *A Genuine Dialogue: Facetious and Pathetic* [etc.] 1736, with this note: "The authorship of this Dialogue is unknown. It may be by Matthew Prior, but on the other hand it may not." That is all he has to say: the British Museum does not catalogue the title under Prior. It ought, of course, to have been put under the name of the prolific Mr. "Anon."

IV

But to explore the vagaries of his bibliographical and editorial methods would require a volume in itself. With the publication of the *Ashley Catalogue* from 1922 onward, Thomas James Wise became a celebrity in the book world. Soon came the academic and other recognitions that were so dear to him. Before recording these, however, one other and little-known activity in his career deserves mention as showing his diversity of interests. In 1922 the firm of Edwin Healey & Co., postage stamp merchants in the City, became Healey and Wise, Ltd. The "Wise" in the firm represented both Thomas James, who acquired a substantial share, and his younger brother, retired from the ranks of the Army. The dealer and collector in rare books was no stranger in the trade catering for that other collecting hobby—stamps. Mr. Gorfin states that after setting up as a bookseller, he did a little side business in foreign stamps for the firm in which Wise and his brother came to be interested. He recalls many visits to the General Post Office to fetch parcels of stamps from Harry Buxton Forman for Wise.

In 1924 Wise was elected to an Honorary Fellowship of Worcester College, Oxford.

In 1925 appeared his first and (as shown) inaccurate entry in *Who's Who*.

The year 1926 saw him elected an Honorary Master of Arts of Oxford University.

In 1927 he was elected a member of the Roxburghe Club (founded 1813), the most exclusive institution of book collectors in the world.

After the death of Edmund Gosse, Wise did much toward making the sale of his library (1928-9) a success. He showed his commercial acumen in advising the insertion of autograph letters received by Gosse in relevant copies of their authors' books.

In 1929 Wise made over to the Bibliographical Society his

copyright in the Ashley catalogues and others of his biblio-graphical works. His membership of the Society dated from 1907; he was nominated to the Council in 1908; was made vice-president, 1919; and was president from March, 1922, to March, 1924.

In 1930 appeared the long *Strand* interview with the founder of the Ashley Library that has been quoted. The only point remaining to be noted is the statement: "He clearly remembers his meeting with George Eliot." Consider-ing how fond Wise was of telling in print and conversation of his associations with Browning and Swinburne; recalling also how he tried to get their recognitions of his forged pamphlets bearing their names, it is remarkable that there is no other mention of this meeting with George Eliot. It could only have taken place when Wise was aged 20, or earlier, and before he had got into the Browning and Shelley collecting circles. Here is another of the authors that was the subject of his specialization. The George Eliot *Brother & Sister* pamphlet, dated 1869, is now condemned as one of Wise's forgeries, having been manufactured about 1888. Another George Eliot pamphlet, *Agatha* (1869), is suspect of forgery. He sold Wrenn a copy as a first edition, and passed that description in the Wrenn Catalogue, 1920; but in 1922 he called it the second edition in his own *Ashley Catalogue*.

From 1924 to 1931, Wise also issued a series of ten large catalogues descriptive of his individual collections of the books, MSS, and "-ana" of Shelley, Swinburne, Words-worth and Coleridge (together), Byron, Conrad, Landor, the Brontës, the Brownings, Dryden, and Pope. Again he was fortunate in securing bookmen like Roger Ingpen, C. H. Wilkinson, and H. F. Brett-Smith to write the introductions not supplied by himself. Particularly interesting is that of Mr. Brett-Smith's to *A Pope Library* (1931), supplying this reminiscence: "He [Wise] has been known to describe the library of a famous collector of the last century, in the words of Charles Lamb, as a 'ragged regiment.'" It is not necessarily the prettiest regiment that provides the best soldiers. There was no room in the crack Ashley Regiment for the old warrior such as Lamb described, which reads the better because we know "the topography of its blots and dog's ears and can trace the dirt in it to having read it at Tea with buttered muffins, or over a Pipe, which I think is the maximum." Wise's conversational disparagement was doubtless not intended to reflect on the collector, who can now be revealed as that worthy eighteenth-century scholar, G. A. Aitken. The story becomes more pointed with the explanation that both the Ashley and the Wrenn Libraries owed much to Aitken, who was one of Wise's private clients.

CHAPTER 19

BYRON ROMANTICS

As for the ladies, I have nought to say,
  A wanderer from the British world of fashion,
Where I, like other "dogs, have had my day,"
  Like other men, too, may have had my passion—
But that, like other things, has pass'd away,
  And all her fools whom I could lay the lash on:
Foes, friends, men, women, now are nought to me
  But dreams of what has been, no more to be.

Don Juan: 2, **CLXVI.**

I

Mention has already been made of Wise's partiality for what are called "human documents." He palpitated over the passions of his heroes; his books flourished on their frailties. Of all his "divine sinners," none fascinated him more than Lord Byron, whose scandals (as the cynical Don hinted when in the depth of them) would be the more devoured the more they were damned. And it was while Wise was immersed in the bibliography of Byron that he chanced on what he believed to be a hitherto unrevealed love affair, complete with the baby.

Don Juan and his Julias and his Haidees are beyond the barb of scandal. They are deep in the slumber that wakes to no fresh gust of surging passion. But a new supply of the old intoxicating wine could add flavor to the *Byron Bibliography* and the *Ashley Library Catalogue*. It was sampled by Wise for his first volume of the *Catalogue* in 1922. That taste muddled him then—as we shall see. But it was not until 1931 that the wine went to his head.

It had come from the well-stocked bins of Harry Buxton

Forman's library. One evening, years back, while browsing among Forman's books, Wise found a red-clothed volume entitled *The Unpublished Letters of Lord Byron:* edited by H. S. Schultess-Young, issued by Richard Bentley & Son, Publishers in Ordinary to Her Majesty, 1872. Unpublished letters of Byron? Issued by Bentley? Wise's shrewd eyes glistened; his cheeks flushed and puffed—as was his way when excited. Never heard of it! It was a bolt from the aristocratic blue to him who prided himself that he knew Byron's bibliography from the young poet's first essay in literature, the *Fugitive Pieces* of 1806, to the last of the many piracies of his *Don Juan.*

Now Forman, keen book hunter that he was, knew this to be a volume of rarity and potentiality.[1] Wise knew it also. For him, how potential! So they had one of their usual deals. Forman, who had bought it at the gift price of four guineas from Bertram Dobell (what days those were!), took a nice margin of profit; and still Wise bought cheaply. Thus the book found itself transferred to the Ashley Library. Its heady wine had to mature a little longer before the great libation.

II

It is necessary here to tell a tale within a tale—a romance of publishing. About 1872 a bright young fellow of 20, by name Schultess-Young, went to Richard Bentley, and arranged with him to produce the *Unpublished Letters of Lord Byron.* These letters derived from two mysterious aunts of the young man—Miss Julia Puddicombe, of Bovey Tracey, near Torquay, and a Mrs. Clark "of Scroop House," [place not stated]. Of these ladies it would be most desirable to have further knowledge. Remarkably enough, the enthusiastic editor was able to inscribe his volume, by permission, to Mrs. Thérèse Black, "the Maid of Athens"—his "sincere and

[1] The British Museum Library was lacking a copy until 1937, when it acquired the Ashley Library.

obliged friend." What a link! She, the fourteen-year-old
beauty, of whom Byron had written:

> *Maid of Athens, ere we part,*
> *Give, oh give me back my heart!*
> *Or, since that has left my breast,*
> *Keep it now, and take the rest!*
> *Hear my vow before I go*
> *Ζωή μου, σᾶς ἀγαπῶ.*

A notable book truly. No doubt Richard Bentley, Pub
lisher in Ordinary to Her Majesty, felt a secret pride in
producing such a valuable contribution to Byron literature,
and scoring against his friendly rival, John Murray the
Fourth, grandson of the poet's famous publisher. But while
the printing press was turning out the momentous book,
Bentley struck a horrid snag. He discovered that some of the
letters had already been printed, the Murray copyright in
them having just expired, and that others—new ones—had
been obtained from one of the aunts without permission to
use them. Moreover, nineteen others were spurious—the work
of the notorious forger De Gibler, who about 1848 assumed
the name of George Gordon Byron, declaring himself to be
an illegitimate son of the poet.

As a man of honor, jealous for his high reputation, Bentley
immediately stopped publication. Eventually, of the edition
of 750 copies (of which half had already been bound), 740
were destroyed; and into pulp went the youthful tribute of
Schultess-Young to the now fading beauties of "the Maid of
Athens." Thus, of his ill-begotten book, which is nevertheless
a work of highest interest, only ten copies were preserved of
the entire edition; and of these, one came by way of Harry
Buxton Forman doubly to ensnare Thomas James Wise, the
ardent bibliographer of Byron.

III

Wise, describing the book for the first volume of his *Catalogue* [2] (1922), did two things: he quoted from Schultess-Young two passages from a series of seventeen letters to "dearest L.——" that the editor had copied from the documents of one of the aunts (Mrs. Clark, apparently).

This was practically the first revelation of the "dearest L——" love affair in the life of Byron.[3] But there were features about both it and the Schultess-Young book that perplexed Wise, and called for inquiry. He must go into this new scandal more thoroughly when he came to compile the *Bibliography of Byron* he had so long projected, which was to be the last of his bibliographies. It should be a two-volume work now: the final word on the subject. But, the "last word" in bibliography is never final.

It was in 1931 that Wise again began to study the alleged letters of Byron to "dearest L——." In the whole seventeen, which date from August 2nd, 1811, to August 1st, 1817, there is only one passage which can with certainty be said to hint at a child as the result of their "imprudence."

This passage is given by Wise with two other quotations all run together as if the three were from one letter. I will here give the three extracts, more fully and correctly, under their respective dates:

St. James's St.: Oct 30. 1811

Dearest L——,

I do not understand your letter or your quotations but only know that I *love* you, and you know I shall never marry you, for which you have reason to be thankful. I wonder whom I shall espouse, for I must take up the conjugal *cross* some day, and perpetuate the name of Byron better than by my rhymes. I sent you a copy of the *Childe* which you have never acknowledged. . . .

---

[2] Repeating the details in *A Byron Library* (1928).
[3] Bertram Dobell had contributed a short note about the Schultess-Young book to *Notes & Queries*, November 14th, 1891.

St. James's St. [no date]
... When I leave England I will not forget the things you ask
for, and regret that you cannot accompany me, which is impossible, not for the sake of my character, but yours. . . .

Feb. 29, 1813.
Dear L——,
What do you mean by *ungrateful?* I am not, who ever of your
acquaintance may be, but am damned and dunned to death by
Christians and creditors, though God knows, I am bad and poor
enough; but I did not expect you to be implacable. The child
* * * * * is dead, and I do not regret it, though a bastard Byron
is better than no Byron. You are about the only woman who has
caused me a remorseful moment; and when I say I am sorry for
our mutual imprudence (to say nothing else), I do not express
the compunction I feel. . . .[4]

These were the kind of "human documents" that highly
stimulated Wise. But he must investigate. Now, the first place
to which the researcher naturally turns in such a case is the
House of Murray, 50 Albemarle Street, where are fascinating
relics just as Byron left them, and also archives of inestimable
literary value. The courtesy of the successive Murrays to the
researcher is famous. Their House has become almost as
much a national institution as the British Museum.

Sir John Murray, the fifth John, responded promptly to
Wise's appeal, and was able to refer to the late Richard
Bentley, son of the publisher who had so drastically suppressed the *Unpublished Letters*. And now ensued among the
three parties a correspondence that has something of the
flavor of the Delicate Investigation into the conduct of
Queen Caroline. In the course of two and a half months this
Wise-Murray-Bentley correspondence totaled between two
and three hundred pages. It is lively witness alike to the
kindness and substantial help accorded to the bibliographer
and to his own indefatigability.

Sir John Murray took the view that the letters to "dearest

---

[4] The asterisks in this extract are from Schultess-Young, and apparently indicate excisions.

L——" were suspect. Wise argued (sometimes at the rate of two letters a day) that they were so Byronic, had so much realism in them; that so youthful a person as Schultess-Young could not have invented them. Briefly, he was prepared to accept them as based upon genuine letters, but crudely castrated—manipulated so as to prevent identification of the aunt from whom they were obtained.[5] There is a hint of Wise's psychology in classing the young editor with the poor banished insects in Shelley's *Sensitive Plant:*

> ....*whose intent,*
> *Although they did ill, was innocent.*

And for his part, were he the Schultess-Young of 80 (Wise assured Sir John Murray) he would not be ashamed of having been the Schultess-Young of 20: he would merely regard himself as having been very foolish.

In the meantime, Richard Bentley was busy drawing on his memory and records. In view of the verdict for £16,000 damages in a recent libel action, he counseled prudence, and the summarizing of any account of the delicate matter with much tact. He had discovered that Schultess-Young was alive, and a barrister!

Wise pooh-poohed the risk. He knew how to handle a situation like that.

Sir John Murray, steeped in the traditions of a family so linked with English bards and Scotch reviewers, and gallantly true to his forbears' loyalty to Byron, did not like Wise's quotation of isolated passages from the letters. "Why emphasize Byron's worst qualities?" he asked. He persisted in his belief that the letters to "L——" were suspect, and read like the forgeries of De Gibler. And he made a shrewd hit with the point that not one of the originals had come to light. That is indeed a curious circumstance, considering how well the poet's correspondence has been preserved.

---

[5] This was pure theorizing. The aunt, as also her documents, was then, and remains, a mystery.

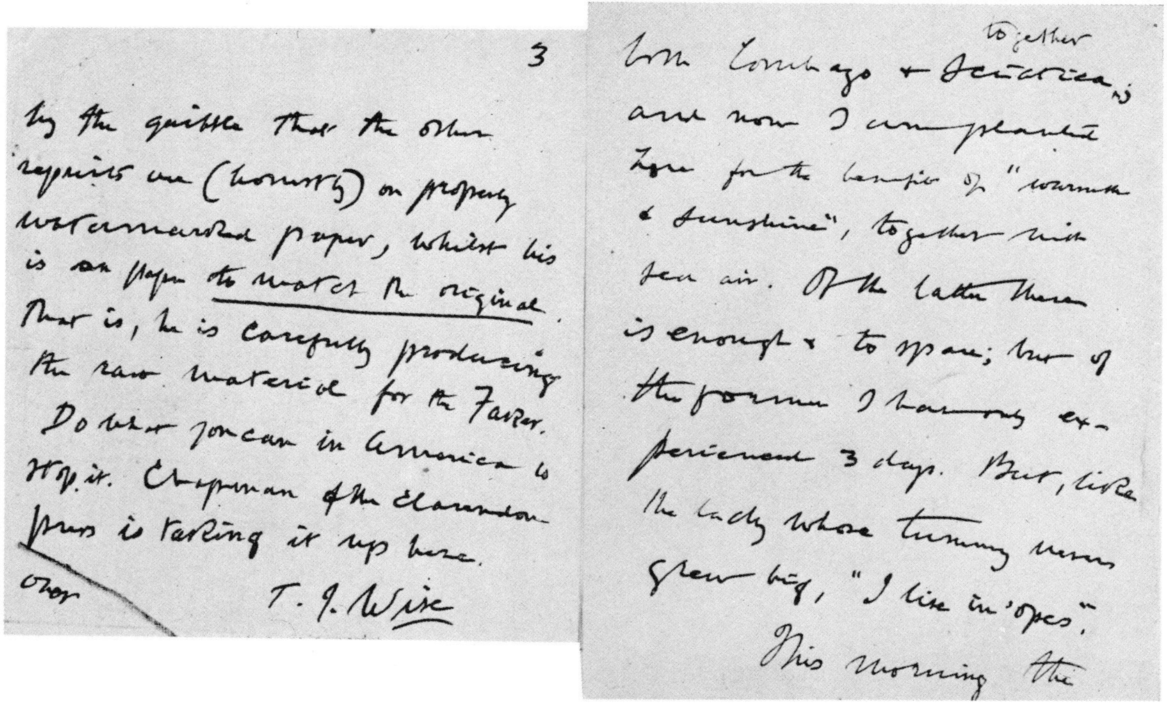

But Wise argued on—insistent but tactful. As to the "bastard Byron better than no Byron" phrase, he pointed out that "bastard" was a favorite word with the poet; who often spoke of his daughter Allegra as "my little bastard," or "the little bastard." So the controversy went on behind the scenes; and the galley proofs of the troublesome pages passed backward and forward, corrected and recorrected, revised and re-revised—until the day came when the three correspondents were more or less agreed—in differing. Wise wrote a joking postscript, conjecturing what a pleasant time the printer's clerk would have marking up his bill for "corrections"!

And the oddest thing of all was Bentley's comment at the end of this Delicate Investigation: "Curious that Wise, Forman,[6] and Schultess-Young should—the three—happen to be living very near each other."

IV

So Wise had his way. A few months later, in 1933, the second volume of his *Bibliography of Byron* came out—complete with the isolated quotations from the letters to "L——": [7] the poet "damned," as he was wont to say, with a new scandal, and fathered with another bastard.

But are the letters to "L——" genuine? Here are some examples of discrepancies that, weighed together, are sufficient to condemn the letters. Those that show date discrepancies are instances of how easily a forger might err through overconfidence in his knowledge of the subject's movements.

(1) In the alleged letter to "L——," dated October 30th, 1811, he speaks of having sent a copy of the *Childe* which had never been acknowledged. Perhaps for good reason.

---

[6] Maurice Buxton Forman, son of Harry Buxton Forman. He had lately retired from the Postal Service in South Africa; and did some research for Wise into the mystery of Schultess-Young's aunts. Schultess-Young died on May 2nd, 1933, aged 83.

[7] After having assured Sir John Murray that he would not dream of printing an opinion in disaccordance with his on the subject.

Childe Harold was not published until February 29th, 1812. Even by November 17th, 1811, only a portion of the first Canto of the poem had been printed.

(2) There are unlikely references to Byron's leaving England. One is in the second extract from an undated letter, which Schultess-Young placed between correspondence dated January 18th, 1812, and February 2nd, 1813. An earlier letter (Nov. 30, 1811) says: "As I should be sorry not to see you again, I will give you a flying visit before I again leave England." But Byron had only returned from his Grand Tour in July, 1811. And he could not have been anticipating the flight of 1816, because he was not then married.

(3) Augusta Leigh was very much in Byron's mind at the time of the separation from his wife. He was her constant correspondent, and keeping a journal for her.

(4) The first of the alleged letters to "L——," addressed from Venice, is dated November 10th, 1816. But Byron did not arrive in Venice until the night of November 11th, 1816.[8]

(5) On his arrival in Venice, disturbing news of Lady Byron's intention to take their daughter out of England awaited him; and his first urgent care was to instruct his solicitor to stop the move.

(6) Almost immediately on his arriving in Venice he was love-making with the libidinous Marianna Segati—the 21-year-old wife of his landlord the draper.

(7) While we know Byron could write cynically enough about his love affairs to his friends (often as a pose), there is a want of gallantry in these letters that would hardly be expected—if they were really written to "about the only woman who has caused me a remorseful moment."

(8) In the letter of January 2nd, 1817, Byron is made to say "you will not accept money from *me*. That cursed pride of yours will ruin you one day." Yet the next epistle says her

---

[8] See Hobhouse's *Recollections of a Long Life.*

"letters are full of complaints about your station, your poverty, and myself." There is some inconsistency here.

(9) In none of the letters or journals of Byron is there reference to a mistress named "L——," notwithstanding his habit of discussing and recording his love affairs.

(10) Wise's only argument to support the authenticity of the letters to "L——" is their Byronic language and cynicism. But the forger De Gibler had sufficient ability to imitate the poet's manner of writing, and plenty of material to derive from.

Bearing these things in mind, and remembering Sir John Murray's further argument that not a single one of the originals has come to light, Wise's judgment in so confidently accepting them as genuine lays him open to criticism. And, considering that he had consulted Sir John Murray and received so persistently his opinion that the letters were suspect, it is surprising that there is no disclosure of the dissentient view, which ought to have been recorded, however much it might have been disavowed.

Wise, however, was not the man to be very tolerant in a conflict of opinion with his own—especially where it concerned his books.

His enthusiasm for "dearest L——" and her unfortunate offspring had a curious sequel. In 1930 a firm of New York publishers produced in elaborate style a book entitled *Seventeen Letters of George Noel Gordon Lord Byron to an Unknown Lady* 1811-1817. Yes! The very same letters to "dearest L——" that our bibliographer first called attention to in the volume of the *Ashley Library Catalogue* (1922). And Wise, in his eleventh and last volume of the *Ashley Library Catalogue* (1936), sniffily called it "this sensational book"—this from the man who had been responsible for its being seized upon as sensational.

V

One other tale to close this chapter of Byron romance. In Vol. I of the *Bibliography of Byron* is described a copy of the second authorized edition of his *English Bards and Scotch Reviewers*. Wise says it was a gift to him from Mr. [now Sir] Sydney Cockerell, the former curator of the Fitzwilliam Museum, Cambridge. This copy of *English Bards* contains the following inscription:

> Byron—Athens—at Theodora Macri's—January 1810. Sun shining Grecianly—Lemon trees in front of the house full of fruit— damn the book! Give me Nature and two eyes opposite.

Now, Theodora Macri was the Vice-Consul's widow, with whom the poet lodged when a young man of 22 in old Athens. The great dark eyes opposite were presumably meant to be those of her daughter—the same "Maid of Athens" to whom reference has already been made as Mrs. Thérèse Black, the dedicatee of Schultess-Young's birth-strangled *Unpublished Letters*. An inscription like that, when in Byron's writing, and linking it with those tender, love-filled days of 1810, makes it the kind of ensouled treasure for which collectors grow sentimental and pay fat checks.

But the sad truth must be told. The inscription is a forgery of De Gibler again. The rascal!

Yet when Wise was first shown this "desirable" association item by Sir Sydney Cockerell, he was enchanted with it. Both the script and the matter of the inscription deceived him; and he promptly offered £100 to call the darling his. Sir Sydney Cockerell, however, being doubtful about its genuineness, declined the offer. Later, on further investigation, his doubts were confirmed. And in the end he presented Wise with the thing as a clever example of the forger's art.

But, just as Homer nowhere admits that he ever nodded, so you may look in vain for any admission by Wise in his catalogue notes that he was so deceived as to offer £100 for this Byron fake. Seven days out of any week he would have scouted the possibility of his being misled by a Byron forgery of De Gibler's. Was he not equally misled by the Byronic color and style of the letters to "dearest L——"?

CHAPTER 20

A REVISED STORY ABOUT MRS. BROWNING'S LOVE SONNETS

This Brat, to him that got it, I return;
Or, to the Parish, where the same was born;
Lest half the misbegotten in the Town,
To finde a father, at my doore be throwne.
Writ by the Knave of Spades, or by his Clerk,
And publisht by the Devil in the Dark.

Major Wither's Disclaimer (1647).

I

THAT WISE should be deceived by one of De Gibler's Byron frauds is curious, for his acquaintance with that clever rogue's art was considerable. The builder of the Ashley Library had come to be regarded as the final court of appeal in matters connected with book collecting. He was generally looked up to as a great judge—one without the least commercial bias—a ruthless enemy of all forgers and fakers. Of his ferocious intolerance of any book or MS suspected of coming from their hands I had more experience than ever from 1931 to 1933, when he gave me useful information for the Rare Book Section I was contributing to the American *Bookman*. His repeated encouragements to me to "block the path of the forger" and his zeal to assist were most impressive.

But what of his own forgeries? Had those offenses become metamorphosed and innocent in the crowded hour of success and adulation? Or was his fierce righteousness a self-goading to drown the whisper of conscience? Or was it a gesture, a superb piece of acting, to bolster his reputation against the day of judgment? Forgotten they could hardly be—those rare little pamphlets by the Brownings, Kipling, Ruskin, R. L.

Stevenson, Swinburne, Tennyson, and the rest, that mocked him from his handsome bookcases and leered at him from other people's catalogues coming into the Ashley Library in a continuous stream.

The day of judgment? He had seen the writing on the wall years ago when Cook and Wedderburn did their duty by Ruskin. More recently there had been Watts-Dunton's threat, and that Mrs. Livingston's probing and querying. Luckily for him, the one had been frightened, and the other had not gone nearly deep enough. But there again had been the disposition to question—to question him, Thomas James Wise, the leading collector and bibliographer of his day! Who else might be probing, investigating? How long before some shrewd and suspicious researcher came across those damning pages in the 39 volumes of Ruskin's Collected Works?

Such questions as these he perhaps often asked himself. Whatever fears he may have had, they were now soon confirmed. But the blow was not to fall immediately.

II

On the 12th of October, 1933, he received a visit from "a young man named Pollard, who fired at me a string of questions about some pamphlets," and a day or two afterward sent a typed questionnaire. This was the gist of the matter as related to me by Wise shortly afterward. The brief account was not complimentary to the visitor, and was curiously vague—a circumstance I put down to the irritability which Wise appeared to be suffering. As he was then recovering from an illness, the subject was not pursued. His agitation was unmistakable, and well it might be: it was his first direct intimation (as I subsequently learned) that his spurious nineteenth-century pamphlets were being subjected to investigation.

Wise had not seen Mr. Gorfin for some years. Their friendship had waned in 1914; and since then the collector had sprung into fame. Now, however, he felt it necessary to renew the friendship: it was so long since they had seen each other. There were urgent letters (once in duplicate) and telegrams of invitation. There was an urgent affair to discuss. He suggested that it affected Gorfin a great deal, and himself slightly! He was so anxious for his former assistant to come to tea. But it was too late—even for his consummate diplomacy.

Later in the autumn of 1933, Wise—accompanied by a lady who remained in the waiting room—called on Mr. Cecil Clay at the firm's London office. The interview between the managing director of the printing firm and its old client took place in the board room. They were alone. Wise soon came to the subject of the investigations into the pamphlets. Mr. Clay knew all about them now. The revelations had naturally come as a great surprise to him. His firm had facilitated the typographical researches of the two investigators, but most unfortunately had not been able to give them just the information that would have immediately revealed the forger's identity.[1]

Mr. Clay, describing the interview, told me:

Wise referred to "those monstrous fellows" and asked: "Can't you say you had nothing to do with these things,"—meaning the pamphlets.
I replied: "How can I when you know we printed them for you. Aren't you rather giving yourself away?"

After this plain indication of the attitude of Clays, the interview quickly came to an end, and Wise returned to his library, to read and reread what he had said in his books about these damned pamphlets which threatened to blast his success. In particular, he turned to the long and romantic

[1] "...They [Messrs. Clay & Sons] admitted readily enough the facts... proved that they had printed the pamphlets. But they were unable to give us any conclusive clue to the identity of their client, because they had preserved no ledgers earlier than 1911—nor is there any reason to suppose that anyone in their employ was privy to the fraud." The *Enquiry*, p. 65. *Op. cit.*

stories he had gathered round one of them—Mrs. Browning's *Sonnets* (Reading: 1847)—because either he had been informed or had guessed that this one would occupy the key position in the impending attack.

Of the group of pamphlets, this purported 1847 Reading edition of the *Sonnets* had always been the most prominent and most highly valued for its rarity and for the famous story behind it. The sonnets were written by Elizabeth Barrett while she lay on her invalid couch, during the clandestine courtship which ended in the elopement and wedding in September, 1846, that has been far-famed by play and film as the romance of *The Barretts of Wimpole Street*. Wise, in his *Bibliography of Mrs. Browning*, had retold Edmund Gosse's now familiar "pretty episode of literary history" (derived from Browning himself) of the coy gift of them a few months after their marriage by the happy Elizabeth to her husband one day early in 1847, in Pisa, while the poet stood looking out of the window after breakfast. To this highly romantic story, Gosse added an account (conceived, it is now obvious, in Wise's ingenious mind) of how Mrs. Browning, at first reluctant to expose her poetical love tributes to the world, was persuaded by her husband to have the sonnets privately printed in the "Reading" pamphlet through the agency of her friend, Miss Mary Russell Mitford.

But Wise was more concerned with the exceedingly interesting account he had given in his *Browning Library* (1929) of how he came into possession of his two copies of this "Reading: 1847" edition. About 1885, he wrote, he became acquainted with Dr. W. C. Bennett, an elderly bachelor and author of some books of verse, who had been a great friend of Miss Mitford. Bennett, an accountant, confided that he possessed copies of the privately printed *Sonnets* received from Miss Mitford when she lived at Three-Mile Cross, near Reading. Wise was invited to Bennett's home at Camberwell to see the treasures; the remainder of the account shall be

given in Wise's own words, both for their own sake and because of the sequel:

> I remember that the meal awaiting us was "high tea," and that
> it consisted of hot buttered toast and sausages. After his land-
> lady had cleared the table, letters and books were brought out,
> among them the much-longed-for *Sonnets*. One of the copies was
> in an old and broken half-calf binding, with the edges fortu-
> nately left untrimmed. But it had inserted the manuscript of the
> additional sonnet, *Future and Past*, which had been sent by Mrs.
> Browning to Miss Mitford to complete the series of forty-four. I
> bought the tiny booklet for £25, and carried it home rejoicing.
> I also purchased one of the unbound copies. . . . Shortly after-
> wards Dr. Bennett sold the remaining copies. They were bought
> by Harry Buxton Forman, Robert Alfred Potts, Sir Edmund
> Gosse, the Rev. Stopford A. Brooke, John Morgan of Aberdeen,
> Mr. Walter Brindley Slater, and other friends to whom I hurried
> the good news. Dr. Bennett received £10 for each.

If Wise's name is substituted for Bennett's in the last
sentence, we shall be nearer the truth. For the fact is that
this further "pretty episode," describing how he discovered
and secured the rare Reading *Sonnets*, is false. And in the
light of what Wise had only recently learned, he knew that
he must shift his tale; for in the autumn of 1932 there had
been published *Letters of Robert Browning Collected by
Thomas James Wise*, the originals of which had been included among the 571 letters sold by Sothebys in 1913 for the
amazing sum of £6,550. A sharp-eyed reviewer in *The Times*
Literary Supplement (Sept. 28, '33) had quoted from one of
these letters collected by Wise (it was to Leigh Hunt) a passage proving that Browning first learned in 1849 of the
existence of his wife's love sonnets to him—i.e., two years
after their purported printing in 1847 at Reading. So thus,
ironically enough, the recent publication of the letters Wise
had collected forced his own hand.

But there was some delay. In November of 1933 he had
a fall—injuring his head, according to a letter to me from Mrs.
Wise, who explained that he had been trying to do too much.

In due course, however, he made sufficient recovery to tackle the greatest problem he had ever encountered.

III

In the spring of 1934 he determined to meet the coming attack upon his spurious pamphlets before it was launched. To this end he wrote a long letter to *The Times* Literary Supplement that appeared on May 24th. The letter is a mixture of stupid and audacious wriggling; and those intimates of his who were anxious for his reputation did not hesitate to express their regret that he had written it. But it is important as being, with the exception of an interview and also another letter on a single phase of the subject, Wise's only public statement on the charges brought against his spurious pamphlets.

The beginning of the letter is curious and characteristic of him:

MRS. BROWNING'S "SONNETS, 1847."

Sir,—The suggestion has been pressed upon me that this book, with an imprint "Reading [Not for Publication]" is an impostor, not printed until many years after 1847.

With cool strategy, he proceeded to anticipate the lines of attack that would shortly be made; though without naming the two investigators. There is an amusing admission that no reference to the 1847 book appeared during Browning's lifetime: he recalled *The Times* reviewer's discovery of the letter establishing that 1849 was the date of the poet's first acquaintance with the *Sonnets;* and this "constitutes a real difficulty in the acceptance of the 1847 book." There followed an ingenious attempt to explain away how Gosse (in his otherwise authentic history) came to include the yarn about the printing of the 1847 edition at Reading through Miss Mitford—a yarn, as has been said above, that was undoubtedly invented and supplied by Wise. After a couple of red-herring hints as to

other unexplored places that might reveal something to save
his face, and some far-fetched supposition—all this wriggling
led to the admission: "I may be driven to the conclusion
that the 1847 book is not authentic." The audacity of it all
is amazing.

But there was still the printing of the spurious 1847 Reading edition to be accounted for. With superbly assumed innocence, he asked:

With whom could this have originated? One name must be
cleared out of the way at once; a name which would never have
been brought into the matter but for a mistake of my own. In the
introduction to "A Browning Library" 1929, writing forty-three
years after the event, I told the story of a visit to W. C. Bennett
in 1886, and said that I acquired my two copies of the 1847 book
from him; and earlier than this, in the first volume of my Ashley
Catalogue, 1922, I said that my copies came to me from W. C.
Bennett. What I actually brought away with me was his own
sonnets, "My Sonnets," privately printed at Greenwich in 1843.
The confusion of two such books may seem incredible, even after
thirty-six years. It is to be explained by the subjects of our conversation. . . . My two copies came to me not from W. C. Bennett
but from Harry Buxton Forman. From whom did he obtain
them? Neither I nor his son Mr. Maurice Buxton Forman can
tell with any certainty, but how he may have obtained them I
hope his son will be able to ascertain from an examination of
his father's correspondence.

With this version Wise threw his reputation for veracity
to the winds. Comparison of this account with his original
one substantially given on page 200 shows to what degree of
mendacity he would go in accounting for his "discovery" of
these spurious pamphlets. After this the rest of his letter
matters little. There were unsuccessful efforts to combat the
technical arguments about paper and type, which he knew
were to be advanced to prove that the "1847 Reading"
Sonnets could only have been printed more than thirty years
after the date on its title page. He concluded: ". . . I will leave
further exposition . . . to those who have a more microscopic

eye than I can boast of." But few would, or could, have boasted a keener eye than Thomas James Wise.

IV

In *The Times* Literary Supplement for the following week appeared two letters on the subject. One was from Mr. Maurice Buxton Forman endeavoring to substantiate Wise's explanation that his copies of the spurious Reading edition (produced by Wise's printers) came from Buxton Forman senior. This was doubtless an effort to help a friend in difficulties; but it does not appear to have done much good to Wise or to anyone else. The other letter was from Mr. Graham Pollard, one of the two investigators into the spurious pamphlets, rebutting Wise's attempt to disprove the technical evidence against the genuineness of the 1847 *Sonnets*. Mr. Pollard concluded by announcing that the *Enquiry* of his fellow investigator and himself would be published within the next few weeks.

In the meantime there had been much activity behind the scenes. Wise, through his agents, bought back the remaining stock of pamphlets, including forgeries and piracies, that he had sold to Mr. Gorfin. The price paid for the recovery of the things was £400, and an assurance was given that they would be destroyed. Mr. Gorfin, in giving me this information, could not remember the number of copies taken back, but estimated the value to him of the pamphlets, on their then market prices, as £2,000.

The stage was now set for the drama.

CHAPTER 21

THE EXPOSURE AND SOME SURPRISING
SEQUELS

The honest men in the Trade usually manage to damp the rogue's powder.

Wise (in an interview), 1930.[1]

I

THE RESULT of the investigation into Wise's spurious pamphlets was published on the 2nd of July, 1934, under the title *An Enquiry into the Nature of Certain Nineteenth Century Pamphlets*. The authors were Messrs. John Carter and Graham Pollard, two professional booksellers; the publishers were Mr. Michael Sadleir's firm of Constable and Co. It must be rare, if not unique, in the annals of controversy for critics to be able to quote their opponents' reply in their original charge. At the end of the volume appeared a "Stop-press" section quoting Wise's extraordinary letter, in which we have just seen him anticipating the attack.

The kind of forgery that the authors set out to expose was new. As shown here in the foregoing chapters, the forger was much too ingenious merely to imitate rarities and to pass them off as genuine. He conceived the idea of printing conveniently small pieces by collected authors, and dating them earlier than any known first editions of them (often as privately printed issues for the authors, with a false imprint, or no imprint at all)—giving them a priority which is the essential of the rare. In this way were created new books that mostly could not be compared with any originals, and required tests other than the usual ones—to prove that they were

[1] *The Strand, op. cit.*

254

not printed at the dates stated, but years later. Thus, both the crime and the methods of detecting it were novel. The *Enquiry* which revealed them was a sensation of the day.

As Wise had foreseen, the pamphlet of Mrs. Browning's *Sonnets* with the "Reading: 1847" imprint, the star piece of his forgeries (one had sold for as much as $1250 at auction), was the focus of attack. The investigators subjected this and over 50 other suspected pamphlets to analyses, chemical (for paper) and typographical. They also applied a third positive test, the familiar use of textual comparison, in addition to certain negative tests. The result was that 29 of the pamphlets were condemned outright as forgeries, 20 as suspect of forgery, and 5 as piratical. Some of the printings were condemned because their paper was of a kind not in use at the dates on which they were purported to have been printed; some because they were printed from type used only by Clay and Sons (Wise's printers) and designed subsequent to the dates of the purported printings; and 5 on textual grounds. (Some were condemned on account of both paper and type; and others on all three positive grounds.) The complete list of them, together with new information, will be found in the Appendix. Various other peculiarities of these pamphlets were revealed. For example, while they purported to have been printed from 1842 onwards, none had appeared for sale before 1889. With one doubtful exception, not a single specimen alleged to have been printed for the author's private distribution bore any presentation inscription or had any other personal association with the author. Neither the British Museum nor any other national collection had received any of the pamphlets before 1888. Most of the pamphlets either had been "discovered" by Wise, or owed their reputation as collectors' items to his published works. And finally, extensive marketing of the spurious things was traced to Wise, who eventually sold stocks of some of them to his agent, Mr. Herbert Gorfin.

The *Enquiry's* conclusions were built up on detail, most

of it highly technical. The work was a testimony to the patience and skill of its compilers. Two parties were vindicated: the printers—as we have seen (footnote page 248), and Wise's office colleague, Herbert. The investigators said that at first they imagined it possible that the forger was Mr. Gorfin. But he was only ten years old when the earliest independent evidence of their existence is found; and all of them had been produced by the time he was 21. "A few minutes' conversation was sufficient to convince us not only that Mr. Gorfin was not the forger, but that he had not the slightest idea that he was selling forgeries"; and tribute is paid to the high value of his assistance and information.

As for the master: in spite of the book's clear inferences, the Enquirers, for obvious reasons, nowhere charged Wise with the responsibility for the forgeries. They were content to show the fraudulent nature of the pamphlets, and to emphasize his extraordinary commercial interest in them, and his patronage of them as rarities. The nearest they came to sharps was: "We find it difficult to believe that Mr. Wise cannot now guess the identity of the forger; but, as long as it remains a guess, he has followed a very proper course in making no suggestion."

II

The sensational character of the revelations, for all their bibliographical technicalities, made big-headline news for the more popular dailies, and evoked long and careful reviews from the staider journals. An interviewer posted down to Hastings, where Wise was recuperating. Wise is reported to have said (*Daily Herald,* June 30th, 1934):

A large proportion of the books condemned are genuine. Those that are wrong were apparently printed in the middle and late 'eighties of last century.

At that time I was a young man in the 20's, hunting for books and seeking for knowledge about them.

These things were accepted as genuine at that time by such men as Buxton Forman, Sir Edmund Gosse, William Rossetti, Dr. Garnett of the British Museum, The Rev. Stopford Brooke, and others.

If these men of age and experience accepted them as genuine, why should I, their junior, suppose them to be spurious?

He went on to say that Harry Buxton Forman had a habit of buying and "salting down" small remainders of pamphlets, etc., of authors he believed in, and disposed of these largely by exchange—a considerable number thus coming to him (Wise) in return for manuscripts, others being taken in payment of Forman's Shelley Society subscriptions. These pamphlets, Wise averred, were disposed of through Mr. Gorfin, who apparently wanted more:

Forman said he could have them all, and I passed them over. I was only the vehicle. I was the messenger lad who took the goods for delivery. They were planted on Forman, and not on me.

Remembering that the last two years he had heard "subterranean rumours and remarks," he recalled the visit to him of Mr. Pollard, who said they had found some wrong things.

I replied that I was very interested, and said I would be pleased to assist them in any way I could. He instantly said "No, we don't want any help, but we would like to know when and from whom you purchased your own copies of certain pamphlets?"—a list of which he produced.

I replied that to tell him offhand where and when I purchased the pamphlets, which cost a few shillings each between 30 and 50 years ago, was an impossibility because the copies I had in my library were frequently not the copies I received from Buxton Forman.

The next day Mr. Pollard sent me a typed list of about 30 or more pamphlets, and asked that I should fill in the source from which my copies came. This I should have done had I not heard, just at that moment, rumours of what was going on.

Next he offered his opinion that "the things that are really wrong were produced by Richard Herne Shepherd" [2]—for-

2 See Chapter 14. On August 19th, 1934, Wise wrote to Mr. Wm. Roberts saying that he did not think Augustus Howell could have had much to do

getting that the two Kipling pamphlets were produced two
and four years after Shepherd's death, and several of the others
in 1895, when the unfortunate man died in an asylum. Wise
wound up this public and self-contradictory statement with
the irrelevant outburst:

"All my life I have been preaching against bad copies of books
and teaching people to leave bad copies alone. That has done
small booksellers a lot of harm and so they curse and hate me."

On the 12th of July, Wise wrote again to *The Times* Literary Supplement, saying that he had glanced hastily through
the pages of the *Enquiry,* and "I lose no time in writing to
explain my position with regard to the pamphlets of which
the authenticity is challenged." But all he did was to deny
that he ever "held stock" of any one of the condemned
or questioned pamphlets, and to give an embroidered version of what he had said in the interview as to Harry Buxton Forman's remainders, and how they passed via himself (Wise) to Gorfin. Within his letter he quoted a longer
letter to him from Maurice Buxton Forman naming some
of the people from whom the elder Forman acquired remainders and items for "salting down." Good son Maurice,
after echoing Wise's stupid and vindictive hint that Shepherd
might be the culprit,[3] wound up by fearing that he had been
rather long-winded, but "I type as I think, and my typing is
not very expert!"

III

After this Wise retired into stubborn silence. But there
were heard some strong voices in *The Times* Literary Supplement. To begin with, Mr. Herbert Gorfin gave the lie direct
to the only "position" Wise had taken up in defense of himself. He wrote (July 19, '34):

with the forged pamphlets, unless it was with the early Swinburnes or
Ruskins.
[3] See page 187.

Sir,—Mr. Wise states, in a letter in your issue of July 12, that he got his copies of those pamphlets which are shown in Messrs. Carter and Pollard's book to be forged, from H. Buxton Forman. Among other material, I was selling these regularly on commission for Mr. Wise from 1898 onwards, and I purchased from him what I understood to be the entire remainder in 1909-1911. In all our many transactions this connexion of the pamphlets with H. Buxton Forman was never mentioned, even by implication; and the suggestion that he was the source from which they came was only made to me, by Mr. Wise himself, on October 14, 1933— two days after Mr. Pollard had visited him and explained that they were forgeries. Mr. Wise had previously given me a totally different account of their origin.

Another correspondent, in the same issue of the Supplement, pointed out *inter alia* that neither Wise nor Mr. Maurice Buxton Forman stated explicitly whether the 54 pamphlets examined in the *Enquiry* were among the "swaps" which Forman senior was said to have made with Wise.

In the next issue Sir Sydney Cockerell rapped the knuckles of Mr. Maurice Buxton Forman for an unnecessary and erroneous observation about Charles Fairfax Murray—an aspersion subsequently withdrawn.

But it was the letter from the Viscount Esher in the issue of August 23rd, 1934, that effectively voiced the opinions of many thoughtful readers:

Sir—Book collectors throughout the world are still waiting to hear from Mr. Wise an explanation of the forgeries exposed by Mr. Carter and Mr. Pollard in their "Enquiry into the Nature of Certain Nineteenth-Century Pamphlets." Those of us who have bought the forged pamphlets for large sums of money cannot consent to leave the matter where it is.

Mr. Wise has said in an interview that "a large proportion of the books are genuine." It is only fair that Mr. Wise should tell us collectors which are the genuine ones, and why. He must have evidence to refute the careful examination made by Mr. Carter and Mr. Pollard. That evidence should be produced. It is clear from the book that Mr. Wise played a great part in the distribution of the forged pamphlets, and therefore must be more anxious than any of us to pursue the enquiry. He presented twenty-three of them to the British Museum, and fifteen to the Cambridge University Library....

[The letter proceeds to state facts already familiar to readers of this book, and continues:]

So far, therefore, the only explanation made by Mr. Wise is to throw back the provenance of the pamphlets on to Mr. Buxton Forman. Does he suggest that Mr. Buxton Forman was the forger? Or, if they were "planted" on Mr. Buxton Forman, whom does he suggest they were planted by? Mr. Buxton Forman was a distinguished man of letters, and his relatives will no doubt be able to tell us whether he was likely to have forged the pamphlets or whether he was likely to have accepted as genuine from somebody else (without mentioning his name or credentials) over a long period of years a mass of unknown and valuable pamphlets. Some evidence of these prolonged transactions must exist and should be produced.

We collectors have been accustomed to look upon Mr. Wise as an expert bibliographer. Indeed he has been president of the Bibliographical Society and is a member of the Roxburghe Club. He has stated that on a more careful reading of Mr. Carter and Mr. Pollard's book, he will have something further to say. A considerable time has elapsed, and the collectors who have followed Mr. Wise have a right to know how they stand in the matter.

Nothing could be more explicit than that. It is perhaps not strange, in view of what has been brought out here, that Wise never broke his silence. But that Mr. Maurice Buxton Forman did not respond to the invitation of Lord Esher's letter is more surprising. An explanation of why no immediate reply was forthcoming from Wise was supplied in the following issue of the Supplement by Mrs. Wise, who wrote briefly explaining that her husband was unfit to carry on any public correspondence, and that his doctor had strictly forbidden him to do so.

There followed in the Literary Supplement [4] a valuable series of letters, some of which were as unexpected as they

[4] Of *The Times*—8, 15, and 22 Nov., 1934.

were timely. The *Enquiry* had erred very unhappily in dismissing as "wholly fictitious" Edmund Gosse's story of the idyllic episode (i.e., of Mrs. Browning's surprise gift to her husband of the love sonnets) just because he had been unwise enough to add on to it Wise's invention about the "1847 Reading" edition and Miss Mitford's part in it. The letters amply substantiated that the first part of Gosse's account of the episode derived from Browning himself; and Mr. John Carter made the proper amende. He could do so without affecting the exposure of the unidyllic nature of the "Reading" *Sonnets* pamphlet: that remained damned and done for.

Later the same year, on December 10th, 1934, Thomas James Wise, at the suggestion of two members, resigned his membership of the Roxburghe Club. The grounds given for the resignation were "ill health." He had been asked for an explanation of the matters in the incriminating *Enquiry*, and made it clear that he did not admit any of the implications.

IV

If the popular Press could find hot news in the exposure of Wise's nineteenth-century pamphlets by such novel methods as analysis of paper and typographical detection (through the broken-backed f, the "button-hook" j, and the tilting question mark), the sensation caused in the book world can be well imagined. It came as a particularly painful shock to distinguished friends and acquaintances of Wise, to those who had lauded his impressive performances as a collector and bibliographer, and to his wealthy clients.

Some criticized the publication of the exposure during his lifetime—illogically ignoring the arguments that frauds ought to be exposed, and that at least the *Enquiry* gave Wise the opportunity to vindicate himself if he could. Among his other friends there was a disposition to suspend judgment, to wait for the oracle to speak. It was unthinkable that the wealthy collector, the builder of the finest private library of its kind, the stern chastiser of fakers, could have stooped to such practices.

In the meantime one leading firm of rare-book experts, who had had considerable dealings of an unimpeachable character with Wise, conducted a private and independent investigation "just in case . . ." They went to the expense of having some of the pamphlets analytically tested for the paper content. But the verdict was just as damning.

And I cannot forget the charming naïveté of a leading and esteemed official of the British Museum Library, who rounded a discussion about Wise and the scandal, and the future of the Ashley Library, by observing to me: "You know him well. Can't you get him to make a confession of exactly what he has done? It would get the dreadful business off his chest, and leave him in peace."

It was easier to imagine a zoo spectator entering the cage of a surly bear racked with toothache, and trying to extract the molar with a wrench.

V

Nevertheless there actually was some sort of attempt at the desperate remedy; it was made, however, by one who could claim the privilege of greater age and closer friendship. Mr. Gabriel Wells, the bookseller of New York and London, discussing the affair with me, recalled that his friendship with Wise had lasted for twenty-five years.

One day [he said] I went to Heath Drive with the idea of making an end of the unsatisfactory position. Tom was very excited. He was willing to do anything. And I even drew up a statement, a confession, for him to sign, of his part in the business, and of his willingness to make recompense for any direct loss sustained through him. But the final decision was not to touch it—that it was best left alone.

Myself: But was Wise willing to sign this document?
Mr. Wells: Oh, yes!

Myself: You are certain he understood it was a confession?
Mr. Wells: Certain! But it was thought best to leave it alone; and there I left it.

Subsequently I sent Mr. Wells a copy of the above note of our conversation, asking if he had any objection to my using it. At an interview, which he requested to discuss the suggestion, he said that the only objection he had was to the use of the word "confession," and that all else was accurate. He averred that there had been no confession, and that I must have misunderstood him. But my note was written within an hour of the conversation. While I believe it to be an accurate record of what was said, it is only fair to give equal prominence to Mr. Wells's objection to the one word.

There were, of course, some friends whose faith in Wise remained unshaken. One of these was a well-known North-of-England man whose library contains not a few purchases and gifts from Wise. Mr. ********* supplied me with a series of notes from which I quote:

Mr. Thomas J. Wise I knew quite well. I always called upon him when in London, and spent many happy hours in his company ... [referring to the attacked pamphlets]. Some of these he admitted to me were false; some he contended were genuine. But what hurt him was the implied accusation that he was responsible for the fakes. As he said, the book would have served a useful purpose had its chief motive not been an attack upon him. As it was he determined to investigate the whole problem, which would have involved an enormous amount of labour and research, going back some thirty years. His doctor at once told his wife that in his state of health such an attempt would kill him. His friends begged him to postpone it until his health improved, and after a few interviews in which he vainly called upon his memory for all the necessary details he had to give in, hoping to regain sufficient strength to tackle the work later. By that time his letters to me were in his wife's handwriting; he had a nurse who also acted as secretary; and on the two or three occasions I was allowed to see him the time was limited to a quarter of an hour. It was really a tragedy, for his failure to refute the charges has left in the minds of those who did not know him well, or at all, the impression that they were justified. And it must be said that there were some who exulted in knocking him off his pedestal. To those who really knew him the charges are unbelievable.... He was proved to be fallible—like every other bibliographer. But that he would live his laborious life knowing that some of the items in his Collection were frauds—and *his* frauds—is unthinkable....

This, then, is the testimony of a personal friend of Wise—of one who, down to 1938, believed in his innocence.

VI

It is an unpleasant task to have to write of Wise's disabilities from the viewpoint of whether they prevented him from doing what was naturally expected of him; but in a biography of this sort the implications of the letter just quoted ought not to be passed over. It is the case that Wise unfortunately was incapacitated for several periods after the spring of 1932, the chief of which have been indicated.

I saw Wise on two occasions when he was confined to bed, but able to converse freely, dictate letters, and read. On one occasion he was suffering from some epidermal trouble about which he told me; and, with bibliographic-like zeal for demonstration, he proceeded to show the locale of the trouble. On another occasion he related a distressing experience of his. A nurse whose services he greatly appreciated was, he said, "just attending to my backside, when she stopped. I heard a thud. Turning round, I saw that she had fallen to the floor in a fit. She died a few hours later. I was much upset."

In spite of his disabilities, however, it is also the case that from 1933 (when he knew of the investigations being made) to 1936 there were periods when he was able to devote himself very effectively to tasks he had on hand. This aspect of Wise's last years was the subject of a note by "Bibliographer" in *The Times* for May 19th, 1937. In the previous day's issue there had appeared a letter signed "A Personal Friend" (the pseudonym, as he informed me himself, of one to whom over many years the Ashley Library meant a great volume of work), protesting that Wise was a very sick man "unable to enter into any controversy, in which condition he remained until he died." In reply, "Bibliographer" wrote:

> With all due respect to "A Personal Friend," there was no need for Mr. Wise to "enter into any controversy" about the forged pamphlets. He was well enough at the time to write a long (though largely irrelevant) letter to *The Times Literary Supplement* (July 12, 1934) on the subject, and subsequently to see through the press the eleventh volume of the Ashley Catalogue. It did (and still does) seem to many people that he might have made the very brief statement of the facts which was all that was required.

As has been shown in the foregoing pages, Wise actually wrote twice to *The Times* Literary Supplement about the forgeries. And on my last visit to him in 1936 he was up and about his library—obviously not the lively man he had been, but able to discuss bibliographical matters with his old keenness. On no occasion did he ever make direct reference to the *Enquiry*'s exposure,[5] though the casual showing of a book containing a Tennyson inscription now caused him to forget the temporary ban on the subject; and he exclaimed bitterly: "They will be saying next that that is wrong." Mrs. Wise uttered a gentle warning . . . and for the next few seconds the stillness in the Ashley Library was disconcerting.

So that when Wise retired in obstinate silence behind the watchful and able care of his wife, he was not, for all his unfortunate periods of disability, always so handicapped that he could not deal with the challenge of the *Enquiry* if he would. The protest of "Bibliographer" in *The Times* was

[5] He wrote a brief indignant letter to me about it on July 6th, 1934, but later, August 16th, 1936, wrote in his own hand forbidding the printing of this letter for "a good reason." His script in 1936, as evidenced by his inscription on Vol. XI of his Catalogue presented to the British Museum, is at least as good as it was ten or twenty years earlier.

justified. Although in his three public statements Wise affected to ignore that the *Enquiry* was an unformulated attack on him, it is now clear that he was fully conscious of its implications against his honor. He could not help being otherwise. In spite of the care of the authors to avoid risks, the book was damaging to Wise's character and reputation: its inferences were obvious. And it is difficult to believe that it did not provide the opportunity for a successful action at law if he was innocent or if the inferences were unfair or based on serious errors of fact.

VII

The British Museum's copy of Wise's catalogue, *A Browning Library,* has become particularly interesting by reason of certain anonymous manuscript corrections made in defiance of one of that institution's most stringent rules. These corrections are concerned with the famous forged "1847 Reading" edition of Mrs. Browning's *Sonnets,* and are designed by minimum alterations to make the text agree in parts with facts that Wise subsequently had to admit (see Chapter 20). On page 83 of *A Browning Library* is the following passage as originally printed by Wise:

This copy of Mrs. Browning's *Sonnets* [i.e., Wise's own copy] was formerly in the possession of Dr. W. C. Bennett. It was given to him by Mary Russell Mitford, to whom had been entrusted by the authoress the task of seeing the book through the press. By Dr. Bennett it was sold to me.

By insertion in script of the word "not" the last sentence has been made to read: "By Dr. Bennett is was NOT sold to me."

———

Page 84 bears this printed passage in continuation of the description of Wise's own copy of the forged *Sonnets:*

———— Sonnets. / By / E. B. B. / Reading: / [Not for Publication.] / 1847.

Collation: Foolscap octavo, pp. 47; consisting of Half-title (with blank reverse) pp. 1—2; Title-page, as above (with blank reverse) pp. 3—4; and Text of the forty-three *Sonnets* pp. 5—47. The reverse of p. 47 is blank. There is no printer's imprint. The head-line is *Sonnets* throughout, upon both sides of the page. The signatures are A to C (3 sheets, each 8 leaves).

The *First Edition*. Bound in dark brown levant morocco by Riviere, with panelled sides and gilt top, the remaining edges entirely untrimmed. The leaves measure 7 × 4½ inches.

This copy of Mrs. Browning's *Sonnets* was formerly in the possession of Dr. W. C. Bennett. It was given to him by Mary Russell Mitford, to whom had been entrusted by the authoress the task of seeing the book through the press. By Dr. Bennett it was sold to me.
ᶫ *NOT*
Inserted at the commencement is an interesting A. L. S. of 4 pp. 8vo, addressed by Miss Mitford to Dr. Bennett, containing much chatty news about the Brownings :—

═══

Inserted also is the Manuscript of *Future and Past*, now No. 43 of the *Sonnets from the Portuguese*. This sonnet was not included in the original series of forty-three printed in the volume of 1847, but was added in the edition of 1856. The MS. had been forwarded by Mrs Browning to her friend at the time of its composition, in order that it might be added to the original forty-three and so complete the series. ∫ ~~Miss Mitford~~ inserted it in her copy of the booklet, where it still remained when I purchased the volume from Dr Bennett in 1886.

Corrections, on different pages, made by Wise in the British Museum's copy of his work *A Browning Library* after the exposure of his spurious 1847 edition of Mrs. Browning's famous *Sonnets*. The making of these corrections is one of the strange features of the story.

Inserted also is the Manuscript of *Future and Past*, now No. 43 of the *Sonnets from the Portuguese.* . . . The MS had been forwarded by Mrs. Browning to her friend at the time of its composition, in order that it might be added to the original forty-three and so complete the series. Miss Mitford inserted it in her copy of the booklet, where it still remained when I purchased the volume from Dr. Bennett in 1886.

Here by the crossing-out of Miss Mitford's name in the last sentence, and the substitution in script of "I," the sentence is made to read: "I inserted it in her copy of the booklet, where it still remained when I purchased the volume from Dr. Bennett in 1886." The anonymous corrector forgot to repeat in the last part of this sentence the correction previously made on page 83.

———

On pages 84 and 85 is this passage:

A third set of MSS, comprising the whole forty-four sonnets complete, was given by the poet's son, R. W. B. Browning, to Mrs. George Smith, and is now in the possession of her daughter, Miss Ethel Murray Smith. When making this gift Pen Browning stated that the MSS had been handed by his mother to her husband in 1849. But the statement was inaccurate.

The last sentence has been altered in script by crossing out "in" in the final word, making it read: "But the statement was accurate."

These corrections, though completely reversing the meaning of the original text, are slight, it is true. But from their manner and matter, I have no hesitation in attributing them to Wise, with whose script and way of correcting proofs I am familiar. To have altered the text more completely would have involved extensive script corrections, thus providing more identification of the anonymous breaker of the British Museum's rule. There is no doubt, however, that at some period subsequent to the exposure of the forgeries, Thomas

James Wise went to the British Museum Library, secured its copy of his own book, and there made the amendment repudiating the fiction with which he bolstered up the account of his "discovery" of the spurious "Reading" *Sonnets*. This eleventh-hour gesture, made in the silence of the British Museum Library, is not the least curious part of the story.

CHAPTER 22

WHY WERE THE FORGERIES DONE?

When bright the brimming goblet gleamed,
And lightly laughed the eager wine;
The glow of Pleasure softly streamed,
And in its sparkles seemed to shine;
But when the cup was passed and drained,
And lay unheeded on the board,
With dark Remorse my heart was stained,
As was the vase with Liber's hoard.

From *Verses.* By Thomas J. Wise.

I

THOMAS JAMES WISE died at his home in Heath Drive, Hampstead, on the 13th of May, 1937. His age was 77 years and 7 months.

For the most part the obituary notices of him were inadequate and contained errors of fact about his family and early career. True to its tradition, however, *The Times* (May 14, '37) gave a short memoir that was a careful and informed summary of his achievement as the builder of the Ashley Library. After an appreciation of Wise's skill as a collector, the notice said that in 1934 his credit as a bibliographer was gravely damaged when a large number of rare and valued pamphlets, whose reputation depended almost exclusively on his elaborate descriptions, histories, or discoveries of them, were proved beyond dispute to be spurious and manufactured many years after their purported dates. *The Times* continued:

Many people in the book world were not satisfied that this was just a case of Jove having nodded. Wise was shown to have been intimately involved with the sale and distribution of the pamphlets to collectors and to libraries in Great Britain and America. In response to a general demand for an explanation of the source of the forgeries and of his repeated attestations of their genuineness, Wise first attempted to throw responsibility on to men no longer alive who had been his friends and co-collectors, and then, challenged to produce evidence for his statements, withdrew into obstinate silence.

This reference to the exposure of the pamphlets and its immediate consequences was resented by some of Wise's friends, although beyond the pseudonymous plea of "A Personal Friend" (see ante, p. 265) their protests lacked the courage of public expression. The obituary columns of *The Times* are among the most valuable contributions to journalism. The reference to the nineteenth-century forged pamphlets was as essential in any true record of Wise as the mention of his honors. But the disposition to shirk the truth is symptomatic of an age when theft is called kleptomania and politely excused; when the lash is deemed cruel for those who batter and rob the helpless; when befoulers of children escape more lightly than offenders against property rights; and when storming dictators are countered with mildly reproving umbrellas.

II

After Wise's death there was naturally much inquiry regarding the future of the superb collection of books and MSS in his Ashley Library: the curiosity of the Press was but a reflection of the wide speculation in the book world. Before 1921 a few of those closely in touch with him had gathered the impression that he intended to leave his Library to the nation. In that year his friend, Mr. Coulson Kernahan, submitted an article to me in which occurred the passage: "Mr. Wise's collection will one day go, I understand, to the nation." I thought it fair to show an important statement of that kind to Wise, who expressed his wish that such an announcement should not be made public because in the then

financial situation it was difficult to estimate what the circumstances would be when he "cleared off the scene." But what
his wishes were and would continue to be, nothing could
change, he assured me. After a subsequent conversation, I
believed that the Ashley Library was destined to be given to
either the British Museum or one of the two Universities—
Oxford or Cambridge.

Wise, who had no children (but was survived by his wife
and his brother), left a fortune of £138,000 gross. In his last
will made in 1926 he lets it be known that by his previous
will he had left to the British Museum some rare and valuable
books that its library either did not contain or only possessed
in poor copies. But he regretted that, owing to the extent
that high rates of the death duty and income tax would
lower the net amount of his estate, he did not feel warranted
in fulfilling his original design. His directions, therefore, were
that his Library was to be sold; but he expressly forbade its
removal to and auctioning in America. By a codicil dated
the 6th of January, 1933,[1] he further directed that his Library
was first to be offered for sale to the British Museum at a
price to be determined by his wife.

In due course negotiations were opened with the Trustees
of the British Museum. The price to be paid was not readily
arrived at, but Mr. Gabriel Wells played a useful and conciliatory part in the negotiations. It was eventually announced
that the Trustees had undertaken to buy the Library from
the executors at a price which was not made public, but
which the official announcement said "is very much less than
its estimated value." Whereupon Wise's widow, who had
throughout the negotiations been anxious for the Library to
be acquired by the nation even at some sacrifice of her particular interest, gave to the Museum the handsome set of
bookcases in which the Ashley books and manuscripts were
contained.

[1] By which date, according to Wise's own statement (see page 257) he knew
of the investigations being made into his spurious pamphlets.

The purchase price agreed is said to have been £60,000, to be paid over a number of years.

The decision received considerable notice in the Press, which for the most part recognized the importance and desirability of the acquisition. There were some exceptions, however. For example, the *Daily Express* announced in a large streamer headline: "BRITISH MUSEUM TO GIVE BOOK FAKER MEMORIAL." Those who had expected the Library to be given to the nation were naturally much surprised at the news.

But whether purchase or gift, scholars and experts welcomed the national acquisition of the Ashley books and MSS. It has already been stated in these pages that many of the Museum's rare Elizabethan first editions, copies of which Wise possessed in superb condition, were very much the worse for wear—hence the desire of the authorities to secure the Ashley Library's specimens, and also its items that the national institution lacked. Moreover, there was the collector's wealth of MSS—the part of the acquisition that received much less notice, though it may well prove the more fruitful. A *Times* leader echoed the approval of responsible opinion with a nicety when it said:

Wise's shortcomings in connexion with that unfortunate business [the series of forgeries], whether they were of omission or commission, are no doubt of considerable psychological interest, but it does not affect in the slightest the value and importance of the great library which he amassed with unrivalled acumen and taste.

Of the approximately 7,000 books and manuscripts a considerable number would be needless duplicates of copies already in the British Museum—especially those of the "-ana" Wise collected and the copies presented to him. The Museum with its 4,000,000 volumes does not require mere duplicates, of which it has many. This was a factor that weighed in the negotiations, and eventually enabled the Trustees to assure the tax-paying public that they had paid less than the estimated value of the collection. Had they run the risk of letting it be dispersed at auction, it is doubtful whether the particular books they needed, and all the manuscripts and letters that it was at least equally desirable for them to have, could have been secured against open competition which might have meant unduly high prices. On the other hand, the vendor's natural preference for the Library's finding a home in the British Museum, on acceptable terms, can well be understood. That had been the wish of its founder, who doubtless calculated the course of events.

In all the circumstances, therefore, it was better that the authorities should take over the whole collection, so that the wealth of material in print and script should be available to the future generations of biographers, researchers, and students, who will be glad of it. The value of the Ashley Library has been estimated at various figures from £100,000 to as much as £250,000—the higher figures based on the high prices of the boom. What it would actually have realized at auction is now purely a matter of guess. It is also a matter of speculation what its original cost was to Wise. It is most probable that even at the Museum's figure the sale price showed a profit. Such a result is not surprising in the case of a man whose genius for collecting was superimposed on great commercial ability and foresight, and who had made not a small part of his fortune out of dealing in books and manuscripts.

III

In the case of a library of any considerable size, it is a frequent experience that when it comes to be checked or moved, discrepancies between its contents on the shelves and as detailed in its catalogues are found. Items get lent out and not returned—though this is less likely to happen in the case of rare and valuable books. When the Ashley collection came to be checked for the purpose of negotiating its sale to the British Museum, it was discovered that over 200 books and manuscripts described in its eleven-volume Catalogue were missing. Some of these, naturally, were of minor interest; but there were 47 of the first importance whose absence—especially in one case—could not be otherwise than disappointing and surprising to the British Museum officials responsible for the checking, removal, and safe custody of the collection, which is now housed in its own room at the Bloomsbury institution.

The missing items included the original letter from Mr. Asquith offering Swinburne a Civil List Pension of £250 a year. "As an old Balliol man, it would be a peculiar privilege to me to secure this slight acknowledgment of the genius of the greatest of our Balliol Poets"—an offer which was promptly declined by Swinburne. Among other manuscripts lacking were eight by Joseph Conrad, four by Swinburne (including that of the *Laus Veneris*—indexed but not described), and two by Thomas Hardy. Of missing printed books, were ten seventeenth-century first editions, including two by John Dryden, two by Thomas Shadwell, Thomas D'Urfey's *The Progress of Honesty* (1681), and gallant Congreve's *The Mourning Bride* (1697), in which the famous line, "Music hath Charms to soothe a savage Beast," first appeared.

Naturally, when the Library came to be checked by the British Museum officials, there was much interest regarding the fate of Wise's condemned or suspected nineteenth-century pamphlets. It was found that fourteen of them (four by Ruskin, one by Swinburne, seven by Tennyson, and two by Thackeray) were missing. The officials were informed by Mr. Maurice Buxton Forman, who as an intimate friend of the Wise family assisted in the final business, that three of the Tennysons were "definitely destroyed" by Wise, and others in the list "may also have been destroyed."

But there was missing one book at whose loss the public, no less than the British Museum, may well feel the profoundest regret. The removal of it from the collection may be likened to the abstracting of one of the central and most lustrous gems in a king's crown. This was the MS of John Keats's sonnet, "A Dream after reading Dante's Episode of Paolo & Francesca" [1819], written on a flyleaf of a copy of Cary's *Dante* (1814). This volume was made still more precious by bearing poor Keats's inscription to his sweetheart, Fanny Brawne, and his monogram drawn by himself; and also by containing a transcription by Fanny of the last sonnet written by the dying poet. No wonder Wise said of this treasure, whose value may be put at several thousands of pounds, "A more fascinating 'association book' it would be difficult to imagine," and was wont to display it to his friends with intense pride. And now it will not be seen in the Ashley Library acquired by the nation after it was revealed that such a large number of rarities was missing; although not with the knowledge that the collection contained important books since proved to be fakes (e.g., pages 40 and 157).

Knowing of the interest of Mr. Maurice Buxton Forman, who is himself a specialist on Keats, I asked him if he could throw any light on the unfortunate disappearance of the treasure. He replied (Sept. 14, '38) informing me that until he went through the *Ashley Catalogue* with the Museum officials on Mrs. Wise's behalf, he did not know that the Dante with the Keats sonnet had ever been there. He regretted that he did not know what had become of it; adding that he wished he did know.

The explanation of these missing books and manuscripts, it is presumed, is that they were sold by Wise. That so many important first editions and highly desirable MSS were thus disposed of is not merely evidence of the extent of his business as a rare-book dealer, but of the fact that (in these cases, at all events) his commercial transactions were of more account to him than the leaving of the Library as described in the *Ashley Catalogue*—which is therefore not now a true record of the collection acquired by the British Museum.

IV

The fact that the range of forgeries perpetrated in the eighties and nineties remained so long unexposed (with the exception of the two in the *Athenaeum* in 1889, and the four Ruskins by Cook and Wedderburn) is remarkable. The damning evidence of the diary of Mr. Y. Z. has shown that Wise's "wild career" was known in 1888 to one man—if not to a few others. But the full extent of that career could not be realized because it had not run its course; also, it could not have been guessed what prices the "wrong things" would reach as the result largely of his subsequent clever publicizing. Moreover, as has been shown in Chapter 6, although some of the things indicated were in fact spurious, they were apparently regarded as piratings; a piracy does not sound nearly so dreadful as a forgery. Wise even then had the reputation of being a prosperous merchant-collector. His "wild career" was perhaps dismissed as an unwise escapade, of which the less said the better. The Diary was a reliable confidant.

But it is now evident that in the course of time the authenticity of some of these rare nineteenth-century pamphlets that kept coming into the market in such remarkably fresh condition became questioned among the more careful and observant booksellers. An expert well qualified by long experience has told me that some of the better-informed booksellers have always been shy of handling certain items because they had suspicions. Wise, as a private dealer, was as well-informed as any in the rare-book trade: he himself demonstrated his intimate knowledge of it. So we have this extraordinary position: that all the time his fame as a collector, as a bibliographer, and even as a scholar, was increasing, and while he was honored for his achievements, he knew there were those who knew that some of the rare pamphlets he had "discovered," and whose reputation he had established so interestingly in his catalogues, were suspect. What is more, he knew there were those who knew that he had had a connection with these pamphlets that was at least suspicious.

Suspicion is one thing, however: proof is another.

Wise proceeded on his way with superb confidence. A cynical appreciator of snobbery, he realized how useful a shield was a reputation for wealth. He was always believed to be very rich. In his younger days, as we have seen, he was a reputedly well-to-do young "merchant"—on a salary of under £6 a week and at times admittedly hard pressed to meet his book bills. At the London offices of his printers he was known as "the millionaire who brought those funny little things enclosed in beautiful leather cases to be printed." There was no anxiety to correct these useful impressions except when circumstances demanded otherwise: as when a well-known poet and critic, hard-pressed and badgered, unsuccessfully sought his financial aid for a literary venture—a worthy enough cause, as Wise regretfully agreed, pushing across the whisky decanter to the disappointed petitioner. The imposing catalogues, the discriminating gifts of them, the scornful denunciations of poor copies, suspect books, and fakes—all these were like defensive weapons. He became a formidable object to attack—if he could be attacked; for, really, there was so little evidence about the origins of these pamphlets of which some rare-book dealers were so shy.

On the other hand, there were some booksellers, and even collectors, who at times felt that Wise carried too far his dictatorial assumption of infallibility, his domineering insistence that his own books or arguments, and not theirs, were the right ones. His bibliographical standpoints were sometimes seriously disadvantageous to others. But the antiquarian book trade is one that seems to bring to its close fraternity a prescience and patient philosophy—if not always from the insides of books. The attitude of the antiquarian critics of Wise was that "We shall see all in good time."

And in good time, inspired by the clues left by the literary editors, Cook and Wedderburn, it was two of the younger generation of booksellers who so brilliantly instanced the

truth of Wise's saying with which I have headed Chapter 21.
His was a haunting secret that he carried for nearly 50 years,
never knowing when might be exploded the mine whose
train he knew was laid in the *Collected Works* of John
Ruskin. The more amazing, therefore, were his aplomb and
strategy which produced that *faux bonhomme* of Mr. Payen-
Payne's description.

V

Why did Wise perpetrate these forgeries and piracies? This
is a question on which there has been much speculation.
Various theories have been advanced. The weakest is that
he did them as a joke. But Wise, from the outset of his
career, was far too purposeful a man to waste his energies
in acquiring the necessary perfection of technique, in pursuing such a systematic course, for the mere pleasure of
caprice.

Another and more favorite theory is the vague one that it
was an aberration—that he manufactured these spurious
pamphlets and piracies for the satisfaction of "putting them
over" experts. But this explanation is almost an insult to
his keen intelligence and shrewd instinct. The same reason
that cancels the "joke" excuse applies here.

Other explanations are that he manufactured the things
to use as levers for ingratiating himself with their authors,
and that he desired the triumphs of "discovering" the rarities.
It has been shown that he did appear to use some of them for
the first purpose; and he probably also gloried over his
triumphs. But these were the results or sequels of the enterprises rather than the original purposes of them. Not all
the falsifications were usable for these ends. Moreover, if
these were the reasons that prompted him, he could have
lessened his offense by refusing to make money out of them.

The latter consideration brings us to the argument most
frequently heard from Wise's apologists—namely, that the

profit he made out of the forgeries was so small that he would have not risked for it his fame as a collector and his reputation as a bibliographer. This is putting the cart before the horse. The forgeries were begun when he was about 27 years of age and only learning his bibliography from Furnivall, Herne Shepherd, and Harry Buxton Forman—when he had not compiled a single bibliographical work, and when he was only known as one of the numerous enthusiastic book collectors of the Browning and Shelley circles. The theory involves the premise that the young cashier, when he began the forging and piratings, envisaged the high and unique position he was to attain in his mature years. This is a very improbable assumption; because, although purposeful and persevering as he was, it is not difficult to show that his subsequent celebrity and success were not unfortuitous.

And were the profits so small on things that Mr. Y. Z.'s diary shows him producing at a cost of about half a crown apiece? When Wise said that Dr. Bennett sold the "discovered" Reading *Sonnets* at £10 apiece, it is not unreasonable to conjecture that this figure represents his own sale prices to Forman, Gosse, and the rest to whom he "hurried the good news." When his clever publicizing resulted in this forgery realizing as high a price as £250 and Ruskin's *Scythian Guest* for £42, it cannot be supposed that he, with his keen commercial mind, did not benefit by the high prices he worked up.[2] True, for reasons that have been shown (see Chapter 6), he at first sold the things cheaply enough to get them into circulation. But he had reserve stocks on which to draw when their market prices rose; for, as late as 1910—after he had satisfied his own private clientele and also sold through Mr. Gorfin—we find him selling as many as 41 copies of one

---

[2] Mr. Graham Pollard is quoted in the *Daily Express* of August 17th, 1937, as saying: "We do know that he [Wise] would put a forgery in a sale, get two booksellers, unknown to each other, to bid for it. It would be sold to him for, say, £50. He would have to pay the fees to auctioneer and bookseller. But then, with a price fixed for a pamphlet, he would produce other copies to collectors—fakes too—and sell them."

spurious pamphlet to his agent. The numbers printed must
in some cases have been out of all proportion to their purported "rarity." Recalling that the Wrenn librarian has estimated the cost to John H. Wrenn of the forgeries and piracies
at over £1,000, that Wise had other wealthy clients on his
private list, that after years of skimming the cream he sold
off remaining stocks of the "wrong" things to Mr. Gorfin in
1909 and 1910 alone, for some £289,[3] it is obvious that the
profits must have been very appreciable—running into thousands of pounds, apart from the kudos he gained for the
"discoveries." The full total will probably never be known.
But in years to come, when the locale of more copies is
known, it will be possible for industrious researchers to form
a better idea of the extent and financial results of the forging
and pirating of the nineteenth-century pamphlets.

He was, as we have seen, originally prompted to it by his
experiments in facsimile reprintings. But, although he prided
himself on his success in making these indistinguishable from
the rare originals, he saw the dangers of detection. It was then
that he conceived the highly ingenious plan of manufacturing small pieces and antedating them as first editions which
could not be compared with any originals. They soon began
to make profits, and at a time when the young cashier wanted
all the money he could make.

It is my carefully considered judgment that the basic
motive of the long system of frauds was gain, to which later,
possibly, was added desire for the kudos of "discovering" the
exciting rarities—kudos dear to the vanity of the ambitious
collector-dealer. The psychological interest in the case is not
why he fell, but how he rose to fame after the fall.

Consider the superb audacity with which we have seen this
Jekyll of the produce market and Hyde of the printing press
carrying himself during the many years he held the secret
that, partly known as he knew it was, must one day be re-

---

[3] This was the sum of an incomplete list of purchases. There were other
sales of stock to Mr. Gorfin.

vealed. Consider the clever way in which he ingratiated himself with men whom he thought would serve his purposes, how usually he steered clear of controversy, how tactfully he handled suspicious critics, and how his explanations involving friends and acquaintances in some of the wrong things were not put forward until after the deaths of these men. Consider how, living through this anxious and tortuous scheme of things, he magnificently realized the triple accomplishment of making his fortune, building a fine library, and rearing his flashily brilliant (if not very sound) reputation. And considering these things, we see behind the varied achievements an uncanny genius.

Not the least strange of many curious features of the story is the coincidence of the quotation made in 1930 by Mr. C. H. Wilkinson, Dean and Librarian of Worcester College, Oxford, in one of the admirable introductions to the Ashley Catalogues. Did Wise wince, feel a chilly premonition, when he found his kindly introducer quoting, as a sort of text, this from *The Rambler*, No. 4?:

There have been Men indeed splendidly wicked, whose Endowments throw a Brightness on their Crimes . . . because they never could be wholly divested of their Excellencies; but such have been in all Ages the great Corrupters of the World.

Whether, remembering the ruthlessness and vindictiveness that Wise's books reveal, the way he used and abused useful friends, his "wickedness" is regarded as "splendid," depends upon the individual regard for truth and honesty and the sacredness of friendship. But that there were many "Excellencies" in his achievement as a collector, that his "Endowments" had their own "Brightness," cannot be denied to Thomas James Wise, who staked for himself a threefold claim in the annals of fame: as the builder of the Ashley Library; as the most prolific and interesting of British bibliographers; and as the forger of the nineteenth-century pamphlets.

APPENDIX

THE BIBLIOGRAPHY OF
THE BIBLIOGRAPHER

THE BIBLIOGRAPHY OF THE BIBLIOGRAPHER

A Record of his Compilations, Privately Printed Publications, Edited Works, Forgeries, Piracies, Etc.

BIBLIOGRAPHIES BY THOMAS JAMES WISE OF

John Ruskin (in collaboration with James P. Smart). 1893. Two vols. Crown quarto. Pages (vol. I) 358 and (II) 276. Illustrations extra. Copies 250.

Robert Browning. 1897. F'cap 4to. Pp. 252. Illus. ext. Copies 50.

Algernon Charles Swinburne (List of the Scarcer Works). 1897. F'cap 4to. Pp. 118. Illus. ext. Copies 50.

Alfred, Lord Tennyson. 1908. Two vols. F'cap 4to. Pp. (I) 382 and (II) 220. Illus. on vellum ext. Copies 100 plus 5 on handmade paper.

Samuel Taylor Coleridge. Printed for the Bibliographical Society. 1913. F'cap 4to. Pp. 328. Copies 500.

Coleridgeiana. Being a Supplement [to the Coleridge Bibliography]. 1919. F'cap 4to. Pages 40. Copies 500.

George Henry Borrow. 1914. F'cap 4to. Pp. 342. With Errata slip. Copies 100.

William Wordsworth. 1916. F'cap 4to. Pp. 288. Copies 100.

The Brontë Family. 1917. F'cap 4to. Pp. 276. Copies 100.

Elizabeth Barrett Browning. 1918. F'cap 4to. Pp. 268. Copies 100.

Walter Savage Landor (in collaboration with Stephen Wheeler). Printed for the Bibliographical Society. 1919. F'cap 4to. Pp. 448. With twelve facs. extra.

Algernon Charles Swinburne. 1919-1920. Two vols. F'cap 4to. Pp. (I) 528 and (II) 428. Copies 125.

Joseph Conrad. 1920. F'cap 4to. Pp. 128. Copies 150.

Joseph Conrad. Second edition revised and enlarged. 1921. F'cap 4to. Pp. 136. Copies 170.

John Keats. Included in the *John Keats Memorial Volume* issued by the Keats House Committee, Hampstead 1921. 4to. (Pp. 209-215.)

George Gordon Noel, Baron Byron. 1932-1933. Two vols. Crn. 4to. Pp. (I) 170 and (II) 166. Illus. ext.

CATALOGUES BY THOMAS JAMES WISE OF

The Ashley Library A List of Books Printed for Private Circulation.... 1895. Crn. Octavo. Pp. 18.

The Ashley Library. 1905-1908. Two vols. Demy 4to. Pp. (vol. I) 286, with 122 facs. on vellum ext; and (II) 182, with 74 facs. on vellum ext. No certificate of issue or printer's imprint.

The Ashley Library. 1922-1936. Eleven vols. Crn. 4to. Dunedin Press. Vol. I (1922) intro. by Richard Curle. Pp. 286, Vol. II (1922) intro. by Augustine Birrell. Pp. 230; Vol. III (1923) intro. by Edmund Gosse. Pp. 226; Vol. IV (1923) intro. by John Drinkwater. Pp. 232; Vol. V (1924) intro. by E. V. Lucas. Pp. 226; Vol. VI (1925) intro. by A. E. Newton. Pp. 234; Vol. VII (1925) intro. by R. W. Chapman. Pp. 238; Vol. VIII (1926) intro. by David Nichol Smith. Pp. 224; Vol. IX (1927) intro. by Alfred W. Pollard. Pp. 350; Vol. X (1930) intro. by J. C. Squire. Pp. 238; Vol. XI (1936) intro. by Arundell Esdaile. Pp. 228. Illus. ext. in each vol. Copies 200 on antique plus 50 on handmade paper.

A Shelley Library. Intro. by Roger Ingpen. 1924. Crn. 4to. Pp. 184. Illus. ext. Copies 160 plus 20.

A Swinburne Library. Intro. by T. J. Wise. 1925. Crn. 4to. Pp. 314. Illus. ext. Copies 160 plus 30.

Two Lake Poets. William Wordsworth and Samuel Taylor Coleridge. Intro. by T. J. Wise. 1927. Crn. 4to. Pp. 160. Illus. ext. Copies 160 plus 30.

A Byron Library. Intro. by Ethel Colburn Mayne. 1928. Crn. 4to. Pp. 174. Illus. ext. Copies 160 plus 30.

A Conrad Library. Intro. by Richard Curle. 1928. Crn. 4to. Pp. 88. Illus. ext. Copies 160 plus 25.

A Landor Library. Intro. by T. J. Wise. 1928. Crn. 4to. Pp. 128. Illus. ext. Copies 160 plus 25.

A Brontë Library. Intro. by C. W. Hatfield. 1929. Crn. 4to. Pp. 108. Illus. ext. Copies 160 plus 30.

A Browning Library. Intro. by T. J. Wise. 1929. Crn. 4to. Pp. 160. Illus. ext. Copies 160 plus 30.

A Dryden Library. Intro. by C. H. Wilkinson. 1930. Crn. 4to. Pp. 116. Illus. ext. Copies 160.

A Pope Library. Intro. by H. F. B. Brett-Smith. 1931. Crn. 4to. Pp. 130. Illus. ext. Copies 160.

NOTE: Wise's *Bibliographies* and *Library* catalogues concerned with the same author are not identical. Although the principal contents are much the same, each gives material not contained in the corresponding volume.

PRIVATELY PRINTED BOOKS, PAMPHLETS, ETC.
ISSUED BY THOMAS JAMES WISE

An asterisk at the beginning of a title denotes that the publication does not bear either Wise's imprint, or the Ashley Library bookmark at the end of the volume, or any other acknowledgment of its having been issued by him.

Where the description "1st edn." is appended, this is taken from Wise; although in a few cases the claim is here challenged. Where there is no such description, the printing is not recorded by Wise as a first, but nevertheless generally is—unless otherwise classified: e.g., as a reprint.

Nearly all the publications bear statements that they were printed for private circulation or distribution. Except in the cases where other printers' imprints are indicated, the printers were Richard Clay & Sons, whose imprint is often omitted. Where their imprint or that of another printer, appears on a publication, the name of the firm is given shortly. In the absence of a name, therefore, the printers may be understood to be Clays—except in the few cases specified in the footnotes.

With the exception of those specially noted, the publications bear unsigned statements saying that the issues were limited to thirty copies each. In some cases—like four of the collections of letters from Shelley—three, four, or five copies were printed upon vellum in addition. Where the number of copies issued is stated, the figures are those of Wise.

The letters S.S.P. at the end of items indicates that these pamphlets were printed from the Shelley Society Papers; and from the same type reimposed, plus the addition of preliminaries. It appears to have been Wise's practice to make these off-prints, giving some, if not all, the authors of the Papers half a dozen copies. In some cases he sent a copy to the British Museum Library; but in other cases the required copyright copy was not supplied. In at least one case the author of a Paper did not consider it worth issuing separately in this form, and declined to accede to the request of Wise, who nevertheless produced it (see correspondence from Dr. Garnett, John Todhunter, H. Buxton Forman, etc., in the British Museum Department of

Manuscripts). All these off-prints appear in Wise's 1895 *List of Books Printed for Private Circulation* (see Chapter 10).

The pagination figures indicate the numbers of leaves printed on, but do not include paper covers or boards.

Matthew Arnold. **Alaric at Rome. A Prize Poem.* Type-facsimile reprint. Edited and with Preface by Wise. 1893. Clays. Octavo Pp. 24. Limited "to a few copies"—which Wise stated in his 1895 *List* numbered 35.

> * *Letters from Matthew Arnold to John Churton Collins.* 1910. Crn. 8vo. Pp. 12. Copies 20. First edition.

Edward and E. Marx Aveling. **Shelley's Socialism,* 1888. Dy. 8vo. Pp. 30. Copies 28. S.S.P.

Sir James Matthew Barrie. *Scotland's Lament.* 1894. Octavo. Pp. 8. Copies 12. 1st edn.

Mathilde Blind. **Shelley's View of Nature Contrasted with Darwin's.* 1886. Clays. Dy. 8vo. Pp. 22. Copies 28. S.S.P.

George Borrow. *A Supplementary Chapter to the Bible in Spain.* 1913. 4to. Pp. 48. 1st edn.

> *Letters to his Wife Mary Borrow.* 1913. Crn. 8vo. Pp. 40. 1st edn.
>
> *Marsk Stig. A Ballad.* 1913. Crn. 8vo. Pp. 40. 1st edn.
>
> *The Serpent Knight & Other Ballads.* 1913. 4to. Pp. 36. 1st edn.
>
> *The King's Wake & Other Ballads.* 1913. 4to. Pp. 24. 1st edn.
>
> *The Dalby Bear & Other Ballads.* 1913. 4to. Pp. 20. 1st edn.
>
> *The Mermaid's Prophecy & Other Songs,* etc. 1913. 4to. Pp. 32. 1st edn.
>
> *Hafbur & Signe. A Ballad.* 1913. 4to. Pp. 24. 1st edn.
>
> *The Story of Yvashka with the Bear's Ear.* 1913. 4to. Pp. 24. 1st edn.
>
> *The Verner Raven . . . & Other Ballads.* 1913. 4to. Pp. 28. 1st edn.
>
> *The Return of the Dead & Other Ballads.* 1913. 4to. Pp. 24. 1st edn.
>
> *Axel Thordson & Fair Valborg. A Ballad.* 1913. 4to. Pp. 46. 1st edn.
>
> *King Hacon's Death.* etc. 1913. 8vo. Pp. 16. 1st edn.
>
> *Marsk Stig's Daughters & Other Songs,* etc. 1913. 8vo. Pp. 24. 1st edn.
>
> *The Tale of Brynild,* etc. 1913. 4to. Pp. 36. 1st edn.

Proud Signild & Other Ballads. 1913. 4to. Pp. 28. 1st edn.
Ulf Van Yern & Other Ballads. 1913. 4to. Pp. 28. 1st edn.
Ellen of Villenskov, etc. 1913. 4to. Pp. 24. 1st edn.
The Songs of Ranild. 1913. 4to. Pp. 28. 1st edn.
Niels Ebbesen, etc. 1913. 4to. Pp. 32. 1st edn.
Child Maidevold, etc. 1913. 4to. Pp. 28. 1st edn.
Ermeline. A Ballad. 1913. 4to. Pp. 24. 1st edn.
The Giant of Bern, etc. 1913. 8vo. Pp. 16. 1st edn.
Little Engel, etc. 1913. 4to. Pp. 28. 1st edn.
Alf the Freebooter, etc. 1913. 4to. Pp. 28. 1st edn.
King Diderik, etc. 1913. 4to. Pp. 28. 1st edn.
The Nightingale, etc. 1913. 4to. Pp. 28. 1st edn.
Grimmer and Kamper, etc. 1913. 4to. Pp. 28. 1st edn.
The Fountain of Maribo, etc. 1913. 4to. Pp. 28. 1st edn.
Queen Berngerd, etc. 1913. 4to. Pp. 32. 1st edn.
Finnish Arts, etc. 1913. 4to. Pp. 28. 1st edn.
Brown William, etc. 1913. 4to. Pp. 32. 1st edn.
The Song of Dierdra, etc. 1913. 4to. Pp. 28. 1st edn.
Signelil, etc. 1913. 4to. Pp. 28. 1st edn.
Young Swaigder, etc. 1913. 4to. Pp. 28. 1st edn.
Emelian the Fool, etc. 1913. 8vo. Pp. 40. 1st edn.
The Story of Tim, etc. 1913. 8vo. Pp. 32. 1st edn.
Mollie Charane, etc. 1913. 4to. Pp. 28. 1st edn.
Grimhild's Vengeance, etc. Intro. by Edmund Gosse. 1913.
4to. Pp. 40. 1st edn.
Letters to his mother Ann Borrow, etc. 1913. 8vo. Pp. 40.
1st edn.
The Brother Avenged, etc. 1913. 4to. Pp. 32. 1st edn.
The Gold Horns, etc. Edited by Edmund Gosse. 1913. 4to.
Pp. 28. 1st edn.
Tord of Hafsborough, etc. 1914. 4to. Pp. 32. 1st edn.
The Expedition to Birting's Land, etc. 1914. 4to. Pp. 28.
1st edn.

Anne Brontë. *Self-Communion. A Poem.* Edited by Thomas J.
Wise. 1900. Clays. 8vo. Pp. 50. Two leaves of facs. ext. 1st edn.
   Dreams and Other Poems. 1917. F'cap 4to. Pp. 24. 1st edn.

Charlotte Brontë. *The Adventures of Ernest Alembert. A Fairy
Tale....* Edited by Thomas J. Wise. 1896. 8vo. Pp. 40. 1st edn.[1]
   Richard Cœur de Lion & Blondel A Poem. 1912. Crn. 8vo.
Pp. 20. 1st edn.

[1] An off-print from the type used for the printing of the tale in *Literary
Anecdotes of the Nineteenth Century* (1895-6).

Saul and Other Poems. 1913. Crn. 8vo. Pp. 20. 1st edn.
Letters Recounting the Deaths of Emily Anne and Branwell Brontë ... 1913. Crn. 8vo. Pp. 24. 1st edn.
The Love Letters of Charlotte Brontë to Constantin Heger. 1914. [Pref. note by Wise.] Crn. 8vo. Pp. 44. 1st edn.
The Red Cross Knight & Other Poems. 1917. F'cap 4to. Pp. 20. 1st edn.
The Swiss Emigrant's Return & Other Poems. 1917. F'cap 4to. Pp. 20. 1st edn.
Darius Codomannus A Poem. 1920. Clays. F'cap 4to. Pp. 16. 1st edn.

The Brontës. *The Orphans & Other Poems.* By Charlotte, Emily, and Branwell Brontë. F'cap 4to. Pp. 20. 1917. 1st edn.

Rev. Stopford A. Brooke. **Inaugural Address to the Shelley Society.* 1886. Clays. 8vo. Pp. 26. Copies 28. S.S.P.

Elizabeth Barrett Browning. **The Battle of Marathon A Poem Written in Early Youth.* . . . Reprinted in Type-Facsimile with an Introduction by H. Buxton Forman. 1891. Dy. 8vo. Pp. 104. Copies 54.
The Religious Opinions of Elizabeth Barrett Browning. 1896. 8vo. Pp. 30. 1st edn.
*A Song. 1907. Post 8vo. Pp. 4. Copies 20. 1st edn.
The Enchantress & Other Poems. 1913. Crn. 8vo. Pp. 30. 1st edn.
Epistle to a Canary 1837. Edited by Edmund Gosse, C. B. 1913. Crn. 8vo. Pp. 20. 1st edn.
Lelia A Tale. 1913. Crn. 8vo. Pp. 36. 1st edn.
Letters to Robert Browning and Other Correspondents. Edited by Thomas J. Wise. 1916. Crn. 8vo. Pp. 56. 1st edn.
Edgar Allan Poe, A Criticism, etc. 1919. Clays. Crn. 8vo. Pp. 16. 1st edn.
Alfred Tennyson With a Defence of "The Dead Pan." 1919. Clays. Crn. 8vo. Pp. 20. 1st edn.
A Note on William Wordsworth, etc. 1919. Clays. Crn. 8vo. Pp. 20. 1st edn.
Charles Dickens & Other 'Spirits of the Age,' etc. 1919. Clays. 8vo. Pp. 20. 1st edn.

Robert Browning. *Letters from Robert Browning to Various Correspondents.* Edited by Thomas J. Wise. 1895-96. Two vols. Crn. 8vo. Pp. (I) 112 and (II) 112. Limited to "a few copies for Private Circulation." 1st edn.

Letters from Robert Browning to Various Correspondents. Edited by Thomas J. Wise. Second Series. 1907-8. Two vols. Crn. 8vo. Pp. (I) 108 and (II) 94. 1st edn.

Letters from Robert Browning to T. J. Wise and Other Correspondents. 1912. 8vo. Pp. 44. 1st edn.

The Death of Elizabeth Barrett Browning. 1916. Clays. Crn. 4to. Pp. 24. 1st edn.

The Last Hours of Elizabeth Barrett Browning. 1919. Clays. 8vo. Pp. 14. 1st edn.

Critical Comments on Algernon Charles Swinburne & D. G. Rossetti, etc. 1919. Clays. 8vo. Pp. 16. 1st edn.

Letters from Le Croisic. [Intro. by Edmund Gosse.] 1919. Crn. 8vo. Pp. 20. 1st edn.

Edward Fitzgerald and Elizabeth Barrett Browning. [Intro. by T. J. Wise.] 1919. Crn. 8vo. Pp. 16. 1st edn.

Some Records of Walter Savage Landor. 1919. Clays. Crn. 8vo. Pp. 16. 1st edn.

Reflections on the Franco-Prussian War, etc. 1919. Clays. 8vo. Pp. 16. 1st edn.

An Opinion on the Writings of Alfred, Lord Tennyson, etc. 1920. Clays. 8vo. Pp. 20. 1st edn.

Letters to his Son Robert Wiedemann Barrett Browning, etc. 1920. Clays. 4to. Pp. 16. 1st edn.

An Account of the Illness and Death of his Father, etc. 1921. Clays. 8vo. Pp. 16. 1st edn.

Samuel Taylor Coleridge. *Letters Hitherto Uncollected.* . . Edited with a Prefatory Note by Colonel W. F. Prideaux . . . 1913. 8vo. Pp. 68. 1st edn.

Two Addresses on Sir Robert Peel's Bill, etc. Intro. by Edmund Gosse. 1913. 8vo. Pp. 40. 1st edn.[2]

Marriage. 1919. 8vo. Pp. 24. 1st edn.

Joseph Conrad. *The Shock of War Through Germany to Cracow.* 1919. 8vo. Pp. 20. Copies 25. 1st edn.

To Poland in War-time . . . 1919. 8vo. Pp. 20. Copies 25. 1st edn.

The North Sea on the Eve of War. 1919. 8vo. Pp. 20. Copies 25. 1st edn.

My Return to Cracow. 1919. 8vo. Pp. 24. Copies 25. 1st edn.

Tradition. 1919. 8vo. Pp. 20. Copies 25. 1st edn.

2 Not a first edition although catalogued as such by Wise (see p. 89).

Some Reflections Seamanlike and Otherwise on the Loss of the Titanic. 1919. 8vo. Pp. 36. Copies 25. 1st edn.

Some Aspects of the Admirable Inquiry into the Loss of the Titanic. 1919. 8 vo. Pp. 44. Copies 25. 1st edn.

Autocracy and War. 1919. 8vo. Pp. 66. Copies 25. 1st edn.

Guy de Maupassant, 1919. 8vo. Pp. 20. Copies 25. 1st edn.

Henry James. An Appreciation. 1919. 8vo. Pp. 20. Copies 25. 1st edn.

*Anatole France. 1919. Clays. F'cap 4to. Pp. 20. Copies 25. 1st edn.

*Tales of the Sea. 1919. Clays. F'cap 4to. Pp. 12. Copies 25. 1st edn.

*The Lesson of the Collision [etc.]. 1919. Clays. F'cap 4to. Pp. 16. Copies 25. 1st edn.

*An Observer in Malay. 1920. Clays. F'cap 4to. Pp. 12. Copies 25. 1st edn.

*Books. 1920. Clays. F'cap 4to. Pp. 16. Copies 25. 1st edn.

*Alphonse Daudet. 1920. Clays. F'cap 4to. Pp. 12. Copies 25. 1st edn.

*Prince Roman. 1920. Clays. F'cap 4to. Pp. 44. Copies 25. 1st edn.

*The Warrior's Soul, 1920. Clays. F'cap 4to. Pp. 40. Copies 25. 1st edn.

*Confidence. 1920. Clays. F'cap 4to. Pp. 16. Copies 25. 1st edn.

*Anatole France. ("L'Ile des Pingouins.") 1920. Clays. F'cap 4to. Pp. 16. Copies 25. 1st edn.[3]

Charles Dickens. *Letters to Mark Lemon.* [Preface by T. J. Wise.] 1917. Dy. 8vo. Pp. 20. 1st edn.

An account of the First Performance of Lytton's Comedy "Not so Bad as We Seem," etc. 1919. Clays. 8vo. Pp. 16. 1st edn.

Notes and Comments on Certain Writings ... by Richard Henry Horne, etc. 1920. Clays. 4to. Pp. 16. 1st edn.

Arthur Dillon. **Shelley's Philosophy of Love.* 1888. Clays. Dy. 8vo. Pp. 20. Copies 28. S.S.P.

Edward Fitzgerald. *The Rubaiyat of Omar Khayyam.* A type-facsimile reprint of the rare first edition. 1887.

---

[3] The last ten of the 20 Conrad privately printed pamphlets bear the imprint of the author. But they were all printed for and issued by Wise—as explained on page 212.

H. Buxton Forman. *The Vicissitudes of Shelley's Queen Mab A Chapter in the History of Reform.* 1887. Clays. Dy. 8vo. Pp. 24. Copies 28. S.S.P.

The Hermit of Marlow A Chapter in the History of Reform. 1887. Clays. Dy. 8vo. Pp. 30. Copies 28. S.S.P.

Shelley "Peterloo" and "The Mask of Anarchy." 1887. Clays. Dy. 8vo. Pp. 32. Copies 28. S.S.P.

Rosalind and Helen. 1888. Clays. Dy. 8vo. Pp. 26. Copies 28. S.S.P.

Elizabeth Barrett Browning and Her Scarcer Books. A Bio-Bibliographical Note. 1896. 8vo. Pp. 32.[4]

Richard Garnett. *Shelley and Lord Beaconsfield.* 1887. Clays. Dy. 8vo. Pp. 24. Copies 28. S.S.P.

George Gissing. *Letters to Edward Clodd....* 1914. 8vo. Pp. 60. 1st edn.

Autobiographical Notes. With Comments upon Tennyson and Huxley...In Three letters to Edward Clodd. The Dunedin Press. 1930. Dy. 8vo. Pp. 16. 1st edn.[5]

Thomas Hardy. *A Defence of Jude the Obscure. In Three Letters to Sir Edmund Gosse, C.B.* The Dunedin Press. 1928. Dy. 8vo. Pp. 16. 1st edn.

Notes on "The Dynasts." In Four Letters to Edward Clodd. The Dunedin Press. 1929. Dy. 8vo. Pp. 16. Copies 20. 1st edn.

John Keats. *Ode to a Nightingale.* Edited with an Intro. by Thomas J. Wise. Fullford Printer. 1884. F'cap 8vo. Pp. 26. Copies 29. Reprint.

Walter Savage Landor. *An Address to the Fellows of Trinity College Oxford,* etc., 1917. Crn. 4to. Pp. 20. 1st edn.[6]

To Elizabeth Barrett Browning and Other Verses. 1917. Crn. 8vo. Pp. 24. 1st edn.[6]

A Modern Greek Idyll. 1917. Crn. 4to. Pp. 16. 1st edn.[6]

Garibaldi and the President of the Sicilian State. 1917. Crn. 4to. Pp. 16. 1st edn.[6]

[4] An off-print from the type used for the printing in *Literary Anecdotes of the Nineteenth Century.* (1895-6).

[5] Not a first edition although so catalogued by Wise (see p. 89).

[6] Although these pamphlets bear no printer's imprint, the typography resembles that in items produced by Eyre & Spottiswoode.

[Andrew Lang.] *Lines on the Inaugural Meeting of the Shelley Society. 1886. Clays. 8vo. Pp. 26.
The Tercentenary of Izaak Walton. 1893. Clays. Crn. 4to. Pp. 16. Copies [?30]. 1st edn.

Joseph Bickersteth Mayor. *A Classification of Shelley's Metres. 1888. Clays. Dy. 8vo. Pp. 48. Copies 28. S.S.P.

George Meredith. Letters from George Meredith to Edward Clodd & Clement K. Shorter. 1913. Crn. 8vo. Pp. 40. 1st edn.

William Morris. Letters on Socialism. 1894. Crn. 8vo. Pp. 40. Copies 34. 1st edn.

W. Kineton Parkes. *Shelley's Faith. Its Development and Relativity. 1888. Clays. Dy. 8vo. Pp. 24. Copies 28. S.S.P.

Dante Gabriel Rossetti. John Keats Criticism and Comment. 1919. Clays. Crn. 8vo. Pp. 24. 1st edn.
Letters from Dante Gabriel Rossetti to Algernon Charles Swinburne, etc. 1921. Clays. Dy. 8vo. Pp. 16. 1st edn.

William M. Rossetti. Shelley's Prometheus Unbound. 1886. Clays. Dy. 8vo. Pp. 32. Copies 28. 1st edn. S.S.P.
Shelley's Prometheus Unbound Considered as a Poem. 1887. [Pt. I only.] Clays. Dy. 8vo. Pp. 50. Copies 28. 1st edn. S.S.P.

John Ruskin. *Two Letters concerning "Notes on the Construction of Sheepfolds..." 1890. Clays. Crn. 8vo. Pp. 32. No statement of copies printed. 1st edn.
*Gold. A Dialogue Connected with the subject of "Munera Pulveris." Edited by H. Buxton Forman. 1891. First edn. Clays. Crn. 8vo. Pp. 28. Indefinite certificate [Wise states 40 copies].
*Stray Letters from Professor Ruskin to a London Bibliopole. [i.e., F. S. Ellis]. 1892. Crn. 8vo. Pp. 104. Indefinite certificate. [Wise states 40 copies.] 1st edn.
*Letters upon Subjects of General Interest from John Ruskin to Various Correspondents. 1892. Crn. 8vo. Pp. 114. Indefinite certificate. [Wise states 40 copies.] 1st edn.
*Letters from John Ruskin to William Ward. Edited by Thomas J. Wise... 1893. Two vols. Crn. 8vo. Pp. (I) 120 and (II) 110. Front ext. Indefinite certificate. 1st edn.
Letters on Art and Literature... Edited by Thomas J. Wise. 1894. Crn. 8vo. Pp. 112. Indefinite certificate. 1st edn.

[Note: The Ashley Library bookmark first appeared in the Ruskin series of Wise's publications in this volume. It is found in nearly all the subsequent ones.]

Letters from John Ruskin to Ernest Chesneau. Edited by Thomas J. Wise.... 1894. Crn. 8vo. Pp. 74. Front. ext. Indefinite certificate. 1st edn.

Letters from John Ruskin to Rev. J. P. Faunthorpe, M.A. Edited by Thomas J. Wise... 1895. Two vols. Crn. 8vo. Pp. (I) 116 and (II) 112. Indefinite certificate. 1st edn.

Letters from John Ruskin to Rev. F. A. Malleson, M.A... Edited by Thomas J. Wise... 1896. Crn. 8vo. Pp. 116. Indefinite certificate. 1st edn.

*John Ruskin & Frederick Denison Maurice on "Notes on the Construction of Sheepfolds." Edited by Thomas J. Wise, 1896. Crn. 8vo. Pp. 56. 1st edn.[7]

Letters from John Ruskin to Frederick J. Furnivall, M.A... and Other Correspondents. Edited by Thomas J. Wise. 1897. Crn. 8vo. Pp. 118. Front and another leaf facsimile ext. Certificate of 30 copies issued. 1st edn.

H. S. Salt. **A Study of Shelley's "Julian and Maddalo."* 1881. Clays. Dy. 8vo. Pp. 34. Copies 28. S.S.P.

*An Examination of Hogg's "Life of Shelley." 1889. Clays. Dy. 8vo. Pp. 24. Copies 28. S.S.P.

Harriet Shelley. **Harriet Shelley's Letters to Catherine Nugent.* ... 1889. Crn. 8vo. Pp. 74. No statement of copies printed. 1st edn.

Percy Bysshe Shelley. **Prologue to Hellas.* With an intro. note by Richard Garnett. Edited by Thomas J. Wise. 1886. Clays. Crn. 8vo. Pp. 30. Portrait front. ext. Copies 20. 1st edn.

*Poems and Sonnets. Edited by Charles Alfred Seymour. Philadelphia: 1887. Crn. 4to. Pp. 76. 1st edn.[8]

*Letters from Percy Bysshe Shelley to Jane Clairmont. 1889. Crn. 8vo. Pp. 112. No statement of copies printed. 1st edn.

*Letters from Percy Bysshe Shelley to Elizabeth Hitchener. 1890. Two vols. Crn. 8vo. Pp. (I) 174 and (II) 178. No statement of copies printed. Ashley Lib. Cat. says 34. 1st edn.

---

[7] Reimposed, after corrections, from the type of *Literary Anecdotes.*

[8] A false printer's imprint. It was printed by Clays, as subsequently stated by Wise in the Ashley Catalogues (see Chapter 5).

Letters to William Godwin. 1891. Two vols. Crn. 8vo. Pp. (I) 120 and (II) 118. No statement of copies printed. 1st edn.

Letters from Percy Bysshe Shelley to J. H. Leigh Hunt. Edited by Thomas J. Wise... 1894. Two vols. 8vo. Pp. (I) 86 and (II) 80. 1st edn.

Letters from Percy Bysshe Shelley to Thomas Jefferson Hogg. Vol. 1. 1897. Crn. 8vo. Pp. 110. 1st edn. [Note: No further volumes issued.]

Robert Louis Stevenson. *Familiar Epistle in Verse and Prose.* 1896. Dy. 8vo. Pp. 20. Facs. front. ext. Indefinite certificate [Ashley Lib. Cat. says 27 copies]. 1st edn.

R. L. & Fanny van de Grift Stevenson. *The Hanging Judge A Drama,* etc. With an Intro. by Edmund Gosse, C.B. 1914. Crn. 8vo. Pp. 104. 1st edn.

Henry Sweet. *Shelley's Nature Poetry.* 1888. Clays. Dy. 8vo. Pp. 56. Copies 28. S.S.P.

Algernon Charles Swinburne. *A Sequence of Sonnets On the death of Robert Browning.* 1890. Sm. 4to. Pp. 14. 1st edn. Indefinite certificate.[9]

> *The Ballad of Bulgarie.* 1893. Post 8vo. Pp. 16. Copies 25.[9]
> *Grace Darling,* 1893. Clays. 4to. Pp. 22. Copies 40. 1st edn. (See Chapter 13.)
> *Robert Burns. A Poem.* Printed for the Members of the Burns Centenary Club. 1896. Dy. 8vo. Pp. 12. 1st edn.[9]
> *The Saviour of Society.* [Intro. by Edmund Gosse.] 1909. Crn. 8vo. Pp. 36. Copies 20. 1st edn.
> *Of Liberty and Loyalty.* [Intro. by Edmund Gosse.] 1909. Crn. 8vo. Pp. 24. Copies 20. 1st edn.
> *In the Twilight. A Poem.* 1909. F'cap 8vo. Pp. 16. Copies 10. 1st edn.
> *Letters from Algernon Charles Swinburne to T. J. Wise.* 1909. Crn. 8vo. Pp. 32. Copies 20. 1st edn.
> *To W.T.W.D.* Written upon a flyleaf of a copy of *Sympathy,* etc. [1909]. Post 8vo. Pp. 4. Copies 20. 1st edn.
> *Mr. Prudhomme At the International Exhibition.* [Intro. by Edmund Gosse.] 1909. Crn. 8vo. Pp. 28. Copies 20. 1st edn.

[9] There is not conclusive evidence that these were produced by Wise. But see Chapter 13.

Letters on the Works of George Chapman. [Prefatory note by Edmund Gosse.] 1909. Crn. 8vo. Pp. 44. Copies 20. 1st edn.

**Lord Soulis A Ballad by a Borderer.* 1909. Crn. 8vo. Pp. 22. Copies 7. 1st edn.

**The Marriage of Monna Lisa.* 1909. Crn. 8vo. Pp. 16. Copies 7. 1st edn.

**The Portrait.* 1909. Crn. 8vo. Pp. 20. Copies 20. 1st edn.

**The Chronicle of Queen Fredegond.* 1909. Crn. 8vo. Pp. 74. Copies 20. 1st edn.

**Lord Scales A Ballad of a Borderer.* 1909. Crn. 8vo. Pp. 16. Copies 20. 1st edn.

**Burd Margaret A Ballad by a Borderer.* 1909. Crn. 8vo. Pp. 16. Copies 20. 1st edn.

**The Worm of Spindlestonheugh A Ballad by a Borderer.* 1909. Crn. 8vo. Pp. 24. Copies 20. 1st edn.

**Border Ballads.* 1909. Crn. 8vo. Pp. 24. Copies 20. 1st edn.

Ode to Mazzini. 1909. Crn. 8vo. Pp. 24. Copies 20. 1st edn.[10]

Letters from Algernon Charles Swinburne to Edmund Gosse. 1910. Series I. Crn. 8vo. Pp. 40. Copies 20. 1st edn.

Letters from Algernon Charles Swinburne to Edmund Gosse. Series II. Crn. 8vo. Pp. 52. Copies 20. 1st edn.

Letters from Algernon Charles Swinburne to Edmund Gosse. Series III. Crn. 8vo. Pp. 44. Copies 20. 1st edn.

Letters from Algernon Charles Swinburne to Edmund Gosse. 1910. Series IV. Crn. 8vo. Pp. 40. Copies 20. 1st edn.

Letters from Algernon Charles Swinburne to Edmund Gosse. Series V. Crn. 8vo. Pp. 40. Copies 20. 1st edn.

A Record of Friendship. 1910. Crn. 8vo. Pp. 12. Copies 20. 1st edn.

Letters from Algernon Charles Swinburne to John Churton Collins... [Intro. by Edmund Gosse.] 1910. Crn. 8vo. Pp. 44. Copies 20. 1st edn.

Letters on William Morris, etc. 1910. Crn. 8vo. Pp. 32. Copies 20. 1st edn.

The Ballad of Truthful Charles & Other Poems. 1910. Crn. 8vo. Pp. 32. Copies 20. 1st edn.

Letters on the Elizabethan Dramatists. 1910. Crn. 8vo. Pp. 48. Copies 20. 1st edn.

---

[10] The nine privately printed pamphlets from *Lord Soulis* to *Ode to Mazzini* inclusive bear the imprint of Watts-Dunton. But they were printed for and issued by Wise as recorded in his *Bibliography.*

Letters from Algernon Charles Swinburne to A. H. Bullen. 1910. Crn. 8vo. Pp. 36. Copies 20. 1st edn.

Letters to Thomas Purnell & Other Correspondents. 1910. Crn. 8vo. Pp. 32. Copies 20. 1st edn.

A Criminal Case. 1910. Crn. 8vo. Pp. 16. Copies 20. 1st edn.

Letters Chiefly concerning Edgar Allan Poe from Algernon Charles Swinburne to John Ingram. 1910. Crn. 8vo. Pp. 36. Copies 20. 1st edn.

The Ballade of Villon and Fat Madge. 1910. F'cap 4to. Pp. 22. Copies 20. 1st edn.

Letters from Algernon Charles Swinburne to Edmund Clarence Stedman. 1912. Crn. 8vo. Pp. 64. Copies 20. 1st edn.

Blest and the Centenary of Shelley, etc. 1912. Crn. 8vo. Pp. 8. Copies 20. 1st edn.

Letters from Algernon Charles Swinburne to Sir Richard F. Burton & Other Correspondents. 1912. Crn. 8vo. Pp. 30. Copies 20. 1st edn.

Letters from Algernon Charles Swinburne to Sir Henry Taylor & Other Correspondents. 1912. Crn. 8vo. Pp. 40. Copies 20. 1st edn.

Letters from Algernon Charles Swinburne to Frederick Locker Lampson & Other Correspondents. 1912. Crn. 8vo. Pp. 48. Copies 20. 1st edn.

Letters to the Press. Intro. by Edmund Gosse. 1912. Crn. 8vo. Pp. 132. Copies 32. 1st edn.

The Cannibal Catechism. 1913. Crn. 8vo. Pp. 14. Copies 20. 1st edn.

Les Fleurs du Mal & Other Studies. Intro. by Gosse. 1913. Crn. 8vo. Pp. 114. Copies 32. 1st edn.

Letters to Sir Edward Lytton-Bulwer & Other Correspondents. 1913. Crn. 8vo. Pp. 56. Copies 20. 1st edn.

Letters from Algernon Charles Swinburne to Stéphane Mallarmé. 1913. Crn. 8vo. Pp. 40. Copies 30. 1st edn.

Æolus. 1914. Crn. 8vo. Pp 16. Copies 20. 1st edn.

A Study of "Les Miserables." Intro. by Gosse. 1914. Crn. 8vo. Pp. 60. Copies 30. 1st edn.

Pericles & Other Studies. 1914. Crn. 8vo. Pp. 84. Copies 30. 1st edn.

Letters from Algernon Charles Swinburne to John Morley. 1914. Crn. 8vo. Pp. 52. Copies 20. 1st edn.

Thomas Nabbes. A Critical Monograph. 1914. Crn. 8vo. Pp. 16. Copies 20. 1st edn.

Christopher Marlowe, etc. 1914. Crn. 8vo. Pp. 24. Copies 20. 1st edn.

Letters from Algernon Charles Swinburne to Edward Dowden, etc. 1914. Crn. 8vo. Pp. 44. Copies 20. 1st edn.

Letters from Algernon Charles Swinburne to Richard Monckton Milnes, etc. 1915. Crn. 8vo. Pp. 80. Copies 20. 1st edn.

Lady Maisie's Bairn, etc. 1915. Crn. 8vo. Pp. 44. Copies 20. 1st edn.

Félicien Cossu. A Burlesque. Intro. by Gosse. Crn. 8vo. Pp. 32. Copies 20. 1st edn.

Théophile. Intro. by Gosse. 1915. Crn. 8vo. Pp. 36. Copies 20. 1st edn.

Ernest Clouét. Intro. by Gosse. 1916. Crn. 8vo.. Pp. 24. Copies 20. 1st edn.

A Vision of Bags Intro. by Gosse. 1916. Crn. 8vo. Pp. 16. Copies 20. 1st edn.

The Death of Sir John Franklin. 1916. Crn. 8vo. Pp. 24. Copies 20. 1st edn.

The Triumph of Gloriana. Intro. by Gosse. 1916. Crn. 8vo. Pp. 16. Copies 20. 1st edn.

Early Letters from Algernon Charles Swinburne to John Nichol. 1917. Crn. 8vo. Pp. 40. Copies 30 [but stated to have been suppressed to 10].

Rondeaux Parisiens. 1917. F'cap 4to. Pp. 30. Copies 35. 1st edn.

Weariswa' A Ballad. 1917. Crn. 8vo. Pp. 20. 1st edn.

The Italian Mother and Other Poems. 1918. Crn. 8vo. Pp. 24. 1st edn.

The Ride from Milan and Other Poems. Eyre & Spottiswoode. 1918. Crn. 4to. Pp. 20. 1st edn.

The Two Knights and Other Poems. 1918. Crn. 8vo. Pp. 16. 1st edn.

A Lay of Lilies and Other Poems. 1918. F'cap 4to. Pp. 24. 1st edn.

A Letter to Ralph Waldo Emerson. 1918. Eyre & Spottiswoode. Crn. 4to. Pp. 12. 1st edn.

Queen Yseult A Poem. Intro. by Edmund Gosse. 1918. F'cap 4to. Pp. 84. 1st edn.

Lancelot, The Death of Rudel, And Other Poems. 1918. F'cap 4to. Pp. 32. 1st edn.

Undergraduate Sonnets. 1918. Eyre & Spottiswoode. Crn. 4to. Pp. 16. 1st edn.

The Character and Opinions of Dr. Johnson. 1918. Eyre & Spottiswoode. Crn. 4to. Pp. 12. 1st edn.

The Queen's Tragedy. 1919. F'cap 4to. Pp. 20. 1st edn.

Letters from Algernon Charles Swinburne to Richard Henry Horne. 1920. Clays. 4to. Pp. 20. 1st edn. [Note: Carries the printer's imprint of Clay & Sons for the first time in this Swinburne series of pubns.]

Autobiographical Notes, etc. 1920. Clays. 4to. Pp. 28. 1st edn.

Unpublished Verses. [n. d.] Crn. 8vo. Pp. 4. A piracy. There is not conclusive evidence that this was produced by Wise, but see Chapter 14.

John Todhunter. *Notes on Shelley's Unfinished Poem "The Triumph of Life."* 1887. Clays. Dy. 8vo. Pp. 28. Copies 28. S.S.P.

Shelley and the Marriage Question. 1889. Clays. Dy. 8vo. Pp. 20. Copies 28. S.S.P.

Edward John Trelawny. *The Relations of Percy Bysshe Shelley with his two Wives.* 1920. Clays. 8vo. Pp. 16.

The Relations of Lord Byron and Augusta Leigh. 1920. Clays. 4to. Pp. 16. 1st edn.

William Watson. *Lachrymae Musarum.* 1892. Dy. 8vo. Pp. 18. Copies 100. 1st edn.

Shelley's Century. 1842. Dy. 8vo. Pp. 18. Copies 29.

Thomas J. Wise. *Verses.* 1883. Fullford, Printer. Pp. 36. Copies 41.

William Wordsworth. *The Law of Copyright.* 1916. Crn. 4to. Pp. 12. 1st edn.[11]

Various Authors. *A Romance of Literature.* By Algernon Charles Swinburne and Dante Gabriel Rossetti. Preface by Wise. 1919. Dy. 8vo. Pp. 16. 1st edn.

> *Letters addressed to Algernon Charles Swinburne.* By John Ruskin, William Morris, Sir Philip Burne-Jones, and Dante Gabriel Rossetti. 1919. Clays. Dy. 8vo. Pp. 16. 1st edn.

[11] Bears no printer's imprint. It appears to have been produced by a firm other than Clays.

Publications by Wise and formerly attributed by him to Swinburne, but not by that Poet:

> *Juvenilia.* 1912. Crn. 4to. Pp. 40. Copies 20. [See Chapter 12.]
> *The Arab Chief. A Ballad.* 1912. Crn. 8vo. Pp. 18. Copies 20. [See Chapter 12.]

FORGED, SUSPECT, AND UNAUTHORIZED NINETEENTH-CENTURY PAMPHLETS

Issued by Wise

The following list is from Carter and Pollard's *Enquiry*, which gives details of sales by Wise of all the pamphlets except Tennyson's *Morte D'Arthur* and Wordsworth's *To the Queen*. The statements in heavy type below some of the titles are the censorship comments since appended to the descriptions of the respective pamphlets in the British Museum Catalogue. Of the remaining pamphlets without such statements, the British Museum Library either did not possess copies at the time this book was written, or had not then recorded censorship. All are catalogued by Wise as first editions, except George Eliot's *Agatha*. The concluding words against each item indicate briefly the verdicts of Carter and Pollard respecting the pamphlet. "Condemned" means that the item is classed as a proved forgery; "piratical," that the item is a piracy at least; and the other terms indicate that the respective items are suspected forgeries.

Matthew Arnold. *Saint Brandan.* 1867. **The imprint is probably fictitious [1890?].**—"Highly suspicious."
> *Geist's Grave.* 1881. **[1890?].**—"Highly suspicious."

Elizabeth Barrett Browning. *Sonnets.* 1847.—Condemned.
> *The Runaway Slave.* 1849. **[In Verse]. The imprint is fictitious [1888?].**—Condemned.

Robert Browning. *Cleon.* 1855. **The imprint is fictitious [1895?].**—Condemned.
> *The Statue and the Bust.* 1855. **The imprint is fictitious [1890?].**—Condemned.
> *Gold Hair.* 1864.—"Suspicious."

Charles Dickens. *To Be Read at Dusk.* 1852.—Condemned.

George Eliot. *Brother and Sister*. 1869. The imprint is fictitious [1888?].—Condemned.
> *Agatha*. 1869. (Second Edition). The imprint is probably fictitious [1895?].—"Highly suspicious."

Rudyard Kipling. *White Horses*. 1897. An unauthorized edition. —Piratical.
> *White Man's Burden*. 1899. An unauthorized edition. —Piratical.

William Morris. *Sir Galahad*. 1858. The imprint is fictitious [1890?].—Condemned.

Dante Gabriel Rossetti. *Sister Helen*. 1857. The imprint is fictitious [1890?].—Condemned.
> *Verses*. 1881. The imprint is probably fictitious [1894?]. —[Suspicious], anyhow a piracy.

John Ruskin. *The Scythian Guest*. 1849. The imprint is fictitious [1890?].—Condemned.
> *The National Gallery*, 1852.—Condemned.
> *Catalogue of the Turner Sketches*. 1857.—Condemned.
> *The Queen's Garden*. 1864.—Condemned.
> *Leoni*. 1868.—Condemned.
> *The Future of England*. 1869. [1870?]. This is really another issue of an edition bearing the fictitious imprint Woolwich, 1870.—Condemned.
> *Samuel Prout*. 1870.—[Piratical].
> *The Nature & Authority of Miracle*. 1873. The preface signed J.B.H. The imprint is probably fictitious [1890?]. —"Suspicious."

R. L. Stevenson. *The Thermal Influence of Forests*. 1873.—Condemned.
> *The Story of a Lie*. 1892.—"Extremely suspicious."
> *Some College Memories*. 1866.—Piratical.

A. C. Swinburne. *Dead Love*. 1864. Imperfect, wanting the wrapper. The imprint is fictitious.—Condemned.
> *Laus Veneris*. 1866. The imprint is probably fictitious [1890?].—[Suspicious].
> *Cleopatra*. 1866. The imprint is probably fictitious [1890?].[12]—[Suspicious].

---

[12] The British Museum cataloguer is a little out in suggesting this date for the probable perpetration of the suspect. It was done before April, 1888. See Chapter 6.

An Appeal to England against the Execution of the Condemned Fenians. 1867. The imprint is probably fictitious [1890?].—[Very doubtful].
Dolores. 1867. The imprint is fictitious [1895?].—Condemned.
Siena, 1868. The imprint is fictitious [1890?].—Condemned.

Alfred Tennyson. *Morte D'Arthur,* etc. 1842.—Condemned.
   The Sailor Boy. 1861. The imprint is fictitious [1895?].
   —Condemned.
   Ode for the Opening of the International Exhibition. 1862.
   The imprint is fictitious [1890?].—Condemned.
   Lucretius. 1868. The imprint is fictitious [1890?].—Condemned.
   The Lover's Tale. 1870. The imprint is fictitious [1890?].
   —Condemned.
   The Last Tournament. 1871. The imprint is fictitious
   [1895?].—Condemned.
   A Welcome to Alexandrovna. 1874. The imprint is probably fictitious [1895?].—"Suspicious."
   The Falcon. 1879.—"Suspicious."
   The Cup. 1881.—[Suspicious].
   The Promise of May. 1882.—[Suspicious].
   Carmen Seculare. 1887. The imprint is probably fictitious
   [1895?].—"Very suspicious."
   Child Songs. 1880.—Condemned.

W. M. Thackeray. *An Interesting Event.* 1849.
   A Leaf out of a Sketch Book. 1861. The imprint is fictitious
   [1895?].—Condemned.

William Wordsworth, *To The Queen.* 1846.—Condemned.

Edmund Yates. *Mr. Thackeray, Mr. Yates, and the Garrick Club.*
1859.—Condemned.

ALSO UNDER SUSPICION

William Morris. *The Two Sides of the River.* 1876.
Robert Louis Stevenson. *Thomas Stevenson.* 1887.
   War in Samoa. 1893.—"Probably a Piracy."
Alfred Tennyson. *Ode on the Opening of the Indian and Colonial Exhibition.* 1886.
   England and America. 1872.

WORKS EDITED, OR CONTRIBUTED TO, BY WISE

A Reference Catalogue of British and Foreign Autographs and Manuscripts. 1893. Wise contributed Parts I and II and also edited the work; which was published by the Society of Archivists and Autograph Collectors. [See Chapter 10.]

Edmund Spenser's *Faerie Queene.* George Allen: 1894. Edited.

John Ruskin's *The Harbours of England.* George Allen: 1895. Edited.

Literary Anecdotes of the Nineteenth Century. By W. Robertson Nicoll and Thomas J. Wise. 1895-6. Two vols. Wise contributed new and important bibliographical material; including bibliographies of Swinburne and Robert Browning that were the bases of his later and fuller ones of those authors.

Robert Browning's *Bells and Pomegranates.* Ward, Lock: 1896. Preface and notes by Wise.

Algernon Charles Swinburne's *Border Ballads.* The Bibliophile Society of Boston: Massachusetts. 1912. Edited.

Swinburne's *Posthumous Poems.* Heinemann: 1917. Edited, in collaboration with Edmund Gosse.

Swinburne's *Letters.* Heinemann: 1918. Two vols. Edited. with Gosse.

Swinburne's *Contemporaries of Shakespeare.* Heinemann: 1919. Edited, with Gosse.

Selections from Swinburne. Heinemann: 1919. Edited, with Gosse.

Harold B. Wrenn's *Catalogue of the Library of the late John Henry Wrenn.* 1920. Five vols. Edited.

The Complete Works of Swinburne. Heinemann: 1925. Edited, with Gosse.

The Shakespeare Head Brontë. 1931-36. Edited, with John Alexander Symington.

N.B. in addition to the foregoing, Wise superintended the publication of the Shelley Society's type-facsimile; and also a few of the Browning Society's reprints.

INDEX

"Act of Copulation and . . . Generation in the Womb," 94
Adams, Sarah Flower, 29
Addison, Joseph, 97
Address to the Irish People, 53
Addresses, 89 *(note)*
Adonais, 17, 31, 50
Adventures of Ernest Alembert, 92
"Affair of the Bags," 199
Agatha, 233
A Genuine Dialogue: Facetious and Pathetic, 231
Aitkin, G. A., 79, 108, 234
Alastor, 50
Albemarle Street, 189
Alchemist, The, 131
Alexander, Sir W., 130
Algernon's Flogging, 79
Alhambra, 72
Alice in Wonderland, 204
Allegra (Byron's daughter), 17 *(note)*, 241
Allen, George, 113
Allen and Unwin, xiii
Almayer's Folly, 207
American Art Association Galleries, 209 *(note)*
-ana, 228, 233, 272
Ancient Mariner, 39
Anderson Galleries, 158 *(note)*
Angrian MSS, 100
An Impossible Thing, 229
A Pope Library, 233
Arab Chief, The, A Ballad, 150, 152
Arabian Nights, 143, 198
Arch, J. & A.. 40, 42
Armageddon, 202
Arnold, Matthew, 69, 85, 105, 140 *(note)*, 144; William Harris, 108, 110-
Arrows of the Chace, 136
Ashley Library, 3, 5, 6, 14, 34-5, 48, 56-7, 70, 75, 78, 82, 86-7, 89 *(note)*, 90, 110, 116, 121-2, 127-9, 131

(note), 132, 138, 141 *(note)*, 146, 148, 156, 159, 164, 168, 185, 193 *(note)*, 195-6, 199, 208, 212, 218-9, 221, 223, 226-9, 233, 236 *(note)*, 246-7, 262, 265, 269-70, 272-3, 275, 281
Ashley Library Catalogue, 15, 42, 55, 60, 78, 84, 90-1, 115-9, 133, 138, 158, 184-5, 189, 190 *(note)*, 211, 216, 219-20, 225-6, 229, 231-3, 235, 238, 243, 265, 275, 281
Ashley Road, 82, 97, 116, 120-1
Asquith, H. H., 274
Atalanta in Calydon, 144
Athenaeum, 123-4, 155, 184 *(note)*, 276
Athens, 244
"Athens, Maid of," 236-7, 244
A Trick to 'catch the Old-one, 230
Autobiographical Notes with Comments upon Tennyson and Huxley, 89
Autobiography (Shorter), 99 *(note)*
Avenell, 11
Avowels (Moore), 145

Bacon, 82
Baillie, Joanna, 172
Bald Faced Stag, 182
Bale, John, 131
Ballad of Bulgarie, 117, 155, 159
Banager, Ireland, 99
Bank of England Notes, 87 *(note)*
Barnsbury, 53
Barretts, The, of Wimpole Street, 249
Barrie, J. M., 85, 117; bibliography of, 117
Battell of Alcazar, The, 131
Battle of Marathon, 74, *(note)*
Baudelaire, Pierre Charles, 145
Baxter, Charles, 197
Belshazzar, 127, 138
Ben Jonson (Oxford), 134
Ben Jonson his Volpone, 130

Bennett, Dr. W. C., 9 (note), 64, 249-52, 266-7, 279; Greenwich edition (Sonnets), 252
Bentley, Richard & Son, 236-7, 239; Richard (Jr.), 239-40
Bible, 227
Bible in Spain, 189; supplementary chapter to, 189
Bibliographical Data Relating to a Few of the Publications of Algernon Charles Swinburne, 213
Bibliographical Society, xiv, 188, 232, 260
Bibliography of Barrie, 117; Borrow, 122, 178 (note), 188, 190 (note); Brontë Family, 195; Browning (E. B.), 195, 249; (Robert), 173 (note), 178 (note), 184 (note); Byron, 51 (note), 181, 223, 235, 238, 241, 244; Carlyle, 182; Coleridge, 188; Conrad, 202, 208, 210, 223; Dickens, 182; Keats, 223; Kipling, 214; Landor, 223; Rossetti, 125; Ruskin, 173 (note), 182; Stevenson, 125; Swinburne, 80, 116, 125, 173 (note), 182, 213, 220, 223; Tennyson, 125, 173 (note), 182, 186; Thackeray, 182; Wordsworth, 39, 75, 195
Bibliography (Wise), 117, 153
Biglow Papers, 64
Birrell, Augustine, 225
Bishopsbourne, 215
Black, Mrs. Thérèse, 236, 244
Blackfriars, 132
Blackwood, Wm. and Son, xiv
Blake, William, 149
Blank Verse (Lamb), 134
Blest pamphlet, 163
Blind, Miss Mathilde, 76-7
Bloomsbury, 199, 274
Bodleian Library, 77, 230
Bonnard, Sylvestre, 219
Bookman, 97, 103, (note), 105, 117, 136, (note); American, 4, 5, 6, 246
Bookman's Journal, 4, 31, 117, 212
Border Ballads, 88, 170
Borrow, George, 21, 78, 85, 88-90, 92, 108, 167, 188-9, 195, 198; Mary, 90; Bibliography, 122, 178 (note), 188, 190 (note)
Boswell, James, 8
Bovey, Tracey, 236

Bowles, Caroline, 60
Bowring, Sir John, 21
Bradbury and Evans, 33
Bradford, Yorks, 68
Brantwood, 95
Brawne, Fanny, 275
Brett-Smith, H. F. B., xiii, 233
Bride, Mourning, 274
Bride's Tragedy, 149
British Museum, 14, 40-1, 51, 53, 60, 70, 74, 77, 86, 90, 114 (note), 115-6, 123, 129, 134, 140-1, 160, 182, 193-4, 199, 212-3, 230-1, 239, 255, 260, 265 (note), 267, 271
British Museum Library, xiii, 61, 65, 69, 86, 96 (note), 117, 122, 229, 236 (note), 262, 268
British State Paper Office, 8
British Weekly, 73, 103
Brontë, Branwell, 196; Charlotte, 21, 92, 99-100, 114-5, 194-6
Brontës, 85, 99-100, 194, 233; Bibliography, 195
Brontë Society, xiv
Brooke, Rev. Stopford, 19, 36-7, 49, 72, 177, 250, 257
Brooks, Mr., 68-9
Brother and Sister, 69, 233
Brotherton, Lord, 108, 171
Brotherton Collection Committee, Leeds University, xiii
Browning, Elizabeth Barrett, 25, 64, 69, 73-4, 109, 111, 138, 140-1, 184 (note), 246, 249, 261, 267; Bibliography of, 195, 249
Browning, Elizabeth Barrett, and Her Scarcer Books, 73
Browning, Mrs. Fanny, 34
Browning Library, 27 (note), 35, 180 (note), 249, 251, 266; Browning Papers, 156
Browning, Pen, 267;
Browning, Robert, 25 et seq., 48, 66-7, 74, 77, 88, 111, 125, 138, 157, 178, 180, 198, 233, 249, 261, 279; Bibliography of, 173 (note), 178 (note)
Browning, Robert Wiedemann, 159, 267
Brownings, 85, 184, 190, 233, 246
Browning Society, 19, 25, 28 (note), 30, 32, 48-50, 52, 63 (note), 67, 72, 83, 87, 155

Buchanan, Robert, 144, 183 (note)
"Bulgaria," 117, 155, 159
Bulloch, Dr. J. M., 98
Burne-Jones, Sir Edward, 199
Burns Centenary Club, 122
Burns, Robert, 114
Burton, Sir Richard, 143-4, 153, 182
-3, 215
Bussy d'Ambois, 134
Butler, E. H., of Jamaica Plain, 108
Byron, George Gordon (De Gibler),
9, 237; Mrs., 9 (note)
Byron, Lady, 242
Byron, Lord, 4, 9, 17, 84, 114, 128,
165, 197, 221-2, 233, 235 et seq.,
246; Bibliography of, 51 (note),
181, 223, 235, 238, 241, 244; Un-
published Letters of, 236, 239, 244
Byron Library, 238 (note)

Caelia, 132
Calkin, A. E., xiii, 222
Call, Lt. Col., 21
Cambridge University, 86 (note), 271;
Library, 260
Campbell, James Dykes, 14, 28, 48,
72
Campbell, Mrs. Patrick, 205
Cancellans, 38, 40-1
Cannibal Catechism, The, 168
Carlyle, Bibliography of, 182
Carden, Jennie Donald, 11
Caroline, Queen, 239
Carter and Pollard, 58, 125, 137
(note), 187, 254, 259
Carter, John, xiii, 254, 259-60
Cary, Henry F., 275
Cashmore, H. M., xiii
Casimir Delavigne, 229
Cenci, 14
Chance, 202, 210-1
Chapman, George, 131-2, 134, 144,
182-3; R. W., 225
"Charlotte Brontë's Tragedy," 193
Chatterton, Thomas, 8, 9, 150, 172,
176
Chaucer, Geoffrey, 165
Chaucer Society, 26
Cheltham, Mrs., 21
Cheyne Walk, 149
Childe Harold, 238, 241-2
Christ's Victory over Death, 130

Clairmont, Jane, 4, 17, 21, 53, 197;
Letters to, 57
Clark, Mrs., 236, 238
Clay, Cecil, xiii, 65, 87, 201, 248
Clay, Richard and Sons, xiii, 30, 32,
49-50, 55, 58, 60-2, 65, 86-7, 93, 95,
120 (note), 168, 200, 248 (note),
255
Clement's Inn Passage, 180
Cleon, 35, 105, 111, 138
Cleopatra, 7
Cleopatra, 68-9, 77, 109, 140 (note),
160, 184
Clifton and Grimaux Dictionary, 221
(note)
Clique, 141 (note)
Clodd, Edward, 88
Clyde, Lord, 152
Cockerell, Sir Sydney, xiii, 244, 259
Cockerell, Viscount, xiii
Coleridge, Ernest Hartley, 231
Coleridge, Samuel T., 14, 39, 41, 85,
89 (note), 165, 195, 233; Bibliog-
raphy of, 188
Collected Works, 30
Collection of Contributions in Prose
and Verse, A, 80
Collier, John Payne, 5, 8
Colvin, Sir Sidney, 101
Comus, 229
Congreve, William, 229, 274
Conrad, Joseph, 85, 86 (note), 92,
188, 202, 207-9, 211-3, 215-6, 233,
274; Bibliography, 202, 208, 210,
223; Mrs., 209
Conspiracie and Tragedie of Charles
Duke of Byron, 131
Constable, T. and A., 123-5, 254
Contemporaries of Shakespeare
(Swinburne), 223
"Contributions to Periodical Litera-
ture," 81
Convention of Cintra, 38
Cook, Sir E. T., 135
Cook and Wedderburn, 135-7, 210,
214, 247, 276-7
Cooke, John, 131
Cooper, Miss, 79
Cooper's Well, 79
Copyright Act, 86
Countercuffe, A, given to Martin
Junior, 131

Covici-Friede, Inc., xiv
Cowper, William, 130
Crane, Walter, 113
Crimea, 152
Criminal Case, A, 168
Crouch Hill, 82
Curle, Richard, xiii, 37 *(note)*, 207-9, 212

Daily Express, 137 *(note)*, 272, 279 *(note)*
Daily Herald, 256
Dale, Francis Richard, 12
Daniel, 127
Daniel, Samuel, 130
Dante, 198, 275
Davenport, Sir W., 130-
Day, John, 130
Dead Love, 184
Death Sonnets, 155
De Bruni, 26
Decker, Thomas, and Massinger, Philip, 131
Defense of Guenevere, 125
De Quincey, 39
Des Graz, C. G., xiii
Dekker, Thomas, 182, 229
Devil's Due, 183 *(note)*
Diary (Pepys's), 99 *(note)*
Dickens, Charles, 85, 114, 154, 197; Bibliography of, 182
Dictionary of National Biography, 96 *(note)*, 145, 151-3, 181
di Ricci, Seymour, 129
Dobell, Bertram, 23, 236, 238 *(note)*
Dobson, Allan, xiii; Austin, 179, 215
Dolores, 184
Dombey, 18
Dombey and Son, 153
Domecq, 135 *(note)*
Domecq, Miss Adèle Clotilde, 135
Don Juan, 234, 236-7
Doomsday, 130
Dorchester, 53
Douglas, James, 152
Dowden, Prof., 48, 55-6, 60, 177
Downside Crescent, 128
Drayton and others, 130
Drayton, Michael, 130
Dream, after reading Dante's Episode of Paolo and Francesca, 275
Drinkwater, John, 225-8

Dryden, John, 108, 165, 228, 233
Dulwich College Library, 8
Duncial, The, 131
D'Urfey, Thomas, 274

Early English Text Society, 26
Early Letters . . . Swinburne to Nichol, 90
Eastward hoe, 132-3
Edinburgh University Union, 124
Editiones Principes of Swinburne, 81
Elegy, 147
Eliot, George, 69, 105, 233
Ellis, F. S., 177
Endymion, 17
English Bards and Scotch Reviewers, 244
Enquiry into the Nature of Certain Nineteenth Century Pamphlets, 64, 137 *(note)*, 187, 248, 253 *et seq.*
Enterlude of Welth and Helth, An, 131
Enterlude of Johan the Evangelyst, 131
Epicurean, 14
Epipsychidion, 21
Evans, C. S., xiii
Evans, Frederick H., xiii
Esdaile, Arundell, 225
Esher, Viscount, 259-60
Essay on Blake, 148
Eton, 153
Etty, William, 198
Everie Woman in her Humor, 131

Faerie Queen, 113, 165
Falcon, 111
Farringdon Road, 13
Faunthorpe, Rev. J. P., 93
Ferguson, F. S., xiii, 130 *(note)*
Field, Nathan, 134
First Fowre Bookes of the Civile Wars, The, 130
Fitzgerald, Edward 85, 229
Fitzwilliam Museum, 244
Fletcher, Giles, 130
Florio, 134
Ford, Richard, 188-9
Forewords, 95
Forman, Harry Buxton, 19, 21, 23, 48, 50-1, 55, 62-3, 66, 71-3, 74 *(note)*, 75-6, 79, 84, 87, 100, 105,

126, 139, 156 *(note)*, 157, 158 *(note)*, 175, 177, 232, 235-7, 241 *(note)*, 250, 252-3, 257-60, 279; Mrs., 158
Forman, Maurice Buxton, xiv, 184, 187, 241 *(note)*, 252-3, 258-60, 274
Fortnightly Review, 104, 116, 157-8
Fountaine, The, of Selfe-Love, 131
Fraser's Magazine, 150, 151 *(note)*, 152
Friendship's Offering, 135
Fugitive Pieces (Byron), 50, 236
Fullford, Wm., 15, 16, 30
Furnivall, Dr. Frederick James, 18, 19, 26-8, 46-8, 62-3, 66, 72, 79, 87, 94, 95 *(note)*, 96 *(note)*, 118-9, 177-8, 179 *(note)*, 184 *(note)*, 279
Future and Past, 250, 267

Gammer gurton's Nedle, 131, 228
Garland, Herbert, 117
Garnett, Miss Olivia R., xiii, 48; Dr. Richard, 48, 177, 179, 257
Gaskell, Mrs., 193
Genesis, 78
Gibraltar, 189
Girton College, 28 *(note)*
Gissing, George, 85, 89
Globe, 152
Gladstone, W. E., 210
Godwin, William, *Letters to*, 57
Gold Hair, 35, 105, 111, 138
Gorfin, Herbert E., xiii, 30, 62, 88, 92, 97, 108, 112, 120 *(note)*, 122, 158, 168-9, 186, 190 et seq., 232, 247-8, 253, 255-8, 279-80 *(note)*
Gosse, Sir Edmund, 34, 47, 71-2, 78-80, 88-90, 101, 141, 144, 145 *(note)*, 148, 150-1, 154, 160-2, 164, 166-71, 173, 182-3, 190, 195, 207, 223, 225, 230-2, 249-51, 257, 261, 279
Gosse, Dr. Philip, xiii, 34; Miss Sylvia, xiii, 34, 78; Miss Teresa, 34; Gosse-Wise Correspondence, xiii, 154, 163
Grace Darling, 44, 116-7 155, 159
Gray, Euphemia Chalmers, 118
Gravesend, 12
Green, George à, 131
Greenhalgh, Frances Louise, 127
Green, Robert, 134
Greenes Tu Quoque, 131

Greenwich edition (*Sonnets—Bennett*), 252
Greg, W. W., 177
Groseman, Amelia, 12 *(note)*

Halliwell-Phillips, 13, 134
Halsey, F. R., 54, 106
Handbook for Travellers in Spain, 188-9
Hand and Soul, 68
Hanging Judge, 230
Harbours of England, 113
Hardy, Mrs. Florence, xiv, 98; Thomas, 85, 98, 102, 197-8, 207, 274
Harriet Shelley's Letters to Catherine Nugent, 57
Harvard University, xiii
Have with you to Saffron-walden, 131
Hawkins, Gen. Rush, 106
Haworth, 100
Healey and Wise, 232
Healey, Edwin, & Co., 232
Heath Drive, 128, 146, 172, 221, 262, 269
Héger, Mme., 193; Prof. Constantin, 100, 193
Heinemann, Ltd., xiii, 209; Wm., 148
Hellas, 21, 31, 50, 61
Her Majesty The Queen, 114 *(note)*
Heyward, 182
Hesperia, 185-6
Highgate Cemetery, 12 *(note)*
Hitchener, Elizabeth, 58 *(note)*, 59; *Letters to*, 57, 59-60
Hitler, Adolf, 143
Hobhouse, 242 *(note)*
Hodder & Stoughton, 103
Hodge, Thomas, 54
Hodgson's, 102, 181
Hoe, Robert, 106, 129
Hogarth, 162
Hogg, Thomas Jefferson, *Letters to*, 57
Holloway, 15, 18, 24, 71, 82-3, 172
Holmes, Sherlock, 20, 152, 219
Home Life of Swinburne, 149 *(note)*
Honesty, Progress of, 274
Hood, Dr. Thurman L., 27 *(note)*
Hornsey Rise, 82
Hours, The, 149
House of Lords, 78

Howell, Charles Augustus, 84, 257
(note)
Humour out of Breath, 130
Hunt (James Henry) Leigh, 17, 21,
197, 250; Mrs., 197; Letters to, 57;
Violet, 149 (note)
Huntington, Henry E., 54, 106, 129
Hutchinson, Thomas, 177
Hutt, Charles, 181; Fred, 179-80

Idea, 130
Ilford, Essex, 158
Illium, 79
Illustrated London News, 97, 116
Ingelow, Jean, 144
Ingpen, Roger, 60-1, 233
Inheritors, The, 208
Inns of Court, 218 (note)
Instructions to a Painter, 130
Ireland, Wm. Henry, 5, 7, 8; Sam, 7
Irelands, 7, 8

James, Thomas, 93
"Jewjube," 200
John Inglesant, 210
Johnson, A. S., xiii
Jones and Evans, xiv
Jonson, Ben, 130-2, 134, 144
Jowett, Benjamin, 146
Juvenilia, 150, 152

Keats, John, 16, 17, 30, 31, 73, 114,
128, 196-7, 229, 275; Bibliography
of, 223
Keats Grove, 172
Keepsake, The, 135, 140
Kelly, John, xiv, 75
Kendal, 46
Kernaham, Coulson, 270
Kerr and Richardson, 17
Kimber, P. R., xiv
King's Cross, 15
Kingsley, Charles, 111
Kipling, Rudyard, 64, 116, 207, 214,
216, 246, 248; Bibliography of, 214
Kirkby, John, xiv
Kjaempeviser, 167
Klein, Judge, 108

La Fille du Policeman, 165
Lake Poets, 39, 42
Lamb, Charles, 134, 233

Lambe, John Lawrence, 145 (note)
Lamentable Tragedie . . . of Cam-
bises King of Percia, A, 131, 134
Landor, Walter Savage, 85, 144, 168-9,
192, 198, 233; Bibliography of, 223
Lang, Andrew, 46-8
Lapham, Edwin N., 108
La Touche, Rose, 119 (note)
Laughing Anne, 208 (note), 215-6
Laus Veneris, 164, 184, 274
Lazarus, 7
Leeds University, xiii, 171
Leigh, Augusta, 242
Leighton Grove, 82
Leith, Mrs. Disney, 144
I eoni: a Legend of Italy, 135
Lesbos, Isle of, 166
Letters   Addressed   to   Algernon
Charles Swinburne, 199
Letters from . . . Swineburne to . . .
Sir Richard Burton, 182-3; Ed-
mund Gosse, 182; Milnes and
Other, 84; William Morris, 182; to
Thomas J. Wise, 182
Letters of Robert Browning Collected
by Thomas J. Wise, 27, 250
Letters on the Elizabethan Dram-
atists, 88
Letters on the Works of George
Chapman, with an Introduction by
Edmund Gosse, 183
Letters to Edward Clodd, 89
Letters to Elizabeth Hitchener, 57-8,
91
Letters to Frederick J. Furnivall, 94
Letters to his Mother Ann Borrow
and Other Correspondents, 89
Letters to his Wife (Borrow), 90
Letters to Jane Clairmont, 57
Letters to J. H. Leigh Hunt, 57
Letters to Thomas Jefferson Hogg,
57
Letters to Wm. Godwin, 57
Lewis, Monk, 53
Lewti, or the Circassian's Love Chant,
41 (note)
Liberty and Loyalty, 88
Library Staff of Texas University,
xiii
Liborum Prohibitorum, 199
Life of Shelley, 55-6
"Light Winged Dryad," 31

Lines on the Inaugural Meeting of the Shelley Society, 48
Listener, The, 203
Literary Anecdotes, 73, 95, 96 *(note)*, 150, 151 *(note)*, 156 *(note)*
Literary Anecdotes of the Nineteenth Century, 92 *(note)*
"Literary chiffonier," 184
Livingston, Miss Flora V., xiii, 213-4, 247
Lockhart, George Gibson, 188-9; Miss, 119
Lord Jim, 188
Love Letters of Charlotte Brontë to Constantin Héger, 194
Lover's Tale, 187
Love of King David and Fair Bethsabe, The, 131
Love Sonnets (E. B. Browning), 246, 249-51, 255, 261; Greenwich edition, 252; Reading edition, 11, 249, 251-3, 255, 261
Lowell, James Russell, 64
Lucas, E. V., xiv, 101, 172, 225; Miss Audrey, xiii
Lucretius, 111
Ludwig von Beethoven, 114 *(note)*
Luttrell, Narcissus, 229
Lyly, John, 134
Lyrical Ballads, 39, 40-2

MacCarthy, Justin Huntly, 144
MacOubrey, Mrs., 188-9
Macri, Theodora, 244
McCarthy, Wm. H., xiii, 58, 107, 188
McKerrow, Dr. R. B., xiv
Maggs, Benj., xiv
Maggs Bros., xiv
"Maid of Athens," 236-7, 244
Major Wither's Disclaimer, 246
Malcontent, The, 131
Mallarme, Stephane, 143
Marmion, 153
Marsden, Wilfred A., xiii
Marshbank, W., xiv
Marston, John, 131-2, 144
Mary Magdalene, 7
Massinger, Philip, and Decker, Thomas, 131, 133
Matthew, 225
Matthew and Brooks, 68-9
Maurice, 95 *(note)*, 96

Max Gate, 98
Mazzini, Ode, 170
Meredith, George, 102, 198
Meretriciad, The, 79
Methuen and Co., xiv, 212
Methuen, Sir Algernon, 108
Middleton, Thomas, 230
Midsummer Holiday, A, and Other Poems, 149
Millais, John Everett, 118
Milton, 229
Mitchell, Dr. Alex, xiv; Harold G., xiv
Mitford, Mary Russell, 9 *(note)*, 111, 249-51, 261, 266, 267
"Moonrise by the Seas" (Swinburne), 101
Moore, George, 145; Thomas, 14
Morgan, John, of Aberdeen, 108, 177, 250
Morgan, J. P., 106
Morning Post, 145 *(note)*
Morris, William, 105, 125, 182, 199
Mourning Bride, 274
Moxon, Edward, 33, 43
Muir, Augustus, 219-20
Murray, Charles Fairfax, 93, 259; Sir John, xiii, 20, 79; Sir John, the Fourth, 237, 239; Sir John the Fifth, 239, 241 *(note)*, 243
My Books, 215
"My Dear but Infamous Pote," 199

Napoleon, 202, 219
Napoleonic Wars, 202
Nash, Thomas, 131
Nashes Lenten Stuffe, 131
National Gallery, 136-7, 140 *(note)*
National Portrait Gallery, 198
Nature and Authority of Miracle, The, 140 *(note)*
Nearer, My God, to Thee, 29
Nettleship, J. T., 178
New Amphion, The, 123
New Shakespeare Society, 26
New York Public Library, 114 *(note)*
Nicholls, Rev. Arthur Bell, 99-100, 194
Nicoll, Sir W. Robertson, 73-4, 92, 97, 99, 103, 117-8, 136 *(note)*
Nineteenth Century, 123
Notes and Queries, 238

Nugent, Catherine, 57, 58 *(note);*
  Letters to, 57

O'Connor, T. P., 19
Ode to a Nightingale, 16, 30
Oedipus Tyrannus, 21
Of Marriage, 82
Offer, Dr. R., xiii
Original Poetry, 53
Other, A. N., 62
Ouvray, Mrs., 9 *(note)*
Oxford English Dictionary, 26, 176
Oxford University, 86 *(note),* 232,
  271
Oxford University Press, xiv, 132

Pair of Blue Eyes, A, 207
Pall Mall Gazette, 155, 159
P. and O. *Verona,* 72
Parliamentary Papers, 87 *(note)*
Pasquill of England, 131 *(note)*
Pauline, Lady Trevelyan, 90
Pauline, 25, 27, *et seq.,* 50, 62, 180
Pauline, a Fragrant of a Confession,
  29 *et seq.*
Payen-Payne, de V., xiv, 220, 278
Payne, John, 198, 231
Pearson, John, 36
Peele, George, 131
Pepys, 99 *(note)*
Pericles and Other Studies, 167
Peter Bell, 37
Philadelphia Historical Society, 55-6
Phillips, G. A., 158
Pines, The, 21, 76-7, 100, 142, 144-6,
  147 *(note),* 149, 153-4, 157, 161-2,
  167, 172
Pisa, 147, 249
Pisa *Adonais,* 17, 31, 147
*Pleasant Conceyted Comedie, A, of
  George à Greene,* 131
Poe, Edgar Allan, 165
*Poem upon his Sacred Majestie's
  Most Happy Return,* 130
Poems (Cowper), 130; (Keats), 230
Poems and Ballads (Swinburne), 144,
  186
Poems and Sonnets, 55-6, 67
Pollard and Redgrave, 131 *(note)*
Pollard, Prof. A. W., xiv, 177, 225,
  230; Graham, xiv, 137 *(note),* 247.
  253-4, 257, 259-60, 279 *(note)*

Pompey the Great, 131
Poor, Henry W., 108
Pope, Alexander, 108 *(note),* 114, 131,
  228-9, 233
Portuguese, Sonnets from the, 267
Potts, Robert Alfred, 62-3, 108, 177,
  250
Powell, 30
Praeterita, 135 *(note)*
Pre-Raphaelites, 149 *(note),* 199
Preston, Sydney E., xiv; Thomas, 131,
  134
Priapus, 79
Prideaux, Col. W. F., 74, 108, 125,
  177
Printing House Square, 194
Prior, Matthew, 108, 114, 228, 231
Priory Terrace, 121
Proctor, Robert, 125
Progress of Honesty, 274
Promise of May, The, 111
*Proposals for Association . . . Philan-
  thropists . . . Ireland,* 54
Puddicombe, Julia, 236
Punch, xiv, 98, 101
Putney, 76, 101, 162, 170
Putney Hill, 147, 151, 157

Quaritch and Co., xiii, 129, 130
  (note)
Quarterly Review, 188
Queen Fredegond, 88
Queen Mab, 131
Queen's Garden, The, 136

Rabelais, 198
Raleigh, Sir Walter, 138
Rambler, 281
Read, Henry, 44
"Reading: 1847" (Sonnets—E. B.
  Browning), 111, 249, 251-3, 255,
  261, 266, 268, 279
"Recent Book Prices," 103
Recollections of a Long Life, 242
  (note)
Record Office of Literature, 70
Records (Shelley Society), 62
Redway, W. E., xiv
*Reference Catalogue of British and
  Foreign Manuscripts,* 114
Reich, Mrs., 149
Revenge of Bussy d'Ambois, 134

Ribbentrop, 156
Ricci, de, Seymour, xiv
Rimbaud, Jean Arthur, 143
Ring and the Book, The, 30
Rivières, 222
Robert Burns, A Poem, 122
Roberts, Wm., xiv, 103-4, 105 *(note)*, 116, 257 *(note)*
Rochford, Essex, 127
Rod for Run-awayes, 229
Rogers, Lionel, 120
Roman Catholick Version of the First Psalm for the Use of a Young Lady, 229
Romance, 114
Romance of Chastisement, 80
Romeo and Juliet, 131
Rosenbach, A. S. W., 204
Rosetti, Christina, 155-6, 158, 198; Dante G., 17 *(note)*, 55, 68, 85, 105, 146-7, 149, 198-9, 231; *Bibliography of*, 125; William Michael, 59, 62-3, 66, 125, 158, 177, 198, 257
Rotherhithe, 139
Rowfant Library, 134
"Rowley, Thomas," 9, 172, 176
Roxburghe Club, 232, 260-1
Rubeck & Co., 12, 82, 97, 112
Rubeck, Hermann, 12, 13, 18, 24, 52, 69, 112, 127, 139, 190, 192, 222
Rubeck, Otto P., xiv, 69, 139
Runaway Slave, 30, 33, 35, 65, 69, 74 *(note)*, 109, 111
Ruskin Biography, 93, 120 *(note)*, 135, 173 *(note)*; Bibliography of, 173 *(note)*, 182
Ruskin, Effie, 118
Ruskin, John, 69, 82, 85, 87, 93-4, 95 *(note)*, 103 *(note)*, 105, 113-4, 118, 121, 135-7, 140 *(note)*, 150, 191, 246-7, 258 *(note)*, 274, 276, 278
Ruskin, John James, 135 *(note)*
Ruskin Literary Trustees, xiv
Ruskin, Telford and Domecq, 135
Ruskin's Romance, 120 *(note)*
Russia: An Ode, 231

Sabin, Frank T., xiii, 124, 148; S. F., xiii
Sadlier, Michael, 228, 254
Saint Joan, 227
St. Andrews School Fund, 136

St. Brandon, 69, 140 *(note)*
St. Irvyne, 52
Salt, Dr., 66
Samuel Prout, 164
Sangorski and Sutcliffe, xiv
Sappho, 166
Saturday Review, 47-8
Schlengemann, E., 69
Schultess-Young, H. S., 236-8, 239 *(note)*, 240, 241 *(note)*, 242, 244
Scotland's Lament, 117
Scott, Sir Walter, 17, 118, 140, 153, 176
Scroop House, 236
Scythian Guest, The, 105, 135, 279
Secret Agent, 215
Segati, Marianna, 242
Selections from Shakespeare (Swinburne), 223
Sensitive Plant, 240
Sequence of Sonnets On the Death of Robert Browning, 155-6, 158
Session of the Poets, The, 144
Set of Six, A, 212
Seventeen Letters of . . . Byron to an Unknown Lady, 243
Seymour, Charles Alfred, 55-6
Shadwell, Thomas, 274
Shahrázád, 153
Shahryár, 153
Shakespeare, Wm., 8, 130 *(note)*, 131, 144
"Sharing Eve's Apple," 197
Shaw, Geo. Bernard, xiv, 19, 205, 227
Shelley, Harriet, 55, 58; Lady, 48, 55
Shelley Library, A, 54 *(note)*
Shelley Library, The, an Essay in Bibliography, 73
Shelley, Life of (Dowden), 55
Shelley, Mary, 4, 21, 46, 197
Shelley, Sir Percy, 48
Shelley, Percy Bysshe, 4, 9, 12, 14, 17, 46, 55, 58 *(note)*, 60, 66-7, 73, 76, 84-5, 87, 91, 108 *(note)*, 121, 128, 131, 147, 150, 161, 175-6, 197, 218, 221-2, 228, 233, 240, 279
Shelley Society, 19, 28 *(note)*, 32, 36, 46-50, 52, 61-3, 66-7, 72, 83, 87, 121 *(note)*, 227, 257
Shelley Workers, 49, 62
Shepherd, Richard Herne, 79, 84,

126, 135, 151 *(note)*, 177, 179, 180-1, 183, 184 *(note)*, 185-7, 257-8, 279
Shorter, Clement King, 97 *et seq.*, 116-8, 119 *(note)*, 139, 166-7, 188, 194-5, 212; Dora S., 99 *(note)*
Siena, 68, 184
Sigerson, Dora, 99 *(note)*
Sir Galahad, A Christmas Mystery, 125
Sir John Oldcastle, 130
Simpson, Percy, xiv
Simpson, 134
Slack, H. J., 59
Slater, J. H., 32 *(note)*, 74; Walter Brindley, 177, 250
Smart, James P., 93, 104 *(note)*
Smith, Miss Ethel Murray, 267
Smith, Frederick, 82; Mrs. George, 268; Selina Fanny, 82-3, 97, 120
Smith, W. A. and Co., 139, 173
Society of Archivists and Autograph Collectors, 114, 140
Solomon, Simeon, 200
Some College Memories, 123, 125
Somerset House, 98
Song, A (Elizabeth B. Browning), 140-1
Songs before Sunrise, 100
Sonnets (Elizabeth B. Browning), 26, 34-5, 64, 111, 139, 266; *(from the Portuguese)*, 267; (Shakespeare), 176
Sonnets on Browning, 155-6, 158-9
Sotheby and Co., xiii, 54, 186-7, 250
Southey, Edith, 38; Robert, 38, 41; *Correspondence with Catherine Bowles*, 60; *Letters to*, 60
Spanish Masquerado, 134
Spectator, 97
Spencer, Walter T., 229
Spenser, Edmund, 113, 165
Spielman, M. H., xiv, 194-5
Spilsbury, Sir Bernard, 174
Squire, Sir J. C., 225
Statue and the Bust, The, 32-3, 35, 105, 111
Sterling, Sir Anthony Coningham, 152
Stevenson, John Hall, 79; Robert Louis, 117, 123-4, 173, 197, 216, 230, 247; *Bibliography of*, 125; William, 131 *(note)*

Still, John, 131
Strand Magazine, 175 *(note)*, 233, 254 *(note)*
Strauss, Harold, xiv
Students of Shelley, 49
Sutcliffe, Geo., xiv
Sweet, Prof. Henry, 46-7
Swift, Jonathan, 179, 198
Swinburne, Algernon Charles, 4, 21, 39, 66-7, 69-71, 76-8, 80-1, 84-5, 88, 90, 92, 100, 105, 108 *(note)*, 109, 116-7, 122-3, 125, 134, 140 *(note)*, 142-4, 145 *(note)*, 146, 147 *(note)*, 148-53, 155, 156 *(note)*, 157, 158 *(note)*, 159, 161-71, 181-2, 183 *(note)*, 185, 190, 197-200, 207, 213, 223, 231, 233, 258 *(note)*; Isabel, 153-4, 247, 274; Lady Jane, 144
Swinburne, Bibliography of, 80, 116, 125, 145, 151, 155 *(note)*, 156, 158-9, 161, 166, 169, 173 *(note)*, 183
Swinburne Library, A, 76 *(note)*, 117 *(note); Life of*, 144 *(note)*, 154

Tegetmeier, 66
Telford, 135 *(note)*
Tennyson, Alfred Lord, 105, 108 *(note)*, 110-1, 144, 146, 173 *(note)*, 184, 247, 267, 274; Bibliography of, 125, 173 *(note)*, 182, 186
Texas University, xiii, 54, 58, 107 *(note)*, 109, 188
Thackeray, W. M., 182, 274; Bibliography of, 182
Thacher, John Boyd, 106
Thebais, 144
Thomson, J. C., 212
"Thunderer," 194
Tiberius, 200
Times, The, xiii, 100, 109 *(note)*, 151-2, 193-4, 260 *(note)*, 264-5, 269-70, 272; Literary Supplement, 74, 184, 250-1, 253, 258, 260, 265
Todhunter, John, 62-3
"Tombeau," 155
Torquay, 236
To The Queen, 45, 75
Trelawny, Edward John, 4, 17, 21, 85, 197
Trevelyan, Sir George, 90; Lady Pauline, 90
Trinity College, Hartford, 27

Trollope, Anthony, 228
Tupper, Martin, 13, 47
"Twilight," 155
"Twin Souls," 102
Two Addresses on Sir Robert Peel's Bill, 89 *(note)*, 90
Two Lake Poets, 36 *(note)*
Two Letters . . . "Notes on the Construction of Sheepfolds," 94, 96

Undergraduate Papers, 183 *(note)*
Underwood, Dr., 109 *(note)*
Unpublished Letters of Lord Byron, 236
University College, 47
University of Texas, xiii, 54, 58, 107 *(note)*, 109, 188
University Union Committee, 123
Unpublished Letters of Lord Byron, 236, 239, 244
Unpublished Verses (Swinburne), 185
Unwin, Stanley, xiii

Vatican Venus, 144, 147, 149
Vaticinium Causuale, 130
Velasquez, 202
Ventures of Book Collecting, 110
Verses, 15, 102, 269
"Victor and Cazier," 53
Villette, 193
Villon, Francois, 143
Virgin Martir, The, 131
Volpone or the Foxe, 133-4
Vrain, Lucas, 7

Waldock, Hannah, 11
Waller, Edmund, 130
Walpole, Horace, 9, 172
Warwick Lane, 103
Watts, Theodore, 144
Watts-Dunton, 76-7, 86 *(note)*, 117 *(note)*, 142, 144-, 145 *(note)*, 146 *(note)*, 147 *(note)*, 148-9, 151, 153, 155 *(note)*, 156-63, 169, 171, 247; Miss Clara, xiii, 149 *(note)*
Webster (of Methuen's), 212

Wedderburn, Alexander, 135
Wee Chain of Literature, 98
Wells, Gabriel, 262-3, 271
Wellesley, Wm., 54
Wheatley, H. B., 32 *(note)*, 177
Whippingham Papers, The, 80
White Man's Burden, The, 64, 116
White, William A., 129
White Horses, 214
Who's Who, 12 *(note)*, 232
Wiclif Society, 26
Widener, Harry Elkins, 108
Widener Memorial Library, Harvard University, xiii, 213
Wilkinson, C. H., xiv, 233, 281
Willis, Miss Irene Cooper, xiii
Wilson, J. Dover, 177
Wise, Frances L. G., 127; Henry Dauncey, 11; Herbert Athol, xiv, 11, 271; Julia, 11; Julia Victoria (Dauncey), 11, 12 *(note)*; Selina F. S., 82-3, 97, 115-6, 120; Thomas, 11, 12 *(note)*; Mrs. T. J., xiv, 230, 250, 260, 263, 265, 271, 275
Wither, George, 108, 130
Woman, The, in the Moone, 134
Woman's Shortcomings, A, 141
Worcester College, 227, 232, 281
Wordsworth, Wm., 17, 36 *et seq.*, 75, 85, 128, 233; *Bibliography of*, 39, 75
Works, The, of John Ruskin, 135, 247
World War, 192, 195, 200, 202
Worm of Spindlestonheujh, The, 88
Wrenn, John Henry, 54, 97, 105, 107, 108 *(note)*, 109, 111, 122, 141 *(note)*, 146-8, 161, 222, 233, 280
Wrenn Library, 54, 58, 60, 107 *(note)*, 109, 159, 234; Catalogue, 223, 233
"Writing on the Wall," 93 *(note)*
Wyndham, H. Saxe, 114 *(note)*

Yankees, 207
Yates, Edmund, 28
Y. Z., Mr., 64, 66, 68, 70, 75, 276, 279